THE A - Z OF ALCOHOL AND SOBRIETY

Everything you need to know

Corinna Alderton

Disclimer: This book is for support and guidance purposes only and should not replace any medical support or input. I encourage anyone considering changing their drinking habits to seek medicl advice before they do so.

*In loving memory of my beautiful sober sister, Sober&Sane.
Thank you so much for coming into my life. My world is a richer
place for having known you. Thank you for showing me the
true meaning of strength and courage. You are, and always will
be, my guiding light. I will not drink with you nor for you today.
In my moments of weakness, thoughts of you will give me the
strength to carry on. Goodnight sweet angel.
Fell asleep 15th January 2022, 11 months and 1 day sober.*

*Also, in loving memory of Dan, who, even when he was dying,
made his wife Pollya promise him that she would not drink
again. I am so glad they had two sober years together and I'm
eternally grateful that he supported her in supporting all of us.
While caring for her Dan, Pollya has spent hundreds of hours
supporting others (especially ladies) in their sobriety. It was
lovely to see Dan when he popped on to say "Hello" to us too.
May your TARDIS take you to another realm, where your spirit
can roam free, and may our Pollya find peace when she feels
you in the wind.
Fell asleep 17th June 2022 following a long illness
courageously borne.*

Gorgeous life!
Bow down so I can kiss you
Your forehead made of sun
Many will dismiss your welcome face
But not the hopeful ones...
Yes there'll be mountains
Bone dry fountains
Places where pain persists
But if we believe
Your sun will seek us
Therein lies our gift!

~Epilogue~
Because just as the sun slips night's robe on at the lull of every eve, so shall she clothe from head to toe each day that we receive.

~Footnote~
So in inching through dark, should you shatter apart, catch your pieces as they fall... for each morning's grace can restore our soul vase for flowers after all.

MERMAID MUST NOT DROWN - 1ST MAY 2022
- 4 MONTHS SOBER

INTRODUCTION

At the age of 12, I took my first sip of alcohol. I cannot remember if I liked the taste or not, but I do remember the feeling of fitting in. At 14 I continued this on a more regular basis, and eventually I used it to numb and block emotional and physical pain. For the last 22 years, I drank at least a bottle of wine every night whilst working as a mental health nurse. In 2019, I found myself being retired due to illness and disability. In 2020 the Covid pandemic hit. Prior to the first lockdown, my husband left. Finances were tough but still I found the money for booze. And, like many people, my drinking increased. In the UK, alcohol related deaths increased by nearly 20% in the year of lockdown. One morning, at 3 am, I found an open bottle of wine in the fridge and instead of my cuppa, I had a glass of wine. As I sat there drinking, I knew I was at my rock bottom. I drank everything in the house and at midday, I quit. No planning, no support. A few weeks later, I visited a friend and went on a week's bender. That was the final blow out. I was so bloated and my liver area was so painful. I joined an on-line sober community and my sobriety journey began. I read, connected and listened to podcasts. I discovered that I could rewire my neural pathways (the messaging system between our body and brain). I worked hard on this, and using mindfulness, improved my walking, talking and thinking. Yes, I have physical health issues and disabilities, but I realised I had actually drunk my neural pathways into oblivion. At the start of my journey, I needed a walker all of the time, often a wheelchair, and I struggled to talk and eat without choking. Now I walk short distances without my walker and have even learned to ride a 600cc trike. I also produce podcasts for a worldwide sober website and am an avid promoter of positive living with sobriety and disability both on social media and in person.

There are many great sobriety books out there, but some can be very difficult to read. I have therefore set about writing a book that is both informative and easy to understand. It is from the heart, with my own experiences, previous nursing knowledge and some stories from real people (although their pseudonyms have been used) and contains some swearing. This book also contains referenced facts, research and resources which are up to date at the time of writing, but may well change with time. For ease, there are website addresses (current at time of publishing) at the end of some sections for further information. I have used bold text in places to highlight that you can read more under that heading. There are some examples of activities which you may find helpful, so a pen and notebook or your journal might be handy, or you may prefer to write in the book itself or photocopy the activity pages.

You may not agree with everything I have written. My word is not gospel. But, if anything in particular stirs you up – maybe ask yourself what that is about! This book contains everything I think you need to know to make choices about your alcohol or sobriety journey. It is not necessarily everything you want to know. My intention is to give you hope, help you to feel less alone and inspire you to be more curious.

Reading this, you might picture me as a completely chilled out, relaxed, got-it-all-together kinda sober girl, but be assured, I feel it all with you. But that's the thing, I really do feel now. I can recognise it, identify it, work with it, turn it around and act on it. And, at times, fall completely apart. And that's OK - it's a great way to reset our emotional and physical being. Come journey with me, into the amazing world of exploration and discovery ...

I ride around here often
on my yellow trike and
love the book Share
telephone boxes and am
leaving copies all over the
UK. Please feel free to take
this away but bring it
back again So it may
help others. Copies are available
on Amazon or you can hear
me read it and follow my
recovery vlogs (alcohol, disability
and grief) on YouTube:
Positive Recovery with Corinna

— x —

A

AA (Alcoholics Anonymous) - is one sobriety way but it's not the only way, so don't worry if it's not for you. I did consider it, as I loved the thought of face-to-face meetings, but I quit drinking during lockdown and Zoom really isn't my thing. In this book you will find alternative sources of support to help you through your journey. AA covers **The Twelve Steps** programme in a set order. Many of us find that we naturally progress through these without ever having picked up the 'Big Book'. Some women feel AA is very male-dominant, as it was founded by men and remained male-based for many years, but I know of several women who have found it extremely helpful. Others are deterred by the spiritual aspects of AA and I was too, but then I looked deeper into the meaning of our **Higher Power**. If you want the traditional AA route, you can find meetings in your local area by looking on-line, Citizens Advice or your local library.

https://www.alcoholics-anonymous.org.uk/About-AA/Historical-Data

Abuse - when we are drinking, we are abusing ourselves. We are putting our body under physical and emotional assault but we don't see that until later in our sobriety journey. Often, there is a history of having been abused by others, which for some of us, may still be happening. Abuse is emotional as well as physical and sexual. Emotional abuse is very controlling but can be harder to recognise. Just because we are not being hurt physically it does not mean we are not being abused. Both men and women can be abused. Many abuse centres support people who choose to remain in their abusive relationship, some of whom are too afraid to leave. Abuse centres also help people to flee an abusive home and get to a place of safety.

If you are ever in immediate danger then contact the police on your country's emergency number e.g. 999/911

If you need help from an abuse centre, look up support in your area or contact your national support network which you can find online by searching for the National Domestic Abuse Hotline.

UK

For men: Mankind Telephone: 01823 334244

www.mankind.org.uk

For women:

Refuge: www.nationalhelpline.org.uk

Refuge Helpline: 0808 2000 247

Women's Aid: www.womensaid.org.uk where you can chat on line, find information, contact details and a local directory.

USA

1.800 – 799 – 7233 www.thehotline.org

Acceptance - is a small word with a huge impact and makes for a happier and easier life. Resistance makes us sad, angry, frustrated and depressed. It keeps us stuck. Accept what is. Accept what's done. Accept your areas of control. Accept that we only ever have this moment. I assure you it will be easier by the time you get to the end of this book. For example: you have quit drinking. Others around you continue to drink. You resent this. You think they should quit to support you. It's triggering your **Addict Voice**, 'If you can't beat them join them'. You are battling with yourself. And then you can go into battle with them. If you accept your sobriety as your **Choice**, and the fact that others have the right to their own choices, it will be easier. Let others be. Accept that this is not their journey, it's yours.

Accidents - I remember getting drunk as a teen and falling over, tearing my brand-new satin leggings. I grazed my knees too. But, in true Essex girl style, I was more upset about my trousers. I have a huge lump on my thumb where I took a chunk out of it on a broken tile. I was drunk and cleaning my home. Not a good mix. I have damaged ligaments in my knee from when my drunk husband fell on me and I twisted it. And, I have had a drunk person fall on me, and take me to the ground with them when they fell. I have also pooped myself and my poor teenage son had to sort me out. And as my sober buddy shickey reminded me, many injuries occur when we try to save our drinks rather than ourselves! Does any of this sound cringingly familiar? Sober life is so much less painful!

Acetaldehyde - is an air pollutant which comes mostly from building materials and cigarette smoke. It can cause diseases such as Alzheimer's and cancer. It is also found in food, especially those that are processed and high in sugars. Why am I talking about this? Because alcohol converts to acetaldehyde in the body and the build-up of this causes us to feel sick and dizzy and makes our heart beat faster. Longer term this can cause liver scarring, **Cirrhosis**, stomach and throat **Cancer**. Alcohol really is liquid **Poison**.

https://www.deltanutra.com/pages/where-does-it-come-from

Acknowledge - your mistakes and any arguments you may have caused. Apologies need to be real and we do not need to take the blame for everything! It takes two to cause a situation and to heal it. There will be apologies that we do not feel we can make and old wounds that should not be reopened. This is okay. Everyone's story is different. There are people who will never see, hear, or accept our side. I have learned to apologise to some silently from afar, accepting that we all have our own hurt child inside. And forgiving the other person for the mistakes I tell myself they have made. This has helped me to avoid further rejection, hurt and pain.

Acne - if you already have this, then drinking is going to make it a whole lot worse. The sugars in alcohol directly affect acne, and alcohol itself stimulates the skin regulating gland which can cause more problems. Alcohol also impacts on our liver and immune system, making it harder for the body to get rid of bacteria and impurities. Interestingly, the article I read on this had advice for reducing the effects of alcohol on acne. But it didn't simply say 'stop drinking'.

https://www.manageyourlifenow.com/does-alcohol-cause-acne

ACT (Acceptance and Commitment Therapy) - I had this psychological therapy for pain management, and it's been really helpful in my sobriety too. It can help us look at what our true **Values** are in life and what we can do to help us focus on these. For me, alcohol was never a value. Family, friends and work were, but much of that was blocked by drinking. Sometimes I even resented them because my values got in the way of my drinking. WTAF?! No wonder I was so bloody miserable! ACT also looks at **Acceptance** and **Mindfulness** to help us achieve our values, and these continue to be invaluable in my recovery.

https://www.goodtherapy.org/learn-about-therapy/types/acceptance-commitment-therapy

ACT (Awareness, Clarity, Turnaround) - a phrase and technique coined by Annie Grace in her book *'This Naked Mind. Control Alcohol. Find Freedom, Discover Happiness & Change Your Life'*. Become **A**ware of the situation, your thoughts and feelings, investigate and **C**larify them – what is the actual issue? Challenge them, look at your areas of control, accept what you can and cannot do and **T**urn it around. I'll leave it to another sober buddy to explain how he uses this:

> *'I would be driving home from my night shift and be fine, until a couple of miles from home, when I would be hit by what I call the zombie. I would automatically drive to the liquor store, go in and buy booze. It felt like I was on the outside looking in and I couldn't stop it. I'd read a blog about ACT online, and this one day, I'm driving home, and I'd even purposefully taken a different route. I'm nearing home and I feel the anxiety starting to build as it has a thousand times before. I'm thinking "Oh shit, here it*

comes!" I've always known what I'm going to be feeling, but I've never had a way to get through it. So, I started to become aware. It's starting to hit me and flood me and I clarify. My anxiety is going through the roof and I'm starting to have flashes of walking into the store and buying the beer, taking a drink and it calming me down and relieving the anxiety. My brain is sending me flashes and playing the movie forwards of how great it's going to feel. I'm clarifying that this is what my brain is doing to me; I'm feeling anxious, I'm seeing movies of the beer, going in the store and my brain is telling me to just have one and it will take all the anxiety away. My heart's racing and I'm really uncomfortable, but then I start to turn it around. If I have that drink, I'm not going to just have one or two. It's going to be a blackout. And then I start playing MY movie forwards in my brain. I'm seeing my wife crying. I see drunk texting people. I'm watching a movie of what I've done a thousand times before. Then I get to the point where I wake up the next morning in panic mode, grabbing my phone to see who I drunk text. Having to get up and go to work feeling like shit, promising myself that I would never do this again. By the time I'd got done, playing all that movie in my head, I was pulling into my driveway. I'd driven past the liquor store. I was so excited that I had turned everything around and beaten the monster in my head, that I even forgot the usual pressure and anxiety to go back to the store and get booze. I knew as I pulled up on my driveway, that I was going to make it through the day and not drink. I knew that I had found a tool that worked for me and I got so excited. That day changed everything for me, because that day I realised I could change my thinking. From that day, ACT became my go to. I feel a craving and I go into ACT mode and it has kept on getting me home.' Drifter February 15th 2022 600+ days sober.

Active - we may need to rest during the first few days of quitting, but once the physical withdrawals have gone it's important to stay active. Being active is good for our physical and mental health and is also a great distraction from temptation and our addiction. If you are struggling, you might find it helpful to write an activity schedule each day to help get you motivated. Write the times that you are going to eat, dress and do activities such as go out, read, do housework and relax.

Heres an example:

8.00	Get up and have a cup of tea and engage with my sober **Community**
8.30	Take Fluffy for a walk
9.00	Have breakfast and fill up a water bottle to drink
10.00	Shower and dress
10.30	Meditate
11.00	Do something I've been putting off
12.00	Research a new hobby/or do hobby
13.00	Have lunch and refill water bottle
14.00	Have an afternoon nap
15.30	Listen to a sober **Podcast**, audio book or read **Quit Lit**
17.00	Cook and eat dinner
18.30	Take Fluffy for a walk
19.00	Have a hot drink (no caffeine) and watch tv, read or do hobby.
20.00	Connect with community and talk with friends
21.00	Get ready for bed and have a wind down read or meditate
22.00	In bed. Lights out. Sleep

How would your day look?

Time	Activity
8.00	
8.30	
9.00	
10.00	
10.30	
11.00	
12.00	
13.00	
14.00	
15.30	
17.00	
18.30	
19.00	
20.00	
21.00	
22.00	

Addiction - my favourite definition is the one offered by Dr Gabor Maté on YouTube (I cannot remember the actual film clip) and goes something like this: *'Addiction is anything that gives you temporary relief or happiness but has a long-term negative effect'*. Read that again. Let it sink in.

Addict Voice - it's there, trying to convince us that it's OK to drink. It is our **Ego** and it wants us to fit in and not miss out on anything. Some people give their voice a name: Winnie the Wine Witch, Dementor, Gin Genie, Booze Baron, Stacy, Pennywise ... just know it, recognise it and have a plan for when it comes calling. Because it will.

"You've done so well. Have one to celebrate"

"Go on. Have one. One won't hurt"

"You've not had a drink for a week or two. You can do this. Just drink every now and again"

 I loved this from another of my sober friends, who calls her addict voice Little Bastard:

> 'In the beginning I envisioned this little spoiled Demon/ Gremlin child throwing addiction tantrums. I could see Little Bastard stomping its foot and throwing itself on the ground pounding out its fury. On bad days I would pick that little shit up and spank the hell out of it and send it to the corner. Sounds abusive? ... absolutely! I hated that 'thing' and I was so tired of it trying to convince me that I was better off dead.'

trailgypsey 16th April 2022 500+ days sober

Adrenaline - is a stress hormone that keeps us safe. When we are faced with danger it directs our blood supply to our heart (making it beat faster and stronger), our lungs (so we can adapt our breathing) and our muscles (to give us strength to fight or get the heck outta there!) In so doing it takes the blood supply away from our non-essential areas such as our stomach (butterflies, diarrhoea, nausea, vomiting) and our skin (causing paleness and sweating). It helped our ancestors to hunt and avoid being eaten by their prey. It stops us from walking out in front of traffic. When we see danger, our fire alarm goes off in our brain (**Amygdala**) Dingalingaling! Danger! Danger! Our sprinklers go off, and adrenaline surges into our body creating the fight or flight response (**Anxiety**).

https://healthfully.com/adrenaline-cortisol-4594433.html

Advertising - plants seeds and myths in order to take our money. It does not tell us the truth. I was hooked in by the advertising and fell for it all. I believed that I needed alcohol to celebrate sporting events, holidays and all celebrations. And the frightening thing is, I didn't know the truth about alcohol until I got sober and started researching. Advertising wasn't the only reason I drank, but it was a very big part of it, and alcohol was always at the top of my shopping list. Now, I absolutely love blowing a raspberry, or giving a rude hand signal to the advertisers as I pass the alcohol aisle. It puts the biggest smile on my face, and leaves me feeling in control again.

Affirmations - are positive sayings to help us rewire our way of thinking. Whatever we tell ourselves our mind and body believe. I used to refer to these as **Mantras** but have now discovered these are actually two very different things. Find some positive affirmations that resonate and work for you and use them when you need to. There are lots out there but here are a few to get you going from my sober buddies:

- Play it Forwards/Play the tape forwards
- I make amends to my loved ones everyday just by being sober
- Alcohol never made a good time better
- Don't stop working on sobriety because alcohol will never stop working on you
- I will take my worst day sober over my best drunk day

- One day at a time (ODAAT)
- My craving means I'm further away from where I DON'T want to be
- I never woke up regretting not drinking the night before
- Fun fact: alcohol is poison
- Go do something creative
- Let go and let God
- Move a muscle, change a thought
- There is no such thing as a functional alcoholic, you are a barely functioning alcoholic!
- I never regret waking up sober
- It does not matter how slowly you go, as long as you do not stop - Confucius
- To get to 10 (or wherever) I have to go through days 1,2,3,4 …
- I am either working on being sober or working towards a relapse
- It works if you work it and you are worth it.
- Be kind to yourself always
- Stop looking for happiness in the same place you lost it
- Alcohol steals tomorrow's happiness
- Sobriety delivers what alcohol promises
- Taking small steps, one day at a time, to a happier and healthier future full of endless possibilities
- From every breakdown there is a breakthrough
- Everything happens for a reason
- No sippy, no slippy
- Pour the poison down the sink

- Not another drop, no matter what

https://yogasigns.com/difference-between-mantras-and-affirmations

Alcohol - the alcohol we drink is **Ethanol** and contains formaldehyde, arsenic and multiple cancer-causing chemicals. It is reported to kill over 3 million people a year worldwide. This means that in the first year of Covid, 300,000 more people died from alcohol related disease than from the virus. Alcohol increases the dopamine levels in our brain. It makes us feel good. It gives us confidence. It makes us have fun. Until it doesn't. It is highly addictive and toxic. Gradually, we need more and more to get that buzz and then the effect will just die, and so might we. We become like zombies, the living dead. There is only one way to stop this from happening. Stop drinking. But **Plan and Prepare** and **Work It**.

https://www.who.int/news-room/fact-sheets/detail/alcohol

Alcohol Abuse - alcohol is part of our culture. The majority of us will drink during our lives. But when does it become a problem? I think this is personal, but I like to use Doctor Maté's take on **Addiction** as a guide. Most professionals would probably say alcohol abuse is regular and excessive use of alcohol. Are you drinking a bottle of wine every night or binge drinking every weekend? Have you ever rung in sick because you overdid it the night before? Ever driven when you were over the legal limit? Ever hurt yourself or got into fights when you've been drinking? Ever cancelled plans because you were too drunk or hungover? Time to face it. These are all signs of alcohol abuse. Owning this is our first big step. Take the **FAST** test to discover more:

https://www.gov.uk/government/publications/alcohol-use-screening-tests

Altered/Unhelpful Thinking - there's a lot of this when we quit drinking. When we've blocked it all for so long, it all wants to come out to play. Some of it even encourages us to drink again. Here are some examples of altered thinking:

- Having a gloomy view of the future: How can I never drink again? Meeting friends is going to be awful, what am I going to do with all the time I'm not drinking? Life is going to be dreadful without alcohol, I'm not going to be able to have any fun
- Negative views about how others see us: Everyone will think I have a problem with alcohol, they're going to call me 'alcoholic', they'll think I'm weak because I can't handle my drink (you're not – alcohol is highly addictive), nobody will like the sober me
- Bearing all responsibility: It's all my fault, I'm making this event boring because I'm not drinking, that fight/argument I had 10 years ago (yep, you really are going to go there at times) is all my fault (It's not!)
- Making extreme statements: I ALWAYS upset everyone, I NEVER make people happy, I SHOULD drink and then I'll feel better and everything will be fine (it won't!)

I'm sure we can all relate to this. But what to do with all these thoughts? More under **CBT**.

Ambivalence - it is normal to have lots of mixed feelings about giving up alcohol, and even more once the numbing has stopped. We have our own conflicting views and there will be more from other people. Be prepared, and stay on track. The saying in AA is 'One day at a time' (ODAAT) but, one moment at a time is even better.

Amnesia - is **Memory Loss** which can be related to age, stress, mental health issues (including anxiety and depression), dementia and of course alcohol... What did you do last night?

Amygdala - the most primitive part of our brain formed by two groups of cells, on each side of our brain. It is part of our **Limbic System** and responsible for our emotions, decision making and memory. It is our own personal fire alarm in response to **Fear**, **Anxiety** and **Pain**.

Anaesthetic - alcohol has the same effect on our body and nervous system as anaesthetic and was used for surgery many years ago – but I suspect it caused a lot of vomiting and choking. That's why alcohol numbs and enables us to deal with physical and emotional pain. It reduces our inhibitions, loosens our tongue, and makes us feel so good in the early days. Because WE are not actually there. Our feelings are locked up and our senses numbed. It's easy to deal with stuff when we have anaesthetic inside us, even surgery. And here's the thing, anaesthetic doesn't actually make us unconscious, it just stops the brain from feeling pain and remembering what's happened, just like the date rape drug Ketamine. Alcohol is the life rape drug. If we let it, it will numb us to the point of no return whereby we can see no way out, and wish we were dead. Unfortunately, many of us continue to drink ourselves to death or take our own life. Towards the end of my drinking, I saw it as a slow suicide. I really didn't care if I lived or died. Luckily, I found my way out, and am now so alive that my heart could burst with joy. I want this for each and every one of you.

Anger - *'is the punishment we give to ourselves for someone else's mistake'* Gautama Buddha, but we also punish ourselves for our own mistakes. Anger is a normal human response. There is nothing wrong with anger, it is what we do with it that counts: fights, arguments, breaking things, self-harm. These are our

THE A- Z OF ALCOHOL AND SOBRIETY

behaviours, and separate from the emotion. If we can learn to accept anger, then we can deal with it differently. Anger often has an underlying emotion. It's easier to feel angry than it is to feel hurt, anxious, rejected, unloved, sad etc. Getting sober is like being a detective and an archaeologist all in one. Let's get digging.

Anger Management - is learning new ways to express and let go of this strong emotion. One way of doing this is to write a letter to the person, organisation or thing that is making you feel angry. Get really angry. Pour it all out, read it, cut the letter into pieces and burn it. Then either let it go on the wind or bury it. No-one can actually make us angry; it is we who allow ourselves to feel this way. When we see red, our **Old Brain** kicks in, **Adrenaline** surges and we go into fight mode. 'Take a deep breath and count to 10' really is great advice. By doing this, we allow our **New Brain** time to come into play and deal with things in a more controlled way. And if you can't, go kick a bean bag, beat up a cushion, go for a run or better still - get a punch bag. Exercise and sport are great ways of channelling our anger into something more positive.

Annie Grace - worked in marketing when her drinking career began. Once she recognised this, she found her way to tackle the booze and share this with many others worldwide, with her book *'This Naked Mind: Control Alcohol, Find Freedom, Discover Happiness & Change Your Life'*. She also runs a free, on-line course called The Alcohol Experiment: 30 days without alcohol. You don't have to stop drinking before starting the 30 days, just start from wherever you are right now, even if you are drinking. What a great place to start. Straight away it takes the pressure off and eases the **Fear** caused by the thought of never drinking again.

https://thisnakedmind.com/blog-the-alcohol-experiment/

Antidepressants - increase the available amount of **Serotonin** in between our nerve endings (**Neurons**), which is thought to improve our mood, appetite and sleep. Alcohol decreases our serotonin and this is why it is known as a depressant. Welcome to see-saw land. When we stop drinking, we may not need our current strength of antidepressants. If you are not on them, but feeling depressed, then just stopping alcohol may prevent the need for them. Don't stop or reduce either of these without medical advice, and discuss any signs of mood change with your doctor.

Anxiety - the BIG A! Arghh! Absolutely debilitating. How many of us drink to calm our anxiety and our nerves? We've had a shock – have a brandy. We've had a hard day – crack open a bottle. I honestly forgot what the kettle sounded like. As soon as I put a foot through my front door, I popped a cork or twisted a lid. I can still hear the sound, see the pour and feel the relief of that first sip. And relax. The truth is, it wasn't calming the anxiety, it was stopping the alcohol withdrawal. And then it would cause the chemical imbalances in my body and brain and bring on the **Adrenaline** surges. I was once a great lover of brandy and cola. I drank it in copious amounts, but I had to stop because the **Caffeine** in the cola was causing far too much anxiety and heart palpitations. I then moved onto brandy with fresh orange juice, but guess what? So, I stopped drinking my favourite tipple and moved onto wine and stuck with it for way too many years. Anxiety is normal. It is a warning, and along with adrenaline and **Cortisol**, helps us to keep safe. But our messages can get mixed up and we sense danger when there is none. It is a perceived danger. Usually a thought. That fire alarm gets sensitive and goes off leading to anxiety loops such as this:

Thought: *'I can't handle this. I need to drink'*

Physical response: *Shakes, palpitations, sweats*

Behaviour: *Have a drink.*
Thought: *'That's better'*
Physical response: *Everything calms down*
Behaviour: *Carry on drinking*

Anxiety Management - there are three parts to this: thoughts, physical symptoms and behaviours. Breathing is the most important thing. Sounds simple, but we often hold our breath or breathe too quickly and this brings on physical changes. Practising **Breathing Exercises** will help, but here's what to do in an emergency: make a forced breath out, you will then automatically breath in, control it and slow it. When we are breathing in and out too quickly (hyperventilating) the carbon dioxide and oxygen levels in our blood become imbalanced and lead to tingling and light-headedness. To correct the balance, simply cup your hands over your nose and mouth and slowly breathe in and out. Nothing deep. Just normal breaths. To prevent hyperventilation, know your physical warning signs. Mine's a thump in the chest or a weird spidery feeling over the back of my head. As soon as you get this just breathe. Slow regular breaths. Often, the physical symptoms are the first sign of an anxiety surge or **Panic** attack. If we can control this, it will help us think and behave more rationally and deal with the cause.

Here's an example of what happens if we don't do this:

Physical change: *Thumping in the chest (or whatever your warning sign is)*
Thoughts: *'I'm having a heart attack'*
Behaviour: *Hyperventilating*
Physical change: *Pins and needles and feeling lightheaded*
Thoughts: *'I'm going to die'*
Behaviour: *Calling an ambulance*
Next time it happens, it feels even worse, as we remember how terrifying it was last time.

Here's what happens if we focus on our breathing:

Physical: *Warning sign*
Thoughts: *'I need to breathe'*
Behaviour: *Slow, steady breaths*
Physical: *Our heart and breathing will gradually slow*
Thoughts: *'It's just anxiety. Nothing bad is going to happen'*
Behaviour: *Continue to control the breathing*
Physical: *Everything returns to normal*
Thoughts: *I managed that well. I know what to do in future*

The absolute worst thing that will happen in an anxiety or panic attack is we might faint from not breathing correctly. This will make our breathing return to normal.

Apologise - to yourself and others, but only where it is appropriate. Avoid over-apologising, especially for things that are not your responsibility. An apology goes a long way to paving the way for a happier future, but only if it is not going to cause ourselves or others more hurt.

Appetite - 90% of **Serotonin** is in our **Gut**. We are drinking it away and decreasing our appetite. Along with the vomiting and **Hangovers** from drinking, who wants to eat? When we quit, we crave sugars, and if we're not careful, will replace one addiction with another. I put on 7kg when I quit, craving and eating things I don't usually eat. It's easy to say "Well at least I'm sober" but beware of **Cross-Addiction**.

Appreciation - is enjoying the good we see in others and the things around us. At first, I thought we are not programmed to appreciate things. Instead, we see all the negatives and take things for granted. We even have sayings such as "It's the calm before the storm". When do we ever stop and appreciate the quelling? But then I started thinking about the innocence and fun of childhood, when we were fascinated and appreciated everything around us: the fun of wet and messy play, the awe of noticing all the little grains of sand, the fascination with a blade of grass, and the sheer joy when we found a lady bird (lady bug), caterpillar or worm. If you really want to learn about appreciation, then just go watch kids at work. I now think we start off appreciating things, but experience, time and reprimands get in the way: hurry up, stop dawdling, stop crying, we've got things to do, we're going to be late etc. We start to notice all the bad things, and forget to look for all the good, even though it didn't actually go anywhere. Even on the darkest, dullest day, the sun is actually still there, it's just hiding behind the scenes. We interpret things and take them at face value, forgetting what's underneath and to appreciate what is actually there. And now here we all are, practising, and trying to learn the latest thing of **Mindfulness** and to appreciate things again! And, it would seem, the hardest thing to appreciate is ourselves. I'd like to invite you to just sit for a minute and feel appreciation for yourself. For being here. For showing up. For everything you have done. Everything you are doing and everything you are yet to do.

Arsenic - is actually naturally occurring in rocks and finds its way into our food from the water and soil. It is also manmade and found in pesticides. The amount of arsenic in alcohol depends on how and where the fruit, hops, cereal or vegetables are grown. An independent study of California wines found that some had 4 -5 times more arsenic than the acceptable level for drinking water set by the Environmental Protection Agency. Manufacturers (and especially wine lovers/sellers it would seem) try to convince us that the amount is so low that it is 'Inconsequential' and that other food sources contain more arsenic than wine. It's true, it is found in food (especially rice apparently) but do we eat that food source every single day and to the extremes that we drink alcohol? And, here's the clincher

- alcohol actually stops us being able to process, break down and get rid of the arsenic properly. The short-term effects of arsenic are headache, nausea, vomiting, digestion and stomach problems, bad breath, red skin, muscle cramps and tingling in our fingers and toes. Sound familiar? Repeated exposure to this poison leads to a higher risk of cancer, tumours, diabetes and heart disease. The good news is, it will be out of our body within 48 hours of having it.

https://justwineapp.com/article/what-is-arsenic-should-consumers-be-concerned-about-arsenic-levels-in-wine

https://nationalenvironmentalpro.com/arsenic-in-wine

Aspartame - an artificial sweetener, also marketed as Nutrasweet. It's not technically related to alcohol and sobriety, but the sugar cravings are. Many of us switch to diet and sugar free drinks and soda and, with the sugar tax, aspartame is finding its way into more and more of our foods and drinks. In fact, most of the pubs, cafes and restaurants in the UK now only stock and serve sugar free drinks! Many years ago, I read an article in a Multiple Sclerosis magazine about aspartame and I was horrified by the reports of it causing MS type symptoms and Systemic Lupus. When aspartame reaches body temperature it turns into **Formaldehyde**. I immediately stopped this for myself and my 2-year-old son, and noticed his overactive 'high' symptoms ceased. If he accidentally ingested it, he would say he felt "drunk like mum" and I could see the 'drunken' presentation. The biggest problem was that he loved that feeling. Companies have now changed the name in many product listings to disguise this. But if anything says 'contains a source of phenylalanine' then avoid it like the plague as it has aspartame in it. This has also been linked to cancer and ADHD.

Assertion - I don't know about you, but over the years I have learnt to be passive aggressive and I don't like it. I let people walk all over me and then erupt like a volcano, and for years I drank to subdue it all. Until I didn't. A drunk volcano is far worse than a sober one! When we quit drinking, we start to see all our habits and patterns and realise that we can change and learn to be assertive in a calm and effective way. Not everyone is going to like it as they will no longer be getting their own way all the time. They have tolerated the volcano moments because the doormat ones were far more useful to them. Be prepared for resistance and beware of the saboteurs.

Authenticity - translated from Latin means 'author of your own life'. Now we get to write our own story. Scary and exciting all at the same time. I have spent far too many years letting others write my story for me. I'm not saying my story is a fairy tale, but I'm moving on from the nightmare my life had become. When we are authentic, we can be in control of our happy ever after. Personally, I'm still a work in progress, but I am now aware and I know I have choices.

Autopsy - liver disease, heart disease, cancer, tumours, pulmonary aspiration (vomit in the lungs) and kidney disease are just some of the effects of alcohol causing death. You can go online and see the difference in organs found at autopsy from alcohol. DIY aversion therapy!
https;//www.whereapy.com/downloads/human-body-alcohol-effects-organs

(Vitamin) A - growing up I was told "Eat your carrots, they will help you see in the dark". And this is true. Vitamin A helps with eyesight and skin and helps us fight against infection and illness. As well as in carrots you will find it in green and yellow vegetables, red fruit, dairy, eggs and oily fish. Why do you need to know this? Because alcohol stops absorption and depletes us of vitamins and nutrients.
https://www.nhs.uk/conditions/vitamins-and-minerals/vitamin-a/

AWOL - ever been Absent Without Leave? Know someone who has and the worry that this causes? Alcohol makes us do things we wouldn't usually do when we're thinking straight. It makes us **Vulnerable** and puts us at risk. That aside, alcohol just makes us plain absent in every sense of the word. We are never fully present when we are drinking. Not at the time of drinking, nor for the next 48 hours after. Yep. That's how long it takes to get out of our system. Not the one hour per unit rubbish we are led to believe (this is actually how long it takes to be processed by the liver). Sobriety welcomes you to the wide-awake club!

B

BAL (Blood Alcohol Level) - is the amount of alcohol that is in our bloodstream. It is only now that I stop to ask myself – if there is lots of alcohol in our blood, what is happening to the rest of the blood components that should be flowing freely around our bodies? Alcohol has a big impact on our blood cells including causing our red blood cells to gather closely together, blocking our blood vessels and stopping blood getting to our tissues and organs. Our red blood cells carry oxygen: this clumping together means they cannot carry oxygen freely around our body or to our brain, which can cause us to pass out.
https://healthfully.com/effects-alcohol-oxygen-absorption-8017604.html

Beautiful - this is you. With sobriety we start to see the beauty in everything. Even ourselves. It doesn't come straight away, and it doesn't come naturally. We have to work through a whole load of ugliness to get there. But remember that old saying 'beauty is in the eye of the beholder'? Give yourself and others a chance.

Behaviour - ever done something drunk that you wouldn't dream of doing sober? Freud was a neurologist in the 19th and 20th centuries who created the theory of the **Id** – the little part of our brain that wants it NOW and the only part of our personality that he says is there from birth. It's how babies make their needs known and met. Fortunately, we develop what he called the **Ego** and **Superego** which keep the id in check and our behaviours more socially acceptable. They are the middle men between our id and the world, and make us show up as sensible human beings. Guess what happens to egos when we anaesthetise them? How I love waking up now and remembering everything I did the night before. Not frantically checking my phone and Facebook to see what I've said, who I've called and what I've texted. When we drink, we tend to tell others what we think and blame them for all of our woes. But no-one else can make us feel or behave in a certain way. NO-ONE - only we have the control over how we respond.

Being - as John Lennon famously said *'Life is what happens to you while you're busy making other plans'*. How much do we miss out on by thinking about the past and future, drinking and not being present in the moment? Just being is a wonderful place to be. I find meditation hard. I struggle to focus for long, yet several times a day I notice myself being everywhere else but in the moment. And that's the trick. Just catching yourself, taking a breath and just being. Even for a split second. Just be.

Believe - if we believe that we can achieve, and want it enough, then we will be more likely to succeed. Alcohol fills us with confidence at first and makes us think we can do anything. And then it fills us with self-doubt, self-loathing, anxiety and leaves us feeling worthless and hopeless. Our addict voice will want to keep on telling us these things. As well as our own inner voice, other people's voices may try to sabotage our decision to quit. It happened to me, and I allowed it to delay my quitting for a year. I now realise, if others agreed I had a problem, they would have to admit they had a problem too (and lost their drinking buddy). If we believe quitting is possible then we can do it. Millions of people have proved it is possible and discovered how wonderful sobriety is; they are the best people to get support from. Find a sober **Community** to help, support, encourage and hold the belief for you at the times when you doubt yourself. Post, read, connect, reach out. The I Am Sober app (**IAS**) is the community that helped me.

Belonging - this is something I have struggled with my whole life. I always felt on the outside. The odd one out. I took my first ever puff of a cigarette and drink of a 'snowball' (eggnog) to be like everyone else, fit in and belong. My drinking career began at 14 for this very reason, yet I never really felt I belonged anywhere until I got sober and found a community and friends who fully accept me for who I am; who understand and get it. And realised how many good friends I have always had in my life. And then I heard Brené Brown say 'Belonging is being your authentic self, not changing to please others'. If only I'd known that sooner. That was so freeing. But I am still working on writing my own story.

Beribieri Disease - is caused by Thiamine (vitamin B1) deficiency, one of those nutrients that alcohol knocks out. There are two types:
 Wet: causing issues with the heart, circulation and body organs, leading to pain, confusion, loss of muscle function and sensation, difficulty with walking and talking.
Dry: affecting the nervous system causing a fast heartbeat, feeling breathless and swollen legs.
Hold on a minute. This sounds familiar!
Left untreated, it can also lead to **Wernicke-Korsakoff Syndrome**. If we stop drinking, start eating and take **B Vitamins** then we will be on a much healthier path.
https://byjus.com/biology/beriberi/

Best - are you doing your best? Then that is good enough. No matter where we are on our journey, our best is all we can ask and hope for, and this will change day to day.

Binge Drinking - many of us think we do not have a problem with alcohol as we do not drink every day. The occasional bender is OK right? But the very fact that we cannot stop once we start says there is an issue. And if we do it every weekend, we are just about getting back to a place of mental and physical balance when we go and do it all again. Binge drinking is drinking a lot of alcohol in one go. How many drinks do you think this is? Tip: You will be shocked! The answer can be found under **Units**.

Bite Size Pieces - it helps so much if we can break tasks down. Even our sobriety plan. When we see everything that needs to be done it can be completely overwhelming. Like never drinking again. AA's saying is 'One Day at a Time' for a very good reason. We only ever have this moment, but we are great at causing ourselves stress by thinking ahead, looking back and missing the **Now**. The important thing is not to set ourselves up to fail, or give ourselves so much to do that we avoid the task completely. And then beat ourselves up whilst running around on yet another hamster wheel! If tidying and cleaning the house seems too much, just start with a room. If a room is too much, start with a cupboard. If a cupboard is too much, start with a drawer. If a drawer is too much, just start with the corner …

Blackout - I love my blackout curtains, they really do help me to get a good night's sleep. Unlike the blackouts my brain and body had when I was drinking. When we blackout with alcohol we become our own darkness and cannot remember what we have done. Alcohol interferes with one of our **Memory** chemicals called glutamate and stops our brain from being able to store our memories. We are still awake and moving, we just cannot remember. Heavy amounts of alcohol can reduce the blood and oxygen supply to our brain and the way our cells communicate with each other and could cause us to physically blackout (faint). Many of us will then drift into a fitful sleep. Some of us will not wake up again. Don't become another statistic.

https://pubs.niaaa.nih.gov/publications/arh27-2/186-196.htm

Blame - if we can try not to play the blame game then it really does help. Our actions are ours. Other people's actions are theirs. Sometimes actions have no rhyme or reason. We cannot change it, but if we can accept that only we have control over our response, we can feel free and happy again. Blame leads to anger, hurt and upset and we will mostly never know '**Why**' anyone did what they did. Very often, we don't even know ourselves.

Blind - when we get sober, we realise how blind we have been. But it doesn't help to beat ourselves up about this. The wool was pulled over our eyes for years by those convincing us of the fun and joy of drinking, whilst laughing all the way to the bank with our money. Getting sober is like getting a new pair of glasses, or polishing the lenses, and everything becomes clearer.

Bloating - there are many reasons our tummy can bloat:

- Eating too quickly
- Food intolerances
- Menstruation and pregnancy
- Irritable bowel and bowel diseases
- Eating/drinking fatty, gassy or high fibre foods and drinks (especially alcohol!)
- Dehydration

But bloating could be a sign of a more serious condition (ascites) caused by increased fluid in our tummy lining. This is generally due to liver damage (cirrhosis, cancer or injury) causing the fluids from our blood to leak into our body tissue. Other causes are:

- Cancer – of the stomach, bowel, ovaries, pancreas
- Inflammation of the pancreas
- Kidney disease
- Heart failure

As you read more, you will see alcohol can, and does, cause all of these illnesses.

https://healthjade.net/enlarged-liver/#what_is_a_spleen

https://www.emedicinehealth.com/ascites/article_em.htm

Blood - is made up of a fluid called plasma, red blood cells that contain iron to enable them to carry oxygen around our body and white blood cells that fight off infection and stop the flow of blood when we are bleeding. It is pumped around the body by our **Heart,** taking oxygen and nutrients to every part of us and helping our body to get rid of all the things we no longer need. It does this by a network of blood vessels – our arteries, capillaries and veins. Alcohol can reduce the amount, shape and size of the blood cells that our bodies make, leading to low iron and oxygen levels, infection, bruising and bleeding and in some cases a stroke (a bleed on the brain).

https://pubs.niaaa.nih.gov/publications/arh21-1/42.pdf

Body - no matter what our beliefs, our body is what we have from the beginning of this life journey until the end. It is basically made of fat, water, cells, tissues and bones, all working together through electrical impulses and chemical reactions. Imagine all those components in a test tube. I wonder what would happen if we poured alcohol over it? As it happens, I know just the person to ask …

> '*An experiment we do at school is to put raw liver into a beaker at the beginning of the lesson and cover it with* **Ethanol**. *By the end of the lesson the liver is cooked.*'

Houndless 1st May 2022 - 22 months sober.

Boredom - I thought it was a few months in when I discovered this was a trigger for me. But, on looking back through my I Am Sober posts, I discovered it was only two weeks. On this journey we discover triggers we didn't know were there. It helps to plan for the unexpected and be ready to step in with acceptance, curiosity and a distraction. One of the hardest, but best things, I had to do, was to learn to be with me. I have no time for boredom nowadays and I actually look forward to time alone.

Boring - this is the response some people give when we say we don't drink. Before my partner started chemo, his consultant and nurse encouraged him to have one last blast on the drink. He told the nurse it wasn't an issue as he wasn't particularly bothered and that I didn't drink anyway. Her response was "Boring". Mine was "Not at all, I'm 7 months sober and I've never had so much fun." And, this is the absolute truth. There is absolutely nothing boring about not sitting on the settee every night, half watching TV and then falling asleep there or on the bathroom floor. Get your response ready!

Boundaries - I'm still working on this one. We set boundaries, only for others to push back or ignore them completely. This is human nature. I used to think it was easier to give in and let go because I couldn't be bothered to argue. But I actually got angry and disheartened by the lack of respect, and my own weakness for not standing my ground, and then I would drink to numb these feelings. While getting sober, I really have had to grow up, take lots of deep breaths, stand my ground and fight off the urge to run and hide like a frightened little girl. I am aware that I also give in because I feel sorry for others, want to save them from their own emotions and myself from having to cope with any friction. I now know that feelings are OK, and that others can manage theirs all by themselves. I cannot save the world and am now laughing at my inflated ego for thinking I can. Giving in is not helpful or respectful to others and it sends mixed messages. The anger and frustration still come when I am ignored and boundaries are pushed, but I don't drink, I accept it and then do something about the cause. Someone recently said to me "When it comes to boundaries you have to treat everyone as you would a child. You have to keep on repeating it until it sticks".

Brain - our control centre for everything. It interprets everything we see, hear, feel, smell and touch. It keeps our heart beating and our lungs breathing and everything working as it should be. It is made up of cells, known as **Neurons**, which communicate with each other to send and receive messages to and from every part of our body. Our brain is 60% fat and its main period of development takes place in the last 3 months of pregnancy until we are 24 years old. Alcohol can stop this and actually shrinks and kills off parts of the brain, changing our physical and emotional reactions. It may not be obvious at first, but just think about how all our senses and our logic change when we are drinking. Continue, and the long-term damage will be done. It is for this very reason that withdrawal can feel so rough, and for some, the **Delirium Tremens** will occur. Omega 3 may help to restore some of the fats we have destroyed with alcohol, and Vitamin B12 and a strong vitamin B compound are often prescribed to help restore our **Neural Pathways**. For some, it will be too little too late.

https://www.mentalfloss.com/article/49024/does-drinking-alcohol-kill-brain-cells

Brain Plasticity (Neuroplasticity) - the good news. We can repair and rewire our brain and our nervous system, and this will be the case for most of us. The growth of the brain, its neurons and the nervous system, is how a child learns to walk, talk, eat etc. It was originally thought that these systems then stopped developing and went into decline, but we now know that WE have the power to retrain our neural pathways both physically and emotionally. Repeated actions become **Habits**. We just have to change the habit to make a new one. For a fantastic podcast on this I can thoroughly recommend listening or reading an article by Todd Crafter at www.sobertownpodcast.com If it fires together, it wires together. It completely changed my life. https://www.sobertownpodcast.com/sober-podcast-episodes/ episode-60-fires-together-wires-together

Breakdowns - in communication, the brain, body, mind and life in general. They happen, but for me it helps to repeat my **Affirmations** that from 'every breakdown, there is a breakthrough' and to trust in and learn from the process. If we can accept what is, we will move through it quickly and it won't be as painful. To resist leads to pain, anxiety, anger and upset. And the breakthroughs are wonderful!

Breathing - is life. It controls so much, both physical and emotionally. It keeps all our chemicals balanced in our body leading to wellness and calm. Our breath is something we tend to hold when we are in physical or emotional pain, leading to changes in our blood pressure and oxygen levels and makes us feel quite unwell, especially if we then start to hyperventilate and panic. Breathing is an automatic thing, but it's something we all need to learn to do effectively!

Breathing Exercises - are great to practice for daily calm, health and wellbeing. The more we practice them, the more automatic they become for us to use when we really need them. My favourite is abdominal breathing, great for anxiety, panic, getting in the 'zone' and those with breathing difficulties due to physical illness. For a great example of what we are trying to achieve, watch how a baby breathes, it is actually our natural breathing rhythm but we get out of practice:

- Sit or lay with one hand on your chest and one hand on your tummy and just breathe normally
- Close your eyes and just notice what is happening to your hands as you breathe in and out – when are they moving up and down? The aim of abdominal breathing is for our tummy hand to move and our chest one to be still.
- Breathe in and out through your nose if you can (it doesn't matter if you can't) and with each in- breath focus on filling your tummy with air pushing your hand out and then emptying it so your hand comes back in.
- Take slow steady breaths, it doesn't matter how long for, or if you have gaps in between your in and out breath, just make them calm and regular. I find that focusing on counting and holding for so many seconds puts more pressure on me. We are all individuals and the more we practice this the longer our breaths and gaps will become, to a pace that helps us relax.

Practice this whenever you can, for as long as you can and use it whenever you get the first signs of anxiety, panic or pain. Relax into it and just breathe, slow and steady.

Breathing Issues - I did not know that alcohol affects breathing until my good friend, and sober sister, Pollya advised me of this. She noticed her breathing issues improved when she stopped drinking and looked into this more. As you will see under **BAL**, alcohol impacts on our blood flow and oxygen levels in our blood and body. It is therefore now obvious to me that this will, and does, affect our breathing. Once we know the truth it all slots into place.

https://healthfully.com/effects-alcohol-oxygen-absorption-8017604.html

Brewing - is basically soaking cereal grains in water with yeast and letting it fester and rot. More conservatively known as 'fermentation'.

Buddha - was born Siddhartha Gautama over 2,500 years ago in India. He was a prince who left the palace and all his worldly goods, to try and find an ending to all the suffering that he saw around him. He discovered that the solution was inside of us all, that we can all be happy and find true enlightenment if we tune in and change our way of thinking and behaving. I will mention some of his teachings in this book as they are tried and tested ways of training our mind to gradually find inner peace. A Buddha is someone who has achieved enlightenment, is free from suffering, experiences joy, pleasure and permanent inner peace.

Buddhism - there are many different types around the world but all practice the teachings of the Buddha. Buddhism is not a religion, it is more a spiritual way of being - of change, compassion, transformations and inner peace. Practices include **Meditation, Metta** and **Mindfulness**.

Burdens - a bottle of alcohol may seem light but addiction is the biggest burden we will ever carry. The lies, deceit, anxiety, fear, secrecy, guilt, regret, remorse, insomnia, headaches, depression, anger, frustration, pain and illness. And then we drink some more to block it all out. And it gets heavier and heavier with each waking hour. Until we wish we could just sleep forever. If only I'd known sooner, that by putting that bottle down and working just as hard at sobriety, my life could have been so much happier and lighter. I can't go back but I can go forwards and today I am light and free.

Bus - who's driving yours? Does this idea sound weird? This metaphor really resonated with me during **ACT** (Acceptance and Commitment Therapy). Imagine our life being a bus and we are the driver. The passengers on the bus are people, thoughts, feelings, beliefs etc that we collect in our journey through life and can influence our direction of travel. But one of the profound realisations that I had, was that I wasn't driving my bus, other people were. And because of this, I drank. I made more of a conscious effort to take back the wheel but it was half-hearted until I quit drinking. Now my hands are firmly on the wheel. Others may try to stop me and even eject me from my seat, but I'm heading in my own direction now and choosing my own route. Who's in control of your bus? Remember, it's only us who can allow others into our driving seat.

B Vitamins - are essential for our nerves, heart and blood and help us change food and air into energy. They also help our bodies process alcohol, and are one of the first vitamins to be killed off with regular drinking, causing depression, anaemia, confusion and damage to our nervous system. Most of us who have been drinking for a while are lacking in vitamin B due to alcohol and poor diet. Vitamin B1 and a strong B compound are one of the front-line treatments in clinical settings for alcohol addiction. Research has shown that 80% of heavy drinkers (that's 14 **Units** a week for women and 28 a week for men) do not have enough B1 (Thiamine) which is vital for our brain and nervous system. Lack of this can lead to brain injury, **Dementia**, **Wernicke-Korsakoff's Syndrome** and **Beriberi Disease**. Lack of B12 can also cause damage to our brain and nervous systems and mental health issues such as depression and paranoia. Vitamin B is found in meat, poultry and beans and is usually added to bread, pasta and cereal, but I would always recommend you speak to your doctor about this as you are more than likely to need more than food can provide.

https://pubs.niaaa.nih.gov/publications/arh27-2/134-142.htm

https://healthfully.com/thiamine-alcoholism-5987452.html

https://byjus.com/biology/vitamin-b/

C

Caffeine - increases the **Dopamine** in our brain and gets us buzzing. When we stop alcohol, we stop the buzz that we so desperately want. Many of us become teapots and coffee addicts. Personally, I only have one caffeine a day, the rest is decaf and herbal teas. Caffeine is the only substance in my life that I can moderate. It causes me anxiety, palpitations and several trips to the loo, as it puts pressure on our heart and kidneys. Just like alcohol. This is the reason catheterised people should avoid caffeine and booze. If you do have decaf, make sure it's water-filtered and not stripped with chemicals. And, if you stop suddenly, be prepared to withdraw (headaches, sweats, shakes, bad mood – sound familiar?) I once heard a psychiatrist say that coffee is more foreign to us than heroin/opiates, as it is completely alien to anything naturally occurring in us. Our natural opiates are our **Endorphins**.

Calm - is a sense of peace and wellbeing. To help with this, I recommend checking out the Calm app. You do have to pay a small amount, but it's far less than we would spend on booze. It helps with meditation, relaxation, anxiety, breathing and has bedtime stories for adults to aid sleep.

Cancer - is our body cells growing and reproducing in an uncontrollable manner leading to tumours and illness. The classified cancer risk of alcohol is the same as tobacco and asbestos and every time we drink alcohol, we increase our risk of cancer. Alcohol causes direct scarring and cancer to the mouth, throat, oesophagus (the tube that connects our mouth to our stomach) and liver and is attributed to 20 - 30% of all cases worldwide. Women increase their risk of breast cancer by 30 – 40% with just 2 drinks a day, due to the effects of alcohol on **Oestrogen**. Alcohol has also been linked to cancer of the bowel, pancreas, prostate and skin and a group of Canadian doctors and researchers are campaigning for alcohol to carry cancer warnings.

https://www.ncbi.nlm.nih.gov/pmc/articles/PMC3318874/#1

https://www.verywellhealth.com/types-of-cancer-caused-by-drinking-alcohol-513626

Capacity - is defined by being able to: understand what is being said, remember the information, make an informed choice (even if not a wise one) and communicate that choice/decision. When we drink, we lose a whole lot more than our inhibitions. We lose our right to make choices and decisions about our life in that moment. That's how we ended up in jail. For some of us it will be a physical one, but for many of us the chains of addiction will eventually be on.

https://www.medicalprotection.org/uk/articles/assessing-capacity

Capillaries - are our smallest blood vessels but are vital for the exchange of gases, nutrients and waste in our body. As a general rule, our arteries take nutrients and oxygen to our capillaries and our veins remove carbon dioxide and waste products from them. But alcohol is absorbed from our **Gut** straight into our capillaries and then onto our **Liver** by our veins. Alcohol therefore puts extra pressure on our circulation, raises our blood pressure and can cause our capillaries to burst. Hence the red face and nose, spider veins and **Rosacea** that so many of us get.

https://www.innerbody.com/image_lymp01/card66.html

Care Plan - whilst podcasting one day, I realised how helpful it would be to write a care plan for ourselves when we quit alcohol. It is a big life change and this would really help us to look at the difficulties, what we want to achieve and how. Whilst this is something we need to do for ourselves, it's really important to remember that we do not have to do this all alone and to include everyone and everything we can think of to help us. Here's an example to get you started and then have a go yourself:

What I want to do: *Stop drinking alcohol*
How: Read about what to expect and ways to do it
Decide if I want face to face or online support
Talk to my doctor
Talk to others who have quit for ideas on what to do and what to expect
*Find a sober **Community** to support me and join*
Tell my family and or friends
Who: *Me, doctor, sober community, family and friends*
When: *One week from today I will stop drinking*

What I want to do: *Manage cravings*
How: *Make sure there is no alcohol easily available*
Reach out and talk to people for support
Distract myself; go for a bath, walk, run, watch a movie, play a game
Play it Forwards
*Use **ACT** – become aware, clarify what is happening and turn it around*
Who: *Me, my sober community, friends, family,*
When: *One day at a time*

What I want to do:

How:

Who:

When:

_____

What I want to do:

How:

Who:

When:

Cars - I love King13's analogy of cars in our **Sobertown** podcast; The power In and OF sobriety:

> *'Humans are like cars. The motor is the brain, the chassis is the frame, the body is the body type as we are all different shapes and sizes and we are the driver.*

Sometimes we cannot get going and have malfunctions and sometimes we're in overdrive and on turbo speed and then we crash and burn. Then we become a write- off in our minds. Repairs need to be done but everything can be rebuilt, including us. We need to drive at a cruising speed to achieve the balance in our life and get ultimate pleasure. It's OK sometimes to drive fast and get those bursts of dopamine, and it's also ok to go slow, but cruising is the safest speed because you don't crash and burn'

This has given me a whole new outlook on the concept of pacing and I love it.

Catherine Gray - turned her life around at the age of 33 by stopping drinking and changing her mindset and is the author of one of my favourite **Quit Lit** books '*The Unexpected Joy of Being Sober'*. She has also written:

'*The Unexpected Joy of Being Single'*

'*The Unexpected Joy of the Ordinary'*

'*Sunshine Warm Sober'*

'*Live, Love, Thrive; Inspiring Women's Empowerment'*

https://www.you.co.uk/catherine-gray-how-a-sunset-saved-my-life/

CBT (Cognitive Behavioural Therapy) - works on the understanding that every area in our life impacts on another. If something changes in one area then it will impact on the others. Stopping drinking impacts hugely on this, as does drinking. The difference is, sober we always have the capacity. I love Dr Chris Williams' 5 areas approach to this; situation, thoughts, feelings, behaviours and physical...

Situation: *At a party and everyone is drinking*
Thoughts: *I'm missing out, I don't fit in, a drink will help, I'm sure I can just have one*
Feelings: *Anxious, uncomfortable*
Physical: *Sweaty palms, heart racing, dry mouth, agitation*
Behaviour: *Have a drink*
Physical: *Relief, numb*
Thoughts: *That feels better*
Behaviour: *Drink more*
Physical: *Feel sick, dizzy, pass out*

Next day

Situation: *Wake up on the bathroom floor*
Thoughts: *What did I do that for? What's wrong with me? What did I do last night? Never again*
Feelings: *Embarrassment, shame, worry*
Physical: *Headache, nausea, tired, hung over*
Behaviour: *Checking phone to see what you've done, ringing in sick or going to work but not really performing*

Now maybe go through these five areas and see how it would be if you resisted that one drink.

Situation: At a party and everyone is drinking

Thoughts:

Feelings:

Physical:

Behaviour:

<table>
<tr><td colspan="2" align="center">Next Day</td></tr>
<tr><td>Situation:</td><td></td></tr>
<tr><td>Thoughts:</td><td></td></tr>
<tr><td>Feelings:</td><td></td></tr>
<tr><td>Physical:</td><td></td></tr>
<tr><td>Behaviour:</td><td></td></tr>
</table>

You can find out more about this, and work interactively on your own five areas either on line at Living Life to the Full (llttf.com) or in his workbooks:

'Overcoming Anxiety: A Five Area Approach'

'Overcoming Anxiety, Stress and Panic: A Five Areas Approach'

'Overcoming Depression and Low Mood: A Five Areas Approach'

Celebrate - there are things to celebrate every day but we are mostly used to noticing the not-so-great stuff. Look for the good today. And celebrate. One of the things I really enjoy doing is celebrating my milestones with my sober community. I celebrated each month of my first year with a new charm for my bracelet; the final one being a heart with all the jigsaw pieces fitting together. I no longer feel like the missing piece. I don't wear it. It hangs on the handle of my drawer, a permanent reminder of my achievement and wonderful gift to myself –

sober life.

Chakras - the idea of these originate from India, and means 'wheel of light'. Our chakras are thought to be spinning balls of energy in our body, that regulate and help our body to function. In the western world of science, we know that our bodies work on electricity produced by chemical reactions so it is not too hard to imagine our 7 chakras starting at that point in between our private parts (our root) and working up to our crown. Our chakras are flowing vibrations and each are associated with a different colour, musical note and function.

- Crown Chakra is white or violet, musical note B and is located at the top of our head. It is our spiritual centre, helping with our spiritual connection
- Third Eye Chakra is indigo, note A and is located in-between our eyebrows. It is our mind centre, helping our imagination and intuition (**Gut Instinct**)
- Throat Chakra is blue, note G and unsurprisingly located in our throat. It is our communication centre, helping us to speak our truth and express ourselves
- Heart Chakra is green, note F and located in the centre of our chest - the place we naturally touch when we feel love or emotion. It is our centre for giving and receiving love.
- Solar Plexus is yellow, note E and located above our belly button - in the space between our rib cage. It is our power centre, helping with our confidence and **Self- Esteem**
- Sacral Chakra is orange, note D and located just below our belly button. It is our pleasure centre, helping with our emotions, creative and sexual energy
- Root Chakra is red, note C and located at the base of our spine or the bit between our anus and private parts. It connects us to our body and the world around us,

helping us feel grounded, secure and stable

When our chakras are blocked, it can cause issues with the harmony of our body and mind and vice versa. I am very aware that I feel and hold onto everything in my solar plexus and am currently working on freeing that. Ways to restore and balance our chakras are through meditation, mindfulness, reiki, tai chi, aromatherapy, acupuncture and mindful breathing. For more information and a great chakra meditation go to (117) Chakra Meditation for Balancing and Clearing, Healing Guided Sleep Meditation - YouTube.

https://www.alchemycrystalbowls.co.uk/chakras_notes_singing_bowls/

https://www.7chakracolors.com

Charlie Mackesy - author and illustrator of one of my favourite books 'The Boy, the Mole, the Fox and the Horse'. He is a cartoonist, book illustrator, writer and artist. His work can be seen in many public places in the UK, including Highgate cemetery, prisons and hospitals (I feel a little investigative tour coming on ...)

'Just take this step ... The horizon will look after itself'.

From The Boy, the Mole, the Fox and the Horse 2019.

https://www.charliemackesy.com

Chi - not as in the 22nd letter of the Greek alphabet (first learning of the day for me) but as in the Chinese life force **Qi** (second learning of the day within the space of minutes!) I need to bulk up Q so I'll write about It there!

Children - I always wanted children and when I turned 30, I was pining for them. I would see a baby in a buggy and cry. I got pregnant and stopped drinking as soon as I knew and I didn't really return to my drinking habits until my beautiful baby boy was two. I'd have the occasional binge with friends, but I wasn't a regular drinker then. I had a fear. A fear that my boy was going to die when he was 2. It was so firmly fixed that I even had a date in my mind and had to take the day off of work to protect him (extreme **Altered/Unhelpful Thinking**!) He lived, but I then didn't think he'd make it into teenage years or adulthood. I could not cope with the fear of loss, or the **Anxiety** this caused, and so my drinking began again. In full force. The irony. The fear of losing him made me miss out on so much as I was never fully present. He is now grown up and a daddy and fortunately we have a great relationship. I cannot go back. All I can hope is that by sharing this, others will stop drinking whilst their kids are young. They really do grow up fast. Don't have the regrets I do.

Chocolate - good news. Dark chocolate is good for us. It boosts the feel-good chemicals in our brain; **Serotonin** and **Dopamine**. Just make sure it's over 85% cocoa and don't eat the whole bar in one go!

Choice - we always have a choice. Even if we are kidnapped and chained, we have a choice on how we react and respond. Actually, that's how alcohol made me feel in the end. Kidnapped and chained. We may feel we don't have a choice but we are never as helpless as we feel when it comes to addiction. We do have choices: to continue as things are, continue with change, or leave the situation. Try writing out a for and against list for each option, the answer will become glaringly obvious. Here's an example to get you started and then have a go:

Continue drinking
For: *I can numb, I can forget, I can block pain*
Against*: cost, anxiety, depression, pain, deceit, guilt, dying inside, dying*

Continue drinking with change
For: *I'll give my body a rest by reducing*
Against: *Anxiety around when I can have my next drink, moody, cravings, physical and emotional withdrawal in between drinking times, I will need more and more and be back to full time drinking again*

Stop drinking
For: *save money, health, better mood, work through trauma, be present for others, haves good relationships, less physical and emotional pain, no drinking remorse, regret or guilt, feel happy*
Against: *I will feel my emotions, no comfort blanket, it will be hard work, others won't like it...erm... I can't actually think of anything else...*

Continue Drinking
For:

Against:

Continue Drinking with change
For:

Against:

Stop Drinking
For:

Against:

Circadian Rhythms - comes from the Latin 'Circa Diem' – around the day. And this is what our wonderful body does, 24 hours a day. It keeps everything moving and circulating in rhythm, ticking nicely away, keeping us in time with the night and day. We might not be a great co-ordinator, but our body is. If we'd just leave it to get on with its job! These rhythms are our mental, behavioural and physical adaptations to the night and day. They help with **Sleep**, hormones, eating, and even body temperature. When you drink, do you know what time of day it is? Do you care? Our drunken singing and dancing are not the only things out of tune and time.

https://www.sleepfoundation.org/circadian-rhythm

Cirrhosis - is an advanced stage of **Liver** disease. Our usually smooth liver tissue becomes scarred and bumpy. Many of us are not aware we have cirrhosis as our liver does not become painful until it is quite badly damaged. Feeling generally unwell, nausea, vomiting, tenderness in the upper right side of our tummy, weight loss, spider capillaries above the waist and blotchy red palms are all signs of this. Alcohol causes liver inflammation and disease. Blood tests can show the extent of the damage and the area of the liver affected. By stopping drinking we can slow down, stop and even repair liver damage. If we don't, then this may lead to liver failure and a liver transplant. You can read more about cirrhosis and see a picture of its effect on the liver at Cirrhosis of the liver - British Liver Trust.

https://britishlivertrust.org.uk/information-and-support/living-with-a-liver-condition/liver-conditions/cirrhosis/

Co-dependency - where there is addiction there is often co-dependency, but what is it? A healthy, dependent relationship is where two people rely on each other to equally give support. Co-dependency is unbalanced - one person needs to be wanted and depended on, and the other person is self-gratifying, often entitled, and allows the co-dependant to keep on giving. I decided at an early age not to rely on anyone else for fear of disappointment, desertion and rejection, and not to express myself for fear of repercussions. But this didn't stop me endlessly trying to please and fit in, despite feeling I never achieved this. As an adult, I have continued to people-please, to pander, to tiptoe around, to try and appease and to do anything for a quiet and an easy life and to prevent myself and others from suffering and feeling pain. But I also wanted to be loved and needed, and so started the cycle of co-dependent relationship after relationship. Not just with partners, but with friends, my son, work colleagues and even patients. I would give and they would take, making sure everyone else's needs were met and my own put on the back burner. The bitterness and anger would fester, and the drinking would dampen the flames. Others would also get reliant on my drinking, because the more I drank, the more I didn't care, the more the more I'd say "Yes" and they could do what they liked. At work I became such a martyr that I would go hungry and thirsty and get constipated because I would put my patients' needs first. Even basic self-care was out of the window. In sobriety, boundaries start to change, relationships change (some will end) and there is a lot of pushing back. Be prepared and realise it is ok for others to deal with their own emotions (in fact it is their right), remove yourself from any situation you find uncomfortable, stick to your **Boundaries**, be assertive, be **Self- Centred**, give **Self-Care** and don't forget to breathe!

https://www.mhanational.org/co-dependency

Cognitions - a fancy word for our learning, understanding and thinking. As we've seen, our thoughts can get distorted all on their own, causing worry, stress and anxiety. Add alcohol to the mix and then we really cannot 'think straight'. Many of us drink to stop thinking, but this makes us **Vulnerable** and it only stops the thoughts for a while. When we wake up the next day, the thoughts come back bigger and stronger, with added regret and shame around drinking and the inability to function properly due to a hangover. At first, problems with our cognitions are temporary, but with time drinking can permanently damage our brain and change our cognitions for good, permanently affecting our memory and our ability to learn and understand.

Comfort Blanket - for years many of us have used alcohol as our comfort blanket. To protect us from life and our feelings and keep us emotionally 'safe' whilst putting ourselves and others at great physical and emotional risk. Stopping drinking is like having our comfort blanket whipped away from us and leaving us out in the cold. Another reason why we need our community, to comfort and support us and keep us warm.

Community - this is absolutely key to recovery. If you are considering quitting, or even if you're in full swing, then find a community to support you. This can be face to face or virtual. For me, the I Am Sober app (**IAS**) has been my saviour. Most of our loved ones don't understand what we are going through, and certainly not to the degree that a recovery community does. It is so freeing to belong and be with people who truly get and understand us, accept us for who we are and do not judge us or our choices.

Compassion - we talk a lot about compassion, but what is it really? There is a clue in its Latin version 'Compati' meaning to 'suffer with'. I'm not suggesting we should all suffer, but on the flip side it can help us to find happiness together too. Compassion is walking in someone's footsteps with them, feeling their **Pain**, accepting and **Understanding** how it is for them and helping them to get through it in any way we can. Compassion goes hand-in-hand with **Kindness** and helps us all to feel better about ourselves. As well as being understanding and accepting of others today, try a little self-compassion and accept yourself warts and all. Treat yourself in the way you would wish others to treat you.

https://www.verywellmind.com/what-is-compassion-5207366

Complacency - we can never get complacent in recovery. I now fear ever drinking again but I can never say never. I hope I never drink again, but to say I won't and get cocky about it, could lead to a slippery slope. As time goes on, we don't have to **Work It** every day, but we have to be aware and remember that our **Addict Voice** taps us on the shoulder at the most random of times. Be prepared. We will always be addicts. It is our choice whether we feed and wake up the beast or leave it to sleep.

Compliments - do they make you cringe? Most of us are not good at taking compliments. We seem to think we don't deserve them. Or that we are big headed if we accept them or agree. Try looking at it this way - if someone takes the time to pay us a compliment and we brush it off, then we are actually demeaning and rejecting them. Take it for what it is. Accept it and let it make you both smile. After all, a compliment is a precious gift and it might appear rude if we reject that. Go pay someone a compliment today, and if you receive one, then take it in the vein of which it was delivered. Resist the temptation to respond with "What this old thing?" Instead, try a simple, but gracious "Thank you" and **Smile**.

Computers - just wanted to throw this little analogy in. Our bodies and minds are like computers. Just imagine never cleaning up our hard drive and continually inputting. Our computer is going to crash. And that's just what we do. We overload ourselves, continually taking on more and more and drinking to 'cope' until we just cannot continue. Our body will throw a mental or physical illness at us in order to say "Stop. Enough is enough". I think that illness can be the body's way of getting us to pay attention and clean up our hard drive and reset. Try and listen to your body today.

Confidence - many of us drink to build up our confidence. Pre-drinks were a definite for me before a night out. And if I wasn't getting tipsy quickly enough at the bar, then I could always count on a few shots to do the trick. We think alcohol gives us confidence. But what it actually does, is dampen down our egos and let the uncontrolled **Id** loose. And it anaesthetises and numbs us so we don't feel and we don't therefore care. Alcohol. The confidence booster. Until it isn't. Eventually it completely wipes our confidence out and leaves us an anxious, shrivelling wreck. It is kinda like dealing with the devil. It will give you a few good nights out but secretly rob you of your **Soul**.

Conflict - occurs when two or more people 'know' that they are right. Just imagine, entering a setting or situation with **Curiosity** and being open to change and being wrong. No more arguments or wars. Now wouldn't that be nice? Perhaps we could finally find that elusive world peace.

Conforming - something we are expected to do, otherwise we are seen as 'weird' and just plain 'awkward'. Glennon Doyle writes that we are expected to conform and start to do so around the age of 12. Hmm. Exactly when I had my first drink to try and 'fit in'. As a teenager, I wanted to join the army and train to be a nurse. But my fantasy was to run away with the circus or fairground. Can you imagine? The disgrace and shame of it all. I didn't go into the army, but I did go into nursing and have to admit, I am very grateful and privileged to have met so many wonderful people along the way. At the age of 55 I was forced to retire on medical grounds. That was a hard pill to swallow. I was supposed to work until 67. My husband left but he was supposed to stay 'until death us do part'. I had to sell my house and buy a mobile home but I'm supposed to live in bricks and mortar. Conforming has always gone wrong for me and it's made me miserable, unhappy and depressed. And an addict. I am now sober, spending most of my time in my mobile home by the lake and back with the love of my life. I've got sober, had time to retrain my neural pathways, learnt to walk without falling and eat without choking and I've even learnt to ride a Can Am Ryker, my 3-wheeled motorbike. As **Glennon Doyle** would say "Here I am" (from her book '*Untamed*').

Connection - is key. There is a saying in recovery circles 'connection is the opposite of addiction' and this is so true. Whilst drinking can start out as a social pastime, in the end it mostly becomes a lonely and solitary act. It is a disconnect and makes us withdraw to a point that it is just ourselves and the bottle. It even makes us hide things, sneak around and lie. That's exactly where the alcohol and the addict voice want us. Isolated and easy to manipulate by whispering its sweet nothings. Connection keeps us accountable, in the here and now, supported, loved, valued, cared for and authentic. Connect and write your own story. Don't let the alcohol and addict have control. Connection will make you strong. It will even allow you to show your weaknesses and learn that this is OK.

Control - we all like to be in control. Drugs weren't my thing. I didn't like the thought of taking something, being out of control and not being able to stop it. In my mind, I could stop the amount of alcohol I was drinking and stay in control. Until I couldn't. In the end, like all addictions, it had complete control over me. Do not be fooled, alcohol makes us spiral until we lose our grip and control on everything. Even our emotions. And in my case, my legs and bodily functions. Once addicted, despite not having control of our own life, we try to control others and everything around us. We recognise this more in sobriety, and realise how much we have been resisting in our life and how angry, anxious and frustrated this has made us. The sooner we accept that we cannot control others the easier our lives become. Everyone is walking their own path through life. We just need to stick to our side. We cannot change others, only our response. Try this:

- Put the palms of your hands on the outside of your thighs
- Raise your arms sideways up to shoulder height
- Twist from the waist left to right.

That is your area of control. Nobody else's. That's why we don't like it when people invade our space without invitation. Anything outside of that area is beyond your control. Just like in a **Hula Hoop**.

Cortisol - is our stress hormone. It stimulates that fire alarm that causes **Anxiety** symptoms. It helps regulate our sleep, blood pressure, blood sugar and reduce inflammation. It also gives us an energy boost when we need it to help us deal with **Stress**. It is similar to **Adrenaline** and is part of our fight/ flight/ freeze response. Cortisol is not as reactive though and takes longer to settle down after the event. Whilst it is positive (like adrenaline) the down side includes panic, anxiety and altered thinking so **Breathing Exercises** and **CBT** can help us to control this.

https://healthfully.com/adrenaline-cortisol-4594433.html

Courage - it takes a lot of courage to get sober. Especially in a world where drinking is normal and when we quit, we are seen to be the one with a 'problem'. This is not so; it is just the perception of others. Just like Dorothy's lion, we all have the courage we need if we just look inside. When we get sober, our security blanket has been pulled from us and we feel completely exposed. That is why it's important to plan our sobriety, connect and share. It is amazing how with each hurdle, our courage grows and we get stronger and stronger each day.

Craig Beck - author of *'Alcohol Lied to me: The Intelligent Way to Escape Alcohol Addiction'*. What I took from this is that drinking only pushes the pause button. When we wake up, everything is still as it was and we then have a hangover too. I want to continue pressing play. I also used his suggested supplements to support quitting alcohol. See under **Vitamins**.

Cravings - the yearning and the longing for something that we think will make this moment all OK. Little Shop of Horrors comes to mind as I am typing, *'Feed me Seymour, feed me now!'* A plant that started out all sweet and innocent but ended up as a giant monster feeding on human blood. Giving into a craving does not make anything better, it just fuels the beast to make it bigger and stronger. Distract, divert, **ACT**, breathe and use whatever is in your **Tool Box**.

Create - a new life for yourself and a new you. Create a new future by living in today. Just for today do not drink. Just for today, get in touch with your feelings. Just for today, start to understand who you are. Just for today, think of your direction. Just for today, start to create your future.

Creative - at the end of my drinking all my creativity had gone. I didn't want to write, sing or dance. I did learn to knit, to try and keep my hands flexible, but every morning I'd have to pick up all the dropped stitches. Every afternoon and night were the same. Drinking wine, knitting, watching Netflix and falling asleep on the settee. When we quit alcohol, activity is right up there with **Connection**. Keeping ourselves busy, doing whatever to distract ourselves from the booze, is really key. And then gradually, our **Confidence** grows and we start to enjoy what we are doing. Creativity isn't necessarily about hobbies and being handy, we can be creative with our mind too, especially if we start thinking outside of the box. It is great to become childlike again, to be mindful and enjoy the grass, sand and water and to be creative with time, dance and song. Just being creative with life. It really is ours for the taking. It may sound or feel impossible at first but, I assure you, once your creative juices start flowing, there'll be no stopping you.

Cross-Addiction - is when we replace one addiction with another. It can happen immediately or years later. It stands to reason that when we stop one **Dopamine** stimulating substance, we are going to crave another and want to satisfy our reward system by using something else. For me, it is chocolate and sugar. Right back to my childhood, when even the dentist would give us a lollipop for being good in the surgery! Fall over, have a sweet. Get upset, have a sweet. When I was nursing, if I'd had a particularly heavy session with a patient, I'd go straight to the corner shop and buy lots of childhood sweets so I could stop being an adult for a while. When I gave up drinking, I replaced my dopamine stimulant and sugars with sweets and chocolate. I'm lactose intolerant so the physical pain created from the chocolate distracts me from the emotional pain. Refined sugars also increase pain for me. I gained 7kg and I'm now working on my sugar addiction, but am aware that this is also a form of **Self-Harm** and a way of diverting myself from emotional pain. I refer back to Gabor Mate's on **Addiction** – "Addiction is anything that gives you temporary relief or happiness but has a long-term negative effect".

https://www.psychologytoday.com/us/blog/addiction-and-recovery/201904/the-challenge-cross-addiction

Curiosity - a good friend once told me 'Stay curious' and it really is sound advice. Even when the very worst happens, when it feels as though our world is crumbling around us, it really helps to stay curious. Curiosity helps us to learn, understand and work things out and definitely helps us to **ACT** (become aware, clarify and turn it around). It can also help with **Altered/ Unhelpful Thinking**, **CBT** and other techniques you will read about in this book. Curiosity can help us just be. To just sit with it. Or to hand it over to the universe and **Trust in the Process**.

C Vitamin (Ascorbic Acid) - keeps our bones, teeth, tissue, muscles, skin, and capillaries healthy and helps us to absorb iron. As with most nutrients, drinking alcohol can deplete vitamin C. Craig Beck recommends taking 1000mg a day when we quit drinking, but you should avoid this if you have kidney disease. It is best taken in two separate 500mg doses. Smoking will stop it working effectively. As with anything we put into our body, it has side effects; heartburn and stomach upsets are the most common but there are more serious side effects such as swelling, difficulty breathing, joint pain and fever for which you should seek urgent medical help. If you prefer, you can increase your intake with foods; citrus fruits, leafy vegetables, and tomatoes are all high in C Vitamin.

https://www.everydayhealth.com/drugs/ascorbic-acid#

D

Dancing - One of the best parts of my journey was when my sober buddy Lilo (I Am Sober resident DJ) suggested a tune, that we put a tea towel on our heads and danced around the kitchen. Well, I took this literally, and it was amazing. I started dancing at the age of 2 and continued in lessons until 18. Dancing was my go-to. I felt free and alive and I loved it. Music and dancing had been a big part of my life, until the vertigo and brain-not-working-with-the-body stuff started. I cannot dance in the way I used to, so I stopped. And I stopped listening to my music. It was so lovely to do this again. I recognise that I still avoid this, so I'm going to stop writing now, put on some tunes and have a jig around in my chair. Come join me if you want - put on some tunes, turn up the volume and jig. Tea towel on the head is optional.

Dancing Around the Subject - the elephant in the room. We see it, we don't want to confront it, we feel uneasy, we drink to ignore it and avoid it. But that elephant isn't going anywhere, it's still right there, and when we wake up the next day the uneasiness builds. If we could just find the strength to confront it, but the fear of repercussions puts many of us off. All the negative responses of our past accumulated and built up in **Fear**.

The fear of hurt, rejection, invalidation. Sober me recognises the elephant in the room. I see it there large as life and I no longer numb it. I feel it in my **Solar Plexus**, I take a deep breath. I hold it. And hold it. And hold it. See, we are all work in progress. I will get there one day. Recognising what we need to work on is our strength. Rome was not built in a day and we have a lifetime of foundations to unpick.

Dandelions - this is one of my favourite parables, a traditional Sufi tale, often used in therapy groups. This is my take on it:

There was a man (I'm going to call him Arthur) who loved his lawn. He wanted to have the greenest, most wonderful lawn in town. Arthur spent hours planting and watering and weeding it and all his neighbours complimented him on it. But, one day, he found a few dandelions in it. He pulled them up, but a few days later they came back again. He sprayed them with weed killer the shopkeeper had recommended. This worked for a few days, but eventually the dandelions were back again. Arthur was not happy. He talked to his neighbours, who recommended a different type of grass which was denser and more dandelion-resistant. Arthur replaced his lawn at great expense and was happy for a while. But then the dandelions came back and he became frustrated and angry. He started to blame others and got all his neighbours to replace their lawns with dandelion-resistant grass too. This still didn't work. Finally, he wrote to the Department of Agriculture for some expert guidance and few weeks later he had their response:

"After much discussion and debate, we have decided that the answer to your problem is easy. You must simply learn to love the dandelions"

If we can learn to love all parts of ourselves and the world, even the parts that we see as unpleasant, then life itself will be easier, kinder and fuller of love.

Dash - think about gravestones. On them is a little dedication and the date we are born and the date we die. In-between these dates, is a dash. That dash is your life. Go live it.

Death - like many, I interpreted some **Quit Lit** to mean that alcohol is the third leading cause of death in the world. During my own research, I have discovered that it is actually the third leading cause of preventable death in the USA. But the impact of alcohol on our health and life expectancy is still pretty scary (see **Statistics** for more information). The following is a list of the top 10 causes of death worldwide, taken from the World Health Organisation (**WHO**) website published in 2019:

- Heart Disease caused by poor blood supply
- Stroke
- Chronic Obstructive Pulmonary Disease (COPD) – lung conditions causing breathing problems
- Lower respiratory infections such as Pneumonia
- Neonatal Conditions – first 28 days of life
- Airway and lung cancers
- Alzheimer's disease and other dementias
- Diarrhoeal Diseases
- Diabetes
- Kidney disease

Alcohol can play a hand in all of these causes.

needtoknow.nas.edu/id/threats/global-killers

https://www.ons.gov.uk/peoplepopulationandcommunity/

healthandsocialcare/causesofdeath/articles/
leadingcausesofdeathuk/2001to2018

https://www.who.int/news-room/fact-sheets/detail/the-top-10-causes-of-death

Debt - addiction of any kind, often leaves us in debt. It will not go away or get better on its own but many lenders will support us, as long as we just talk to them. The longer we put it off, the worse it will get. There are also charities out there that help with debt management. In the UK, the one most creditors will ask if you are working with is Step Change. This is a free service and they will help you with budget plans and even contact the lenders to set up a repayment plan. You DO NOT need to pay for a debt management service or plan in the UK.

https://www.stepchange.org/?channel=ppc&gclid

Deceit - towards the end of my drinking days, I would lie to purposely deceive others about how much I was drinking. I would lie about how many I'd had and about the time of day I'd started drinking. I'd drink wine out of a mug or put a drop of squash in it to change the colour. When I went to fill up glasses in company, I'd down some whilst I was out of sight so everyone thought I was drinking the same as them. But the biggest person I was deceiving was myself. Drinking is such hard work. Admitting we have a problem makes life so much easier.

Dehydration - our body needs water to keep us hydrated and functioning as we should. Alcohol is a diuretic which makes us pee lots and get rid of salt, water and nutrients that our body actually needs for us to stay healthy, hydrated and fully functioning. Excess loss of these leads to us becoming dehydrated, causing dry and inelastic skin, headaches, bad breath, heart and blood pressure problems and just feeling generally poo. A bit like a hangover really.

Delirium Tremens (DTs) - are a severe form of alcohol withdrawal which approximately 5% of us will get when we stop drinking. This is another reason for seeking medical support, or at the very least, **Reduce Gradually** our daily intake of alcohol before quitting completely. We are more likely to get DTs if we are drinking heavily and are in poor health. Let's face it, most of us are in poor health towards the end of our drinking career. Poor sleep, poor nutrition and dehydration do not contribute to good health. Agitation, confusion, shaking, sweating, vomiting, hallucinations and seizures are all signs of severe alcohol withdrawal and can lead to vomit in the lungs and airways and death. For this very reason, some of us need a medical **Detox**.

https://americanaddictioncenters.org/alcoholism-treatment/delirium-tremens-symptoms-and-treatment

Delusions - in westernised medical terms, these are firmly fixed thoughts in our mind which no amount of argument or reasoning can shift. We can get paranoid delusions and think that people are after us or spying on us (not too difficult to believe this nowadays I know!), or that someone is trying to poison us. We can have delusions of poverty and think that we are useless and not worthy, or become grandiose and think we are rich, or much grander than we are: "She's got ideas above her station that one". We can think that our heart is not there, or that we have no stomach or that we have actually died and are living in the twilight zone. Does any of this sound familiar? We are all prone to these type of thoughts at times, but can often argue the case and rationalise that they are not true or real. When we cannot, and neither can others convince us, then this is a delusion. Unless you have a smartphone, tablet or computer of course!

Dementia - is due to our brain cells dying causing problems with memory, mood, thinking and eventually physical functioning. There are many different types including, Alzheimer's, Korsakoff's and Lewy body. Alcohol can directly and indirectly cause death of brain cells, memory problems and dementia.

https://www.alzheimers.org.uk/about-dementia/risk-factors-and-prevention/alcohol

https://www.addictiongroup.org/alcohol/effects/dementia

Dependency - is alcohol the key focus of your life? You may initially respond with a resounding 'No' But just think about it for a minute. If someone suggests a day out to the dinosaur park with the kids, is your first thought "Can I get alcohol there?" (Sadly, yes you can!) Do you research or take alcohol with you just in case it's not available? If you're going on a picnic do bottles or cans go in with the food? When you finish work do you rush to the pub, or home to open the bottle? Do you find it hard to stop drinking once you start? Do you have friendships based solely on drinking? This may sound familiar to lots of us, but these are the first signs of alcohol dependence. Continue and you will become fully dependent if you are not already there. I knew I had to stop when I awoke at the cursed 3am and got up for a cup of tea and found wine in the fridge. I couldn't possibly throw it out. Following this I had one final binge, but it was so bad, that I came away with the final signs of dependency; sweating, shaking and nausea. Oh, and terrible pain in my stomach and beneath my right ribs. Liver pain. The only time we get liver pain is when it is that swollen that it presses on other areas of our body. That really did kick my arse into shape.

Depression - this is so much more than low mood. If we have a persistent low mood for more than two weeks, with loss of interest, motivation, appetite and disturbed sleep, then we are likely to have a clinical depression and will need to seek medical help. Although, this does depend on our situation – if we have just lost a loved one for example, then it is quite normal to feel this way. Depression is thought to be due to low serotonin levels in the brain and antidepressants could possibly help with this, but so can CBT, talking, therapy, sunlight, exercise, activity scheduling and quitting drinking.

https://www.nhs.uk/mental-health/conditions/clinical-depression/symptoms

Deserving - alcohol robs us of our self-esteem, our self-worth and our being. If not the alcohol directly, then from the remorse, guilt, deceit and isolation. We beat ourselves up on a regular basis, to a point that we feel we do not even deserve to be alive. But we deserve the same as everyone else. We are not less, we are not more, and if we can allow ourselves to just be, then we will see that we are just as deserving as everyone else. You deserve to be alive and you deserve to live. Not just in the heart beating, breathing sense, but to actually be alive and live. Sobriety gives us that. We are all deserving. Alcohol and addiction are not. They are unjust.

Destiny - what is our destiny? Is it pre-planned or do we make it up as we go? Personally, I think it's a bit of both, that we have a blueprint, with turns along the way, that we can choose to take or ignore. I would not wish addiction on anyone, but I am pleased that alcohol got its hold on me, in the same way that I am grateful for my mental and physical health experiences. They have made me who I am today. I have met so many wonderful people, learned so much and hopefully helped others because of it. Are you at a crossroads or junction? Are there turns you could take? Do you want to carry on the road of drinking and addiction, or turn off and find a brighter, happier and healthier path? I'm not going to lie, it's just as bumpy and winding at times, but we soon learn to ride and smooth the bumps rather than numbing them and pretending they are not there.

Detox - when we stop taking something our body has become reliant on, then we go through a period of detoxification. This varies, depending on how much we have been taking, genetics and our health. Stopping drinking for some can be very dangerous as it can lead to seizures and death. I would always encourage everyone who is stopping alcohol, to discuss this with their medical practitioner first. Some of us need a medical detox in hospital, whilst others can do this safely at home, either with or without medication. We are all different, and medical advice is always recommended. But I didn't practise what I preach, so I get it if you don't want to do this. If you are physically dependent on alcohol (i.e., you need a drink to stop shaking and to be able to function each day) do NOT stop drinking dead. If you cannot talk to someone or access a medical detox, then **Reduce Gradually** the amount you drink each day until you are at a stage where you can then stop.

Diabetes - is caused by lack of insulin in our body leading to unstable amounts of sugars in our blood. Insulin is made in the **Pancreas**, and helps sugar enter our muscles for energy. Diabetes can be caused by damage and inflammation to our pancreas, pancreatic cancer, poor diet, obesity and pregnancy. Treatments vary from changes in diet, tablets and injecting insulin; dependent on the type and cause. Left untreated, this can be very dangerous and lead to coma and death. Small amounts of alcohol increase the sugars in our blood and larger amounts decrease them – making diabetes unstable. Early signs of diabetes are an increase in thirst and peeing, tiredness and unexplained weight loss.

https://www.webmd.com/diabetes/drinking-alcohol#

https://www.healthline.com/health/diabetes-and-pancrea<u>s</u>

Disability - the inability for our body and mind to do as they should, due to restriction. That's my definition anyway! That restriction could be anything; physical injury, our thoughts, our mindset, illness, disease, restraints, chemicals, alcohol …

Disconnection - can be a good thing. What? After all that I said about connection! But sometimes, we are so busy helping others with their life and sobriety, that we forget to connect with ourselves. It is good to turn everything off, hunker down, and learn to be with ourselves every now and again. Too much connection can lead to one of my favourite pastimes – avoidance! (I've lost count of the number of times I've said to my communities "I'm going to be absent for a while as I really need to focus on my book"). I did do a 72-hour phone silence though, which was very enlightening. You can listen to my experience on my **YouTube** channel - (90) Off grid - Diary of 72 hours without a phone/internet - YouTube.

Disease - something that stops our body, or parts of it, working in the way that we expect. I hesitate to use the word 'normal' as we are all different. But when it comes to medical expectations there are general guidelines. The body is expected to do what it is designed to do. Now for the crunch. Is alcohol addiction a disease? Many believe it to be so. We know it causes disease, illness and disability, but is it a disease in itself? Does it really matter? Some feel that referring to it as a disease = being unaccountable and creates an "it's not my fault" mentality. But whether we are addicted, disabled or have a disease, we always have something to bring to the table. There is always something for us to be accountable and responsible for. Even if it's just changing our **Mindset** (which actually, is a huge thing).

Disorder - how confusing! Let's throw it all up into the air! That's basically disorder, anything that interrupts the general running of things. And when alcohol is involved, we can probably add a bit of chaos in as well. When we think of mental health issues and brain disorders, we think of disruptions in our thinking, mood, behaviour, perceptions, interactions, emotions, actions. There's a reason it's called 'Drunk and Disorderly'.

Distraction - I used alcohol for this for way too long - to numb and distract from physical and emotional pain, boredom and loneliness. What is it/was it distracting you from? If you're just starting out, then it's important to identify this so you can be prepared. Listening to a podcast I heard something along the lines of 'Addiction is always there in the corner, doing its press ups and getting ready to flex its muscles. You've got to be ready'. This is so true. Once we quit, we need activities to distract us from our addict voice, so armour up. Exercise, meditation, eating (oh boy did I eat – get healthy snacks in), writing, reading, posting and reaching out, connecting, **Playing it Forwards**, hobbies. Anything you can do to get through, until you get to the stage where you can simply just laugh and tell it to f*** right off!

Done - I've often heard people refer to those with a year's sobriety or more as "Done". But I'm gonna tell you loud and clear, we are never done. We have to work at it every day. But don't panic. Just think of all the work you put into drinking:

When can I get away with my first drink?

Can I rush through this last bit of work to get home early?

If we go there, can I get alcohol? I better check. If not, I'll need to buy some and sneak it in.

What am I going to do/say if I get caught?

And on and on and on. If we put as much effort into our sobriety as we do our drinking, then we are onto a winner. It does get easier; we get to a point where we are thinking about sobriety everyday instead of drinking. And with change we develop and grow our emotions, attitude, reactions, memories and feelings. I have re-written many headings as I have physically, spiritually and emotionally evolved, and I suspect that I could keep on updating until the end of my days but there has to be a cut off and publishing point!

Dopamine - is a reward chemical in our brain that gets a hit and increases when we drink alcohol and caffeine, take drugs, have sex and eat chocolate (to name but a few). It gives us a thrill and a buzz. And then our dopamine drops, hard and fast, to a level lower than it was originally. That's why the aftermath is referred to as 'the come down'. When we stop alcohol, our brain still wants that hit and this is where **Cross-Addiction** can kick in.

https://www.drugrehab.com/addiction/alcohol/alcoholism/alcohol-and-dopamine

Dragonflies - I looked up the meaning when I bought my 9-month dragonfly charm; change and transformation, flexibility, courage and living in the here and now. Perfect little summary of the tools that got me to that milestone (and onwards).

Drama Triangles - occur when people react to a situation in these 3 roles:

- Rescuer who wants to save everyone and everything
- Persecutor who purposefully annoys and attacks others
- Victim whom the Persecutor is attacking

The roles can change as the situation goes on and can lead to despair and upset for everyone involved. If one of us can step outside of the triangle and not get hooked in, the situation will settle and not spiral out of control. You might find it helpful to just recognise this to help you resolve any ongoing feelings or difficulties.

Dreams - hold onto your zzzz's because the dreams ramp up big time when we stop drinking. We can wake up with sweats, palpitations, feeling anxious and holding onto every moment of our dreams. This is because the **Amygdala** (our fire alarm) is very active during sleep. Take a deep breath and focus on the now, but deal with any issues raised and know that these will settle with time. Dreams help us process our thoughts, feelings, trauma and situations without the logic of daytime awareness. They go with the flow. They help us to clear memories, keep important ones and make way for new ones. Our dreams can be our very own therapist and also get our creative juices flowing. I expect you can think of a few movies or books that probably came from the author's dreams!

Drinkaware - is a great website in the UK with information, advice and support. I used the phone app with a day counter for a couple of years, along with a drink measure cup they supply. You can also set an alarm on the app to alert you when you are getting near a trigger pub. I did use this, but often still went in. It did help me to **Moderate** and give up for weeks at a time and, a combination of this and the **IAS** community, helped me realise that I just cannot moderate long term. I'm an all or nothing kinda girl.

https://www.drinkaware.co.uk

Drinking - is hard bloody work when the addiction takes hold.

Yes, it's fun at first. I'm not going to deny that. Drinking can be fun. We've all had some great nights out with friends. It boosts our confidence, makes us see the funny side of things and makes us laugh harder and longer until our sides hurt. But it also causes some very messy nights. Have you ever injured yourself when you've been drinking? How many fights are caused by alcohol? How many suicides? Eventually, drinking can become a lonely, sad and isolated habit where ALL the fun has gone from every aspect of our life. This is something I wrote on my Wordpress blog 10 months before I quit:

> *'So, my whole blog is around Living Positively with Fibromyalgia. But I have slumped. And felt it equally important to share.*
>
> *For the last 10 days I have got up but not gone out. I have done some of my daily maintenance plan but not all. Today I went out with my rollator for a stroll. The motivation? To buy brandy - the worst thing for fibro. My alcohol consumption has been going up and up and today on my walk I asked myself why. Is it because I feel I am dying inside? I am once again trying to numb or maybe speed along the process? I even dreamt last night about all my physical tests being fine, apart from my liver levels. A physical answer to a physical cause. I don't think I could ever take an assertive act to end my life now, but I am not belittling those that do. But maybe I could take a slow way out. Have I not been doing that subtly for 20 years anyway? I feel selfish for saying this, especially when people are out there dying when they don't want to. But aren't we all dying slowly anyway?'*

Thankfully, I no longer recognise that person.

Driving - ever driven with the fear of getting pulled over? Knowing that you are over the legal limit but you just have to get to where you are going? Knowing, but not really caring, that you are not fit to drive because you are too drunk to worry? I am horrified when I think back to my selfishness. The risk to others and leaving Jack without a mum, which was another of my fears - I had to stay alive until Jack could look after himself. The anxiety of this was another thing that fuelled my blocking and numbing and I could have died. Crazy huh? It is so wonderful now being able to get in my car at any time without stress or fear and not living with regret. I cannot change the past. I do not dwell on it. I did wrong. I've thought about it whilst typing this section but now I have to let it go. In 2019, in the UK alone, at least 7,800 people were killed or injured on the roads, whereby one or more drivers had over the legal drink drive limit of **BAL** (80 milligrams per 100 millilitres in the UK, with the exception of Scotland where it is just 50 milligrams).

https://www.gov.uk/drink-drive-limit

https://www.gov.uk/government/statistics/reported-road-casualties-in-great-britain-final-estimates-involving-illegal-alcohol-levels-2019

Drunk - why do we get drunk? I don't mean why do we do it to ourselves time and time again, I mean why does our body react in the way it does? And why does the same amount of alcohol make us drunk sometimes and not others? Alcohol can dissolve in water and therefore some of it enters our blood stream directly from our bowel without even seeing our liver. It is taken straight to our brain, where it slows everything down leading to stumbling, slurring and memory loss. Drinking on an empty stomach really does make alcohol go to our head much quicker than if we have eaten. It can also depend on how hydrated we are, so drinking lots of water can also slow down the effects of alcohol.

https://www.howitworksdaily.com/why-do-we-get-drunk

Dry Drunk - I heard this term a lot when I first started out, but it took me a while to figure out its meaning. Basically, it means quitting the booze but not working on our recovery. When we do this, we continually feel as though we are missing out, leading to misery and pain. When we **Work It**, read, write, listen and connect, recognise and work through our emotions, learn the truth about alcohol and get the right support, our journey is far less painful.

D Vitamin - is great for calcium and helps with our teeth, bones and muscles. Our biggest source is through sunlight and we need at least 30 minutes of unfiltered sun a day on our skin, but remember to put your sun cream on after this. It's reported that 50% of people in the UK are lacking in vitamin D during the winter months, as the sun doesn't give off enough UVB rays for our bodies to make it. But I like to remember that the sun is always there, and every little bit helps. Lack of vitamin D can lead to joint pain, bone thinning and deformities such as rickets. It is added to foods such as cereals and is naturally occurring in oily fish, meat and eggs. The daily recommended dose is 600mg and I would not advise you to take more than this as too much can lead to overdose and nausea, vomiting, leg cramps, dry mouth, weight loss, thirst and diarrhoea.

https://www.nhs.uk/conditions/vitamins-and-minerals/vitamin-d

https://news.sky.com/story/amp/vitamin-d-overdose-warning-after-man-admitted-to-hospital-for-excessive-intake-12646798

Dysfunctional - what is dysfunctional? Society has a way of telling us what should and shouldn't be. But we are who we are. Try not to view this as to where you are in relation to the world and its inhabitants. You are you and you function in the way that you do. Anything that interferes with the way YOU usually function is dysfunctional. I think we can give alcohol a great big tick on this one.

E

Eating - is what keeps us alive. When we drink alcohol, we can often find ourselves overeating or not eating at all. When I was calorie counting, I would eat less so that I could still drink. I did the keto diet because I had read that you could still drink clear spirits and wine on it. I ate organic food because it's better for you, but would continue to pour poison down my throat. I was so excited when I found organic wine. I didn't know then of all the poison in it. Food is our nourishment and our fuel; it keeps us healthy and alive. Alcohol kills us. Yet in addiction we choose the booze over the food every time. It is so lovely to be eating again and actually tasting my food. It really helps if we eat mindfully, no TV or distraction, sitting at a table, eating slowly and chewing our food well. Our mouth is where we start breaking our food down and this is very basic, very simple, but essential **Self-Care**. Eating slowly also allows us to realise when we are full and not overeat. If I catch myself comfort eating, I ask myself this: Am I really hungry? If yes, what is it I really want to eat, and then I have it. If I'm not hungry, then what is it I actually want? It's usually a hug, love or solitude. So, I find my own space, hug myself, rub my arms and remember how great I'm doing.

Eckhart Tolle - is a spiritual teacher and author with a lived experience of mental health issues and homelessness. He focuses very much on living in the present and his book *'The Power of Now: A Guide To Spiritual Enlightenment'* really helped me overcome my addict voice. You can listen to this for free on YouTube.

Ego - one of Freud's theories of the mind. Freud actually called it "Das Ich" – the I. It is realistic and organised and mediates between the part of us that wants something right now (our **Id**) and our more rational side (**Superego**) which is trying to keep us heading in the right direction. This is the part of us responsible for our **Self-Esteem**, confidence and jealousy. It also compares us to others and fills us with the fear of missing out (**FOMO**). It is the little trickster part that tells us that "Just one drink will be OK" when deep down we know that it won't. It is our gossiping **Mind** and constantly trying to confuse us with things that are not actually real. Our ego is the view we have of ourselves and what we build around us to make us feel safe. This is who we think we are and what life has made us, but who are we truly? Some say we can only find this in the silence of meditation. This section may become clearer if you now read about the id and the superego.

Egotistical - when it all becomes about 'me, me, me, me'. We can all get like this, especially when drinking and numbing the rational side of ourselves. This is when we can take on the world and have an increased sense of importance and rights. But of course, drink can make us go the other way too. It's a fine tightrope we walk.

EMDR (Eye Movement Desensitisation and Reprocessing) - is a therapy used for **Trauma**, especially when we have flashbacks and are very stuck in our past experiences. This therapy involves recalling the memory whilst moving our eyes from side to side, a bit like when our sleeping brain is processing our day in dream state. It is thought that, by distracting the brain, it can lower the intensity of our memories and help us to change the way we feel about it.

https://emdrassociation.org.uk/a-inique-and-powerful-therapy/emdr-the-basics

Emotions - are there to tell us something. After years of numbing, it is a bit of a discovery to find out what they are, let alone what they are telling us! Emotions automatically arise from inside of us as opposed to our **Feelings** which are our reactions. Emotions are timely. They help us through. It is not easy to hide our emotions and actually, in so doing, this can lead to physical and mental health issues. Allow them to come without judgement and let them just be.

Empath - many of us are empaths, with so much **Empathy** that we almost want to live the life of others with them, jumping in, making it easier and trying to take their pain and suffering away. Sounds pretty intense and overpowering now I write this. And it is, for all parties concerned. In fact, it is often too much for us empaths, so we open another bottle and make it all go away. Or, we could just get sober and recognise what we are doing. We are not Atlas: We do not have the world on our shoulders. Others' troubles are not ours to bear, and we are actually doing them a disservice by trying to shoulder all the blame and suffering.

https://www.healthline.com/health/what-is-an-empath#high-sensitivity

Empathy - is our ability to understand and relate to someone else's feelings and emotions. It's putting ourselves in someone else's shoes. Obviously, we cannot fully understand someone else's journey as we are not them, but it can help to walk the same path and that is why sober communities are full of empathy.

Empowerment - something **Empaths** take away from others, in our striving to help and do good. I have to admit, whilst I was never great at delegating (or asking for help of any kind) I was pretty good at empowering others in my working life. If someone came up with a good idea, I'd encourage them to roll with it, and support them to do so. This gave me less to do, but most importantly helped build their confidence. If only I could have done this in my own life, I'd be far richer and a lot less stressed! Another area to work on. It goes hand in hand with **Boundaries** I guess.

Empty - there was a time that I only worried about this word when my glass, or even worse my bottle, was empty. I didn't realise how empty my life was. Sure, there were people and things in it but I was not present to appreciate it all. Alcohol takes us to a sad, lonely, withdrawn place and we feel numb and empty. As though we have nothing, we are nothing and have nothing left to offer. In sobriety we have so much more. I was as empty as that bottle, but now I am brimming over. OK, sometimes that bottle is fizzier and more explosive than others, but what's a few alcohol-free bubbles every now and again?

Empty Threats - oh boy! I used to be full of these:

"If you don't behave, we'll go home" when it was somewhere I wanted to be, so clearly, I had no intention of going home.

"If it's not in the wash basket, it doesn't get washed" and then I couldn't stand the dirty washing strewn everywhere, so I'd pick it up and wash it.

"If you so much as kiss another woman, that will be it"

and then I'd let them back in.

And through all of this, I'd feel unloved, unheard and powerless, and crack open another bottle to block it all out.

Do you make empty threats? Does this help with boundary setting? What can you do about it?

Endorphins - are our happy chemicals and natural pain relief. Our body naturally releases them when we hurt ourselves, are in pain, or when we are having a fun experience, such as eating yummy (and usually naughty) foods, drinking, having sex and taking exercise. Endorphins can help reduce pain and inflammation and keep our mood happy and stable. Interestingly, low endorphins can increase our risk of addiction, as well as problems with our mental health, physical health and sleep. Good news; we can boost our endorphins naturally with exercise, music, dancing, laughter, that dark chocolate treat, meditation and sex. Alcohol does increase our endorphins initially, and feeds the **Reward Pathway** of our brain. But over time, like our dopamine, our levels drop and we need more and more alcohol to get that feel good factor again. Eventually we just drink ourselves into misery. As my good friend Pollya often says:

> *"I was stuck at the bottom of a well. Everything was grey and dark. I managed to climb my way out and I never want to go back there"*

Where are you right now? Where were you? Maybe visualise it and use it as your motivation for getting and staying sober.

https://www.eurekalert.org/news-releases/756852#

Energy - I used to hate mornings, but now I love them. I actually wake up early, feeling refreshed and full of energy. Yes, I have an afternoon lull, but I sometimes make time for a lovely afternoon nap. Alcohol sucks the life force out of us. It makes us tired, drained and unable to **Sleep** properly. Hopefully, you are already starting to see the effects alcohol has on your body and the damage it causes. It stands to reason that this is going to make every day harder to wade through.

Envy - can plague us when we are drinking and even when we stop. In the beginning we can be resentful about others' apparent ability to moderate, and so envious of the drinks in their hands! But, with time, we come to realise that we are in a far better place than they are. I now watch people drinking, accepting that it is their right to do so, and think 'If only you knew what I now know'. I have come to realise that if they did know, then they would be the envious ones.

Erica Spiegelman - is a recovering alcohol addict, who wrote her own recovery plan based on her core values and principles whilst focussing on a healthy mind, body and spirit. She is now a drug and alcohol counsellor, motivational speaker and author of *'Rewired; A Bold new approach to Addiction & Recovery'*. This is based on her own experiences of addiction and recovery and that of those that she has helped.

https://www.ericaspiegelman.com

Escape - I realise now that I have been running away my whole life. In the last 30 years, I have lived in 4 different counties, had 10 different cars, married and divorced twice, had 3 other long-term relationships (one with the same person twice) and bought and moved into 8 different homes. I was about 6 months into my sobriety, listening to **Pema Chodron**, when I suddenly fell about laughing. Light bulb moment. No matter how far or fast I ran, I was always still right there! That's when I really started working on me. I still get itchy feet, and my partner and I tour on our bikes, but I am right there. No more running. No more trying to escape the impossible.

Ethanol - is a renewable fuel made from plants and sugar. It is the alcohol that we drink, but it is also mixed with gasoline for our vehicles. E5 fuel contains 5% ethanol, E10 10% and so on. It is a far better fuel for our vehicles than our bodies. It helps them to run and cover many miles, whereas it makes us splutter and clap out far too soon.

https://www.arnoldclark.com/newsroom/347-can-cars-run-on-alcohol#

Everything Happens for a Reason - yes, even death; it will come to us all in the end. Phrases such as *'What goes up must come down', (Sir Isaac Newton),* in Buddhist terms *'Everything that arises passes away'.* 'Everything happens for a reason' and 'from every breakdown there's a breakthrough' have got me through so much. Just before getting sober, I lost my health, my career and my husband who couldn't cope with my disabilities. I then lost the alcohol, my home and my cats. But I gained a grandson, freedom, a different way of living (which is actually far more me, I never was a conventional girl), my Can Am Ryker Trike (AKA Bumblebee) and got back with the love of my life. I don't tell you this for sympathy, it really is not needed, life is great now. I tell you this to give you hope.

E Vitamin - like vitamin A, this helps keep our skin and eyes healthy and helps us fight infection and illness. We get this from olive oil, and other less healthy oils, such as sunflower, rapeseed and corn oil. It is also found in wheat, seeds and nuts.

https://www.nhs.uk/conditions/vitamins-and-minerals/vitamin-e

Excitement - is the same physical feeling as anxiety: butterflies, palpitations, trembling etc. It's just the thinking that's different. I've known this for many years, but it really hit me the morning I was going to meet my beautiful sober friend SJ333 in person for the first time. The physical feelings came on and I thought I was anxious. I reflected on how the old me would have had a drink before I left the house and got to the meeting place early to neck another one. Not doing this enabled me to realise that what I was actually experiencing was excitement, and it was a wonderful feeling. I have numbed this incredible feeling hundreds of times in the past. It is so lovely to now feel it.

Exercise - we all know it's good for us but just the word can be enough to put us off! At one point in my life, I was a gym junkie but I'd still go for a pint of Guinness after my workout. I thought this was a healthy option as it contains iron. How I laugh at that now. I didn't actually drink that much when I was going to the gym. Instead of blocking my feelings, I was easing the pain and making myself feel good by releasing my endorphins. I can no longer do that but, like dancing, it does not mean I cannot exercise at all. We don't have to go for a 2-hour workout, a Zumba class, swim 50 lengths or run 10k. Armchair/wheelchair yoga and a few stretches are OK. The important thing is to have a baseline and get moving. Mine is to do my physio exercises and have a short 200 yard walk each day. If I can do more, then great. And if I can't, then that's OK too. And if I don't do my baseline, I don't beat myself up. I just accept that my pain levels and mood are within my control, and it's down to me to try again tomorrow and accept responsibility.

Expectations - try not to have any! I used to have to know where life was taking me and where I was heading. It would put me in a massive panic if I didn't know and things weren't going to plan. But whoever really knows? Everything is moment by moment. In a split second everything can change. Even life and death. Once we can accept our area of **Control**, we can embrace life more wholeheartedly and enjoy the freedom of 'not knowing'. Afterall, unfulfilled expectations only lead to hurt and disappointment.

F

Fact not Fiction - the truth of alcohol is hidden, it is easier nowadays with the internet, but we still have to work our way through all the fiction: the advertising, romanticising and the convincing of how wonderful it tastes. Ever wondered why gin has been so heavily rebranded with fruit and exotic flavours and tonics? It's because neat it actually tastes shite! I've just googled 'Alcohol' and here's a dictionary meaning by lexico.com:

'A colourless volatile flammable liquid which is produced by the natural fermentation of sugars and is the intoxicating constituent of wine, beer, spirits and other drinks, and is also used as an industrial solvent and as a fuel'

Interesting how even here the use in drinks is the priority. Now here's the fact, if they wrote this on alcohol bottles, they probably wouldn't sell any:

> *'Flammable solvent with arsenic and formaldehyde. Causes liver damage, dementia, cancer and kills over 3 million people a year'*

I've now started a petition to ban advertising and fancy packaging of alcohol and to write the truth on the bottles and cans Petition · Alcohol Truth to be Declared · Change.org. You can sign it no matter where you are in the world as I want to make this a global campaign.

Faith - it's so important to have this. Not necessarily in a religious way, but to have confidence and trust in ourselves and our community. And when we lose sight of this, give some of that power over to our sober tribe or our spiritual guides. They will hold the faith and hope for us, until we feel strong again. If we want something enough, we can do it. We just have to believe in ourselves and our goal, and learn that it's OK to ask for help.

Falling Apart - at the seams when we are drinking, both inside and out. Don't get me wrong, sober we feel like this too. But it's far more controlled. Yes there are the howler episodes, but that's fine. Go to an empty field and shout, scream and cry. Get it all out. Take a deep breath. And resume normal duty. Sober we will still fray, and feel tattered and torn, but the feeling when we start to sew ourselves back together is the best in the world. And don't worry if you drop a stitch or the pattern gets a bit wonky. It really is OK.

False Promises - I try really hard not to promise anything to anyone. Instead, I tell people I will do my absolute best to make it happen. Life can change instantly, and even with good intentions we may not be able to make good our promise. And, when alcohol is involved, then it's even less likely. How many promises do we make when we are drunk? And do we even remember what we said? It is so horrible when people tell us what we said, and we don't even know if it's true. Alcohol can build mistrust and confusion and we let ourselves and others down.

Family - can help make or break us. Our younger years are our foundations for life. But this does not mean we cannot change. Life is like sobriety; it does not follow one straight line, despite that **Dash**. The journey is forever changing and we only graduate when we die. Some of us have had fantastic childhoods and have great family connections, others of us not so. There is a saying that 'Blood is thicker than water' meaning that a blood family bond is stronger, and more important than other relationships. But just look how alcohol can contaminate the blood. There can be toxins in family relationships too. We can try to make the blood run fresher, but if it continues to get contaminated by exposing us to hurt, rejection and pain, then sometimes we just have to let it go. A family can also be a group of people or things with a common theme, such as our sober community. This water can be so refreshing that the love, acceptance and happiness are effervescent.

FAST (Fast Alcohol Screening Test) - this is a great alcohol screening tool and a bit of a stark reminder of our drinking behaviours. If you really want to know if you have a problem with alcohol then search fast alcohol use screening test.gov.uk. It only takes a few minutes to complete.

https://www.who.int/news-room/fact-sheets/detail/alcohol

Fear - is our response to threat or harm and can trigger that fire alarm bringing on all the physical and emotional reactions of **Anxiety**. Remember though, that threat does not have to be real or in the moment. It can be how we see and interpret things, our altered thinking, or a triggered memory from our past. Things I find threatening may not be to you. Things we are fearful of one day, may not bother us the next. Fear is there to keep us safe, but like anxiety, it can get a little overactive.

Fear of Never Drinking Again - this is generally our biggest fear when we quit drinking. It can be absolutely terrifying. I mean how are we ever going to get through Christmas, our birthday or that wedding without alcohol? But ask yourself this - what is the actual threat here? There is none. There is far more threat of harm if we continue to drink. My fear now is of ever drinking again. My first sober birthday was amazing. I was 6 months in, and as I made my morning cuppa, I realised there was no voice saying:

> *'It's my birthday. I wonder what time I can get away with drinking today? Maybe 10am? Or should I wait until 11? I can't wait until lunchtime. It is my birthday after all! I need to celebrate. I can get away with drinking earlier today'.*

The silence was wonderful. I listened to the kettle boil and the birds singing and smiled to myself and enjoyed the dawning of a new day. Where is the fear in that?

Feelings - as my good friend Pollya says "We start feeling the feels" when we put the booze down. I call this my rainbow journey, as I have been every colour: blue with sadness, green with envy, red with rage, tickled pink and bright, smiling, happy yellow sunshine. I cannot remember ever feeling the true happiness and joy that I feel now, and that makes all the less favourable feelings worth it. I'm not going to call them negative feelings because if they are apt, then they are all valid. For example, we may well grieve the loss of our favourite tipple. That's appropriate as it has been our comfort blanket for so long. We may get agitated with withdrawal. That's appropriate too. We may get angry with others, ourselves, alcohol, advertising, the government. Well, why shouldn't we? We have discovered the lie after all these years. Our task is to work out what each feeling is, where it is coming from and what to do with it. The good thing is, feelings come and go and we cannot feel the same way forever. But remember, no-one can make us feel how we feel. That person didn't make us angry, happy or sad. We chose to react that way. Feelings are like rollercoasters at times but be kind to yourself. Sobriety is uncovering a lifetime of situations that we have numbed, and now we have to deal with them once and for all. It is the best thing we can ever do for ourselves. Welcome to the adventure of discovery.

Fermentation - changes the normal structure of food to release sugars or produce alcohol. How is this done? By starving it of oxygen, adding yeast or bacteria and letting it rot and stew. Yep. We are drinking rotten grapes, apples, potatoes ...

Fertility - alcohol affects sperm and women's periods which can cause problems with getting pregnant. It also effects sex drive and can cause issues with erection. If you are wanting to get pregnant, then both parties should stop drinking as even light drinking can cause issues.

https://www.yourfertility.org.au/everyone/drugs-chemicals/alcohol#

https://www.medslike.com/why-is-boozing-harmful-to-your-sexual-life/

Fetal Alcohol Spectrum Disorders (FASD) - a group of 5 disorders associated with birth defects and childhood development caused by drinking whilst pregnant. These include a wide range of physical and neurological issues. No amount of alcohol is safe to the baby at any time during pregnancy. Any amount can cause irreversible damage at any stage. Alcohol can also increase the risk of miscarriage, premature birth and still births.

https://www.ncbi.nlm.nih.gov/books/NBK448178/

Finances - improve with sobriety. There will still be debts (especially from our drinking days), and money will probably still be tight, because we like to spend beyond our means. But think about all the money we can save by not buying alcohol!

How much do you spend a week on alcohol? Times it by 52. Now that's far better than any pay rise you'd ever get. You don't need to buy a lotto ticket in the hopes of winning. Sobriety is a winner. Next time you go to the bottle bank, add up how much you have thrown away.

Fits - or seizures, are due to changes in the way our brain cells work and can be a very real and dangerous effect of alcohol withdrawal. We have been numbing and changing our brain cells for a long time, feeding them with a substance they have come to rely on. Take it away, and there's going to be a thunderstorm up there. I cannot stress enough how important it is to gradually reduce the amount of alcohol you are drinking before you quit and preferably see your medical practitioner.

Flashbacks - remember the fire alarm (**Amygdala**) in our brain? Well, we also have a librarian (**Hippocampus**) which keeps all our memories nicely stored and filed. But when that fire alarm goes off, the librarian gets upset and everything gets muddled up. We can be right there (back at our trauma site) seeing, smelling, hearing, tasting, feeling everything again as if it is happening right now. Anything can trigger this. The smell of perfume, the sound of a car backfiring, a thought... Flashbacks can be a symptom of Post-Traumatic Stress Disorder (**PTSD**).

Floundering - when we are drinking, we can often stumble, struggle to think straight, not know what we are doing or where we are going, and find ourselves in awkward or difficult situations. This is the same for sobriety. So, when you get a moment of struggle and not knowing, just remember that although you will feel it more, it really is easier to do sober. And if you are **Wise**, you will have a sober community to help you.

Flow - go with it. We really do not need to know where we are heading or what the outcome will be. Focussing too much on that stops us from living in the **Now**. Remember, life is what happens whilst we are busy making plans. And, we have no control outside of our arm span, just our response. Conflict occurs when we think we know the outcome and that we are right. Just imagine how it would be, if just for a minute, we stopped and basked in the joy of not knowing.

FOMO - the Fear of Missing Out. Oh boy! This is a real driver for many of us. In fact, alongside wanting to fit in and not be the odd one out, fomo probably played a large part in my drinking, smoking and most things I've done. There's that saying, "The grass is always greener on the other side", but it really isn't. Grass is grass. It's how we treat it and interact with it that makes the difference. And peeing all over it really isn't helpful. Now I have **JOMO** (the Joy of Missing Out) which is so much better.

Forest Bathing - translated from the Japanese idea of shinrin-yoku. It's back to basics and reconnecting with nature. Go sit under a tree, breathe, live in the moment and absorb all the wonderful nature around you and don't forget to turn your phone off!

Forgiveness - forgive yourself and others. What's done is done. We can't go back. We can't change it. All we can do is accept and move on. But first we need to work through the anger, hurt, sadness and frustration. Or, we could just hold a grudge and beat ourselves up forever. It really is our choice. Here are a few questions to get you started. This can be yourself or someone else. It might be helpful to stay curious and read: **Acceptance, Acknowledge, Blame, Compassion, Drama**

Triangles, **Kindness**, **Metta** and **Understanding** before doing this.

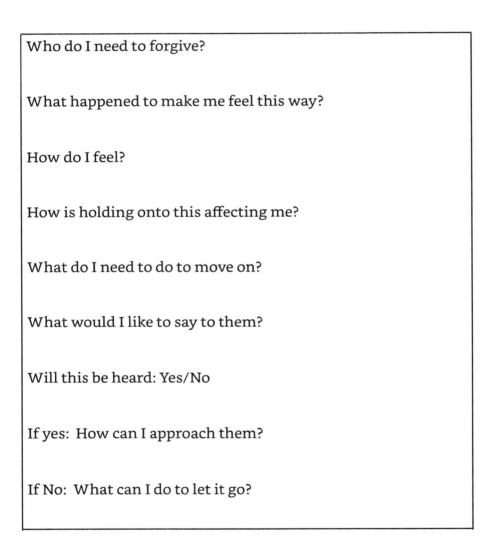

Who do I need to forgive?

What happened to make me feel this way?

How do I feel?

How is holding onto this affecting me?

What do I need to do to move on?

What would I like to say to them?

Will this be heard: Yes/No

If yes: How can I approach them?

If No: What can I do to let it go?

Formaldehyde - is a chemical preservative used in building materials (mostly pressed woods and glues), as a steriliser and for embalming bodies. It is also found in cigarettes, alcohol and food colourants. Formaldehyde has been linked to leukaemia and cancer, and for many years has been linked with alcohol and cancer, but studies about this are conflicting. One systematic study, *'The Margin of Exposure to Formaldehyde in alcoholic Beverages'* by Monakhova, Jendral & Lachenmeier published in 2001, suggests that the cancer-causing risks of formaldehyde in alcohol is negligible. It does however state that there is harmful risk from **Ethanol** and **Acetaldehyde**.

https://www.cancer.gov/about-cancer/causes-prevention/risk/substances/formaldehyde/formaldehyde-fact-sheet

https://pubmed.ncbi.nlm.nih.gov/22728807/

Frank Ostaseski - is a Buddhist teacher, founder of the Metta Institute and co-founder of the Zen Hospice Project (just for starters!) He has worked for many years in end-of-life care and is the author of *'The Five Invitations: Discovering What Death Can Teach Us About Living Fully'* and I absolutely love this book. Whilst it's not a sobriety book, so much of what he says relates to addiction and really helped with my recovery.

Friends - getting sober, we really do find out who our true friends are. Some accept our new found sobriety, support us and are proud of us. Others try to **Sabotage** us and this is completely understandable. The thought of losing a drinking buddy, our partner in crime, is pretty scary. We also discover that there are friends that we really do not have anything in common with once we remove the booze, but we make new friends with whom we have plenty in common, not just sobriety. Just find your virtual or face to face **Community**. I have actually met many of my initially online sober friends face to face. Eight of us recently had a spa weekend away and laughed so much our sides ached. There are also lots of sober socials, clubs and pubs popping up. **Sober** is the new trendy.

Frustration - only comes when we give things meaning. For me it's when I feel I'm not being listened to or heard, or when I feel I keep doing things wrong. But what does that really matter? We can't get things right all of the time, and not everyone wants to listen to what we have to say! We all have our own issues going on. We all have our hang ups and frustrations. We are all scared little children at our core with expectations way too high. For today, accept what is, take a breath and just be.

F*** It Button - pause before you press it. Have you used your **Tool Box**, reached out and connected? Probably not, because the last thing we want is someone to talk us out of it right? But do you really want to press it and release the double f*** it button? Do you really want to give yourself extra pain for an hour or two of peace? You know that when you sober up, everything will be a whole lot worse than it is right now. And the beast would have won yet again. But you have a choice and it is yours alone to make. Maybe **Pause** and try one of these:

- 4D's – delay, drink water, deep breath, do something (I'm going to add a cheeky 5th – discuss)
- What do I need? Blanket? Tears? Boxing bag? Laughter?
- Does this feed my addiction or my recovery?
- What would I say to a friend?

Functional Alcoholic - is the term used to describe people with an addiction who still function; pay the bills, have a roof over their head, continue to work or care for the children. This was me, but was it really? Was I really functioning? Are you? I wasn't feeling, I wasn't present, my mind was focussed on when my next drink was (and I'd get angry if anything got in my way of that). How could I possibly be a good nurse, partner and mother when I was under the effects of long-term **Anaesthetic**?

That is the reality. And then there are the sick days with 'diarrhoea and vomiting' or 'migraine'. Never what it really was - the mother of all hangovers!

Functional Neurological Disorder - this is something I was diagnosed with a couple of years ago. My head and my body do not work well together as there is a messaging problem in my nervous system. There is no structural damage as in Multiple Sclerosis, but the symptoms are very similar. It causes problems with walking, talking, eating, continence and coordination (just for starters). Since getting sober, and learning about **Brain Plasticity**, I have worked really hard with **Mindfulness** to retrain my brain and body signals. It is hard and focussed work, but for the most part, it has really helped me. What I have also learnt is that I was drinking away my **Neural Pathways**. I share this with you to demonstrate the very real damage alcohol can cause.

Future - none of us know what our future holds. But I will put everything into it being a sober one. That way, I know without a doubt that it will be so much better than before. But to have a good future, we have to focus on today. The only day we ever really have, this day will never come again.

G

GABA (Gamma-Aminobutyric Acid) - is a body chemical that reduces our anxiety and fear response by calming our nervous system. When levels are low, it can lead to increased stress, anxiety, depression and even schizophrenia. Imbalances in GABA can also cause epilepsy and movement disorders. And, of course, alcohol affects GABA. It actually stimulates its activity, blocking our nerve messages and creating that warm, calm feeling. But this is only temporary, and eventually we need more and more to create the same feeling of relaxation. Bring on the addiction.

https://www.verywellhealth.com/gaba-5095143

Gambling - I like a little bit of bingo every now and again and the slot machines (although never over 20p a go and usually the 2p cascades) but I've never really been a 'gambler'. My ex-husband was, and I hated it. He wasted thousands of pounds, he was deceitful, he lied, it robbed us of our time together and built a great big rift between us. Oh shit! I clearly was a gambler. I did all of that, and also gambled on the worst thing of all; the life of myself and others.

Genetics - can make us more prone to alcohol addiction and to illnesses caused by alcohol. According to **WHO**, way back in 2004 2 billion of us were drinking alcohol and 76.3 million of us had an alcohol use disorder. That's more than a quarter! I suspect that this has increased since but I cannot currently find more up to date global data. This isn't all down to genetics though, environment and social factors also play a part. But studies with twins, mice and adopted children do highlight genetics as a contributing cause and some even refer to alcohol addiction as a genetic disease.

https://www.ncbi.nlm.nih.gov/pmc/articles/PMC2715956/

https://www.ncbi.nlm.nih.gov/pmc/articles/PMC4056340/

Getting Sober Again – a great YouTube channel hosted by Jae. Tune in at www.YouTube.com/GettingSoberAgain to follow his sober journey and for some great tips, such as:

'22 Tips: The Best ADVICE For Early SOBRIETY!' (Episode 152)"

'What are the 5 ENEMIES of your Sobriety?' (Episode 146)

'15 Signs that you're DRINKING TOO MUCH!' (Episode 149)

'20 benefits of NO ALCOHOL for 30 Days' (Episode 131)

'35 Need to Know Alcohol & Drinking Statistics' (Episode 130)

Gifts - sobriety is the best gift we can give to ourselves and others. It really is a blessing to wake up refreshed and hangover free, to remember what we have said and done, and to be there for ourselves and others. But if we want to treat ourselves then why not? Drinking me would see things that I liked and then ask 'But do I really need it?' and not buy it. Sober me realises I don't really need it, but I now buy things as a treat because it's nice to do so. I equate it to how many bottles of wine it would have been in value but I have got a bit carried away at times!

Glennon Doyle - author of *'Carry on Warrior'*, *'Love Warrior'* and *'Untamed'* in which she writes about her struggle and recovery from addiction and Bulimia. I have read *'Untamed'* and I loved it. In her introduction she talks of a cheetah born in captivity who has known nothing else. The cheetah is looking out of her cage in a yearning way. Glennon feels the Cheetah is longing for the wild and refers to this as our **'Knowing'**. And so, starts her writing of how we too are tamed and how we can break free.

Gold - if we can look for this in everything we see and do, then there will always be far more than a silver lining. Find it, and you will be the richest person alive.

The Parable of the Beggar: The Treasure
You Seek is Within You.
From Eckhart Tolle book 'The Power of
Now' 2005 edition, page 9.

'A beggar had been sitting by the side of a road for over thirty years. One day a stranger walked by.
"Spare some change?" mumbled the beggar, mechanically holding out his old baseball cap.
"I have nothing to give you," said the stranger.
Then he asked: "What's that you are sitting on?"
"Nothing," replied the beggar. "Just an old box. I have been sitting on it for as long as I can remember."
"Ever looked inside?" asked the stranger.
"No," said the beggar. "What's the point? There's nothing in there."
"Have a look inside," insisted the stranger.
The beggar managed to pry open the lid. With astonishment, disbelief, and elation, he saw that the box was filled with gold.'

Good Enough – that's you. Yes, I'm talking to you. There you are. Right there. You are good enough, as is everything you are doing. Good enough is enough. Anything else is very overrated.

Government – if alcohol is so bad then why doesn't the government step in and do something about it? It's a simple answer: money. According to Statista.com the UK tax received from alcohol in 2021/2022 was around £13.1 Billion (up £1 billion from the previous year). During lockdown, Off Licences were seen as essential shops and allowed to stay open and pubs were one of the first venues to re-open, albeit with a 10pm curfew. With exception of the government of course, whose bars were allowed to remain open as our MPs were busy working away into the night whilst anaesthetising themselves through a crisis ...
https://www.statista.com/statistics/284336/united-kingdom-hmrc-tax-receipts-alcohol-duties-by-type/

Gratitude - is the key to happy living. Research has shown that being grateful helps us to feel less alone, lifts our mood, eases pain and can improve our sleep. I am grateful for so much now, including having an addiction. If I hadn't had this, I wouldn't have found so many wonderful, like-minded people from all over the world. At last, I fit in and have learnt that there is nothing wrong with me or who I am. And that is amazing. What are you grateful for today? It could be as simple as seeing the sunshine or hearing the birds sing. Writing a gratitude journal can be really helpful; just write 3 things you are grateful for each day.

https://www.baystatehealth.org/news/2019/11/gratitude-and-your-brain#

Grounding - most of us have probably heard of the new trend of 'grounding' or being 'grounded'. Of stopping what we are doing, feeling our feet on the floor and being in the moment. It's a mindfulness technique but it isn't actually anything new. It's actually a very natural concept that fashion and expectations of the 'norms' has been restraining us from for years. We are electrical beings and very positively charged. The earth is negative and we need the tune of this to keep us in check, get rid of excess energy and be 'grounded'. So, kick off your shoes and go stand on the grass - better still go and lie directly on it. Walk barefoot along the edge of the ocean or through a forest (you could do a bit of **Forest Bathing** whilst you are there) or just around your garden, a local park or street. Or just stand barefoot, in the moment. We don't need to waste money on expensive grounding mats. We just need to strip off and connect with mother nature.

https://pemfcomplete.com/do-we-have-electricity-in-our-bodies

Growing Up - something we have to do in sobriety. We may think we are adults when we are drinking and our body can confirm that we are. But mentally? After blocking, numbing and anaesthetising it for so long? Sober is that feeling when you are looking for the adult in the room, and you suddenly realise it is you. Don't get me wrong, we mostly 'act' as adults every day when we are drinking. We go through the motions but we avoid the emotions. There are times that I really do not like this "grown up sober shit" but I know it is so worth it.

Growth - just as smoking cigarettes stunts our growth; alcohol does this too. It makes everything malfunction, slow down and eventually stop working all together. But remember, what doesn't kill us makes us stronger. What's done is done, but we can use our experiences to help ourselves and others. Sober, we grow emotionally, physically, spiritually, creatively and financially and we can learn to forgive and free ourselves from burden.

Guidance - what better place to go for guidance than from those that are going through something similar? One-to-one therapy is good, but groups of people who have lived the experience are even better. Many **Quit Lit** and self-help books are written by people on a similar journey. We really don't need to reinvent the wheel and it's great if we can accept that others can help. My lifetime mantra of 'I don't need anyone else' had to be thrown out of the window from a great height! I've tried quitting many times before, but it only worked when I found my support communities. I read and got involved with podcasting and supporting others. It is easier to climb a mountain with support and guidance from those that have gone before us. Let others walk by your side. It really is a far less lonely path.

Guilt - we can seem to be an endless hive of guilt, turning ourselves inside out and churning ourselves up. Feeling guilty may have led some of us to drink, and then we feel guilty about our drinking and our behaviour. It really can be a never-ending circle. But only if we allow it to be. The hardest person to forgive is ourselves, but we can do it, and it helps if we can write it all out. Write letters to yourself and to others. And if you think it will help, then write a calmer letter to send to others. Or, if you feel brave enough, then go and talk to them. But only if you think it is going to help both you and them. Don't cause more stress and upset just to relieve your guilty conscience. Some things really are best left unsaid.

Gullible - well I've always been easily persuadable, despite my driving force that 'you can't trust anyone'. Possibly because I've also looked at the world through rose tinted glasses. I'm a romantic at heart, and I believed the stuff of Mills and Boon. What a harsh awakening real life was. But I still wanted it all to be true. So, I drank away my disappointment with the world. And drunk me was even more gullible and persuadable to believe and do things that I probably would have resisted a little bit more if I'd been sober. Alcohol = gullible = vulnerable = risk.

Gut – is our gastrointestinal tract and starts at our mouth and ends at our anus. It includes our mouth, oesophagus (the pipe running from our mouth to our stomach), stomach, appendix and **Intestines**. Our gut is our digestive tract and mostly responsible for breaking down our food, absorbing nutrients and getting rid of food waste and other things we no longer need in the form of poo. We have muscles (sphincters) either side of our stomach which open and close to let food in and out and keep our stomach acid in place. Alcohol can interfere with these, making them slack and allowing stomach acid to seep into our oesophagus causing heartburn. It also affects the lining of our gut directly causing mouth, oesophageal and bowel cancer. Alcohol is absorbed in our small intestine and taken straight to the liver, increasing the risk of liver damage and stops us from absorbing nutrients correctly.

https://patient.info/news-and-features/the-digestive-system#

https://pubs.niaaa.nih.gov/publications/arh21-1/76.pdf#

https://www.verywellhealth.com/types-of-cancer-caused-by-drinking-alcohol-513626

Gut Health – is said to be the future of medicine and I really feel this is true. We have over 50 trillion tiny organisms in our digestive system, and there are a thousand different types. We need to feed them well to keep them healthy and help them to thrive. Out with the alcohol, sugary drinks and junk food: in with the fresh, unprocessed and natural foods. We really are what we eat. For more information on this I can recommend '*The Clever Guts Diet: How to revolutionise your body from the inside out*' by Dr Michael Mosley and '*10% Human: How Your Body's Microbes Hold the Key to Health and Happiness*' by Alanna Collen. They have conflicting views on how much of us is bacteria, but it's at least half!

Gut Instinct - feel it, listen to it and go with it. It really can tell us so much. Even when I was mental health nursing it was okay to go with this, and record that we had done so. There is a very large nervous system (**Vagus Nerve**) in our gut and it is often referred to as our 'second brain'. Listen to your tummy today, it has so much to tell you.

https://www.verywellhealth.com/enteric-nervous-system-5112820

H

Habits - it's generally thought that it takes 66 days to break a habit, but in fact it takes an average of 66 days to form a new habit (less and much longer for some). Don't panic - this is actually good news, as it can take as little as 21 days for an old habit to go and a new one to take its place. And that is the trick. To replace our drinking habit with something new. A hobby, a project, exercise, flavoured tonic water in a posh glass. The joy I now have, when I hear the sound of the kettle and have a lovely cuppa, is far more wonderful than opening that bottle.

https://www.blackmores.com.au/everyday-health/how-long-does-it-really-take-to-break-a-habit

Hallucinations - are when our mind can see, hear, feel, taste or smell things that are not really there. Ever smell gas when there was nothing? Or hear someone call your name? Or had any experience where you've put it down to your mind playing tricks on you? One reason for hallucinations is thought to be high dopamine in the frontal area of the brain. Hang on a minute. Does alcohol not affect that? Hallucinations can become more common when we are intoxicated and also when we stop drinking. When I quit, my skin itched for two months with the sensation of little insects crawling all over it.

HALT (Hungry Angry Lonely Tired) - is something a lot of us use in recovery. When you are feeling out of sorts or craving just stop and think. Are you Hungry, Angry, Lonely or Tired? Take the correct action for what you are feeling. It's a great way to stop us from reaching for that bottle.

Hangovers - another wonderful side-effect of not drinking; no hangovers. No headaches, shaking, nausea, vomiting or tiredness and no drinking anxiety, guilt or regret. How many times have you said 'never again'? And yet, still we do it time and time again. I stopped drinking whisky at the age of 16 because it made me so ill. And then another time it was tequila; when I found myself in the middle of the Nevada desert, on all fours and honking endlessly like a dog. And then brandy because it made me so anxious. And then beer because gluten made me ill. And that's just it. I do not eat gluten because it makes me ill, but still I continued making myself ill day after day with alcohol. Pretty crazy huh? What about you?

https://www.niaaa.nih.gov/publications/brochures-and-fact-sheets/hangovers#

Happiness – is the opposite of **Suffering** and I truly never realised it could feel like this. Happiness is genuine, it is natural and it is of our own making. Initially, I could not remember having ever felt this way, but that's because our memories have a habit of hanging onto sadness and misery. Now, sitting writing this, I am reflecting and remembering many good times from my past which filled me with happiness and joy. Have a little dig around today. Go find some happiness, and remember to share it around, it really is infectious.

Happy - we are all connected by our wish to be happy but we look for things, situations and people to make us feel this way. But it's a bit like the beggar's box of gold; we just have to look inside. Yes, there are lots of emotions inside of us, but numbing them is not the way to make us happy. Working through those emotions, dealing with the situations and feelings, accepting our contributions and areas of control and letting go of the past really does make us happy. **Anger**, greed, resentment and **Jealousy** will just keep us in a dark place. Learning to let them go allows our happy to shine through.

Harmony - is music to our sober ears. When we stop drinking not only are our relationships much calmer and authentic, but our body, brain and mind become much more in tune when we are not numbing all of our senses.

Healing - happens in sobriety. We have so many emotional and physical wounds and scars from battling through life and addiction. Once we put the alcohol down, the physical healing begins. All the withdrawals, shakes, anxiety, nausea and sweating are our body getting rid of toxins and adapting to not being dependent on a substance. That is a great start. Eventually our bodily systems, organs and functions will automatically reset to their healthier and new normal but remember to schedule in a medical review if you can. Eating healthily, drinking plenty of water, pacing ourselves, resting, exercising, sleeping and taking supplements will all help. And then the emotional healing starts. The tricky part is going up against our **Ego** and **Addict Voice**, our **Anxiety** and **Altered/Unhelpful Thinking**, our hurt and **Anger** and resisting the urge to numb it all. There are parts that are so painful we think we will die. Pain cannot kill us, but our actions can. No emotion, feeling or pain can stay the same way forever, it has to change. If we drink, we only numb it for a while and then it comes back again. If we stay sober and actually work with it and through it, then this is one place where the grass can begin to grow greener. And the great thing is, it is all within our control.

Health - well finally, here's to your very good health! I cannot believe that we chink glasses and say 'to good health' before pouring poison down our necks! Quitting alcohol most definitely improves our physical and mental health in the long run. It might not feel like it at first with all the withdrawals and starting to feel, but eventually, not only do we start to feel healthier, we actually feel alive.

Heart - you've probably read (and jumped up and down with joy) the articles saying a glass of wine is good for the heart. This is actually down to all the nutrients in the grapes! The heart is the main muscle of our body. It keeps us alive by pumping our blood around our body, delivering oxygen and nutrients to every organ in our body and taking away the stuff we no longer need. You have already read how alcohol affects the **Blood**, oxygen, nutrients, and circulation. It stands to reason that it is going to affect the heart also. Our heart is a vital organ, if it stops, so do we. If we drink ourselves into a coma, the part of the brain that unconsciously keeps the heart beating, can go to sleep too … RIP.

Heart Disease - is anything that affects the rhythms and pumping of the heart and the blood flow to and from it. This includes strokes (caused by a blood clot or a burst blood vessel in the brain), unusual heart beats, high blood pressure (this is the pressure of our heart pumping the blood around our body – too high and we could have a bleed on the brain) and narrowing of our blood vessels, to name but a few. Alcohol affects all of these things and there is a heart disease that is specifically caused by alcohol weakening and thinning the muscle of our heart. It is called Alcoholic Cardiomyopathy (alcohol causing heart muscle disease). This, like all heart disease, can lead to complications in other areas of our body and heart attack. Again, get yourself checked out, especially if you are getting breathless, dizzy, have pain or have any swelling or fluid collecting in your lower legs and feet.

https://www.cdc.gov/heartdisease/about.htm

https://www.healthline.com/health/alcoholism/
cardiomyopathy#symptoms

Help - we all need it, but it helps if we can ask for it. To ask for help shows strength and courage, and it stops others second-guessing what we need and us getting annoyed with them for not knowing!

Helplessness - a horrible feeling that comes and goes. I have never felt more helpless than when I was drinking. Completely trapped in that hamster wheel. Continuously going round and round. When we break free from alcohol, we really can break free from anything. We just need to **Work It** as much as we do our drinking. And ask for help. Because it actually is OK to feel helpless.

Hereditary - it's our looks, our genes, our traits and behaviours which are passed down to us by our parents. We've already seen that there is thought to be a **Genetic** link to alcohol and addiction so it could all be passed on. But there is always that nature/nurture aspect; was it genetically passed on or did we learn it from our environment? But does it really matter? There is no blame here. Once we can just accept it for what it is, it can make for much smoother sailing.

High - sobriety is the best high we can ever achieve. It is natural and genuine. Yes, there are moments of doubt, sadness, anxiety and darkness but it is a far better comedown than with a hangover. Sober joy, love and laughter are the best highs ever. Be patient, they will come, and the wait is so worth it.

Higher Power - is said to be something greater than us. I think we all have our own greatness; we just need help to find it. My higher power is anything, or anyone who can help me to achieve and recover. My sober communities are my higher power. You are my higher power, for giving me the motivation and inspiration to write this book.

Hippocampus - is part of our **Limbic System** and helps us to work out information from our short and long-term memory. This is our librarian, keeping all of our memories in order. Until our fire alarm goes off or we anaesthetise it. We should not sign legal documents or go to therapy when we are drinking alcohol due to the impact of this on our ability to store and recall correct memories.

https://qbi.uq.edu.au/brain-basics/memory/where-are-memories-stored#

Hobbies - there are so many to choose from. When I first quit, I thought 'What am I going to do with all the time now I'm not drinking? It's going to be so long and boring'. Now, I honestly don't know how I ever had time to drink! What did you enjoy doing before you were drinking? Is there anything you've often thought about doing, but not had the money, confidence, motivation or time? Look round for inspiration today. My Bumblebee motorbike really helped me find the little girl in me again and it is so much fun. I also knit, read, jigsaw, play board games, podcast and write. And, just as I type this, an email has come through from Hobbycraft. Now there's a great place for inspiration …

Honesty - is always the best policy. Learning to be honest with ourselves and others can be difficult but so worth it in the end. Admitting to ourselves that we have a problem with alcohol is tough, but it's a huge step forward. Even if we don't do anything about it at first, or keep trying and then giving up, identifying the problem is good. This is our journey, and we may not want to tell everyone of our issues and problems, but seeing and speaking our truth can be so refreshing. It stops us from tying ourselves up in knots by trying to remember what we have said to whom! In a nutshell - be true to yourself, only tell others what you want to, but don't lie.

Hope - is what helps us to change and succeed. There will be times when we lose it. And that's fine, we just need to let others hold it for us for a while and be our cheerleaders. A good **Community** will always walk by our side and hold our hand. There is no in front or behind. We are all walking side by side and keeping the hope going.

Hula Hoop - similar to our outstretched arms, imagine a hula hoop on the floor and think of yourself sitting or standing in it. This is our area of **Control**. Remember it and recognise when you've stepped outside of it, take a breath, get back in it and relax. The control freak in me sometimes wishes I had an extra-large one, but as others have pointed out, an extra small one would give me less to worry about ... Recently I have found my ego way outside and ready to do battle and I have had to catch it, drag it back inside (kicking and screaming) and nail it firmly to the floor!

Human - we are only this after all is said and done. A mass of tissue, bone, water, chemicals and electricity. And, like all these components shoved in a test tube, we get a bit overloaded at times. I do believe we have spirit and soul encased in our bodies and sometimes it feels as though I am screaming blue murder to be let out! Another case of learning harmony. Alexander Pope wrote 'To err is human, to forgive is divine'. Start today by forgiving and harmonising yourself.

Human Rights Act - gives us the freedom to be who we are, speak out and move freely. There are 30 Human Rights, but how many times do we violate our own rights by drinking?

- The right to live in freedom and safety, to live freely without control and without torture and pain
- The right to our own privacy and keeping our good name
- The freedom to move, travel and go where we want (hmm ... nope, not gonna go there)
- The right to play, rest and relax

Nobody can take these freedoms and rights away from us, nor can we take them away from others. But alcohol does take our freedom away.

https://www.samaritanmag.com/we-have-30-basic-human-rights-do-you-know-them#

https://www.citizensadvice.org.uk/law-and-courts/civil-rights/human-rights/what-are-human-rights/

Humour - can be found, even in stressful situations. Like the gust of wind when we are sprinkling our loved one's ashes, the looking back on that 'Fawlty Towers' or 'Sketchy Grange' stay, the time we reversed the car into a bollard. Oh. Is it just me then? Humour is a bit like the sun, we can't always see it, but it will come and shine on us later. A very good friend once said to me "Will this really matter when you are 80?" I use this all the time now to identify what really matters in life. So, if you are feeling stressed today, try asking yourself if it will matter in years to come and remind yourself that one day this could well be a talking and laughing point.

Hygge - pronounced hoo-gah, this Danish word and concept is all about cosiness, comfort and connection and is a wonderful form of **Self-Care**. It's lighting a candle or a fire, putting on snuggly clothes and curling up with a good book, a pet or a loved one, going out into nature, connecting with friends or picnicking in the park. Don't have a hoo-hah today, have a hoo-gah instead.

Hype - what's it really all about? It's about exaggeration, bombardment, getting us excited and whipped up into a frenzy with the 'I really must have it. NOW'. Oh! It's bringing our **Id** out to play. And then our **Ego** wants to moderate, but there's that **FOMO** to deal with and the relentless **Advertising** that makes it look so inviting, we cannot possibly miss out on feeling so good … Oh bugger. I hit the **F*** It Button** again. Don't be hard on yourself. It's easy to see how we can get so carried away and succumb.

Hypothalamus - is probably the busiest part of our brain, keeping everything balanced and in order. It keeps everything where it should be, including our heart beat, breathing and behaviours. It also controls our response to pain and gratification, such as in our **Reward Pathway**. Alcohol numbs every part of us, including our brain and its functioning and knocks everything out of balance, including our hypothalamus.

https://www.topdoctors.co.uk/medical-dictionary/ hypothalamus

Hypothermia - is when our body gets too cold and it can be fatal. Alcohol directs blood supply to our skin making us feel warm but actually making us cold inside. And then, because we feel warm, we strip off or become tired and confused and fall asleep outside, putting ourselves at great risk. We become pale, our lips may go blue, we shiver, and our breathing slows down …

Some medications, such as antidepressants, anxiety medication, antipsychotics, heart medications and opioids, can also make us more at risk of hypothermia.

What to do: Get help, get inside if you can, have a warm sugary drink or eat chocolate, remove any wet or cold clothes and wrap up warm with blankets. <u>Do not</u> have a hot bath or shower, sit directly in front of a fire or rub yourself warm as this can lead to burns, shock and loss of consciousness. Do not drink alcohol, this will make it worse.

https://www.verywellhealth.com/hypothermia-causes-and-risk-factors-4161049#

https://www.nhs.uk/conditions/hypothermia

I

IAS (I Am Sober) - a free sobriety app with an amazingly supportive **Community**. I own my sobriety, but I credit the wonderful people in this community for helping me get and stay sober. You can remain completely anonymous if you wish, most people use pseudonyms, some of which you will see in here – mine is Corinna Dotty Pot. You can post, read, support, be supported and celebrate. There is also a daily counter, milestone marker and money counter on there. And it covers so much more than alcohol; I'm currently working on my sugar addiction! There are informal daily Zooms which were set up and are run by people from the IAS community. If you would like more information on these, just email me at alcoholandsobriety@gmail.com with your IAS user name and the milestone you last posted at and I will send you up to date information on Zoom times and sign in details.

I Am Woman - I stumbled across this movie and song during my first year of sobriety. For many months the song was my morning go to, and gave me the strength and right attitude for the day. The film is about Helen Reddy's life and her battle as a female singer in a very male dominated industry in the 1970's. With strength and conviction, she became one of the most successful female singers of her time and '*I Am Woman*' became the anthem for the Women's Rights Movement in America in which she played a very active part. Her husband at the time was Jeff Wald and his drug and alcohol use was a catalyst for their divorce in 1983. He has now been sober for over 35 years. Helen Reddy died in 2020 and never saw the equal rights amendment that they had fought so hard for as it has still not been signed. Here are some of the words from her song. You can change the woman to man, sober, or whatever works for you. But if it doesn't, try to find your anthem as it really does help.

'I am woman hear me roar

In numbers too big to ignore

And I know too much to go back and pretend

Cause I've heard it all before

And I've been down there on the floor

And no-one's ever gonna keep me down again

Oh yes, I am wise but its wisdom born of pain

Yes, I've paid the price but look how much I gained

If I have to, I can do anything

I am strong

I am invincible

I am woman

You can bend but never break me

Because it only serves to make me

More determined to achieve my final goal

And I've come back even stronger

Not a novice any longer

Cause you've deepened the conviction in my soul'

Id - From Freud's "Das Es" – The It. The id is not organised and realistic like our **Ego** and **Superego**. It is our unconscious desire and works on instinct; I want it and I want it now. Think of babies and toddlers. We feed them on <u>their</u> demand.

Their id does not know about waiting. With time, explanation and development of our egos, we slowly learn to wait, even if it is begrudgingly. Once we learn **Acceptance**, we don't mind waiting. No more anger or frustration. It just is. But beware, our id also likes to do push ups in the corner and make us spit our dummy out!

Identity Crisis - a term used by psychoanalyst Erik Erikson, along with Mid-Life crisis. Our biggest identity crisis is in our adolescence, when we start figuring out where we fit in the world. This can be a tricky time for all, with a tug of war between our parents, our peers and our conscience. I started drinking when I was 14. Not every day, but a few days a week. My friends and I would work our way around our parents' drink cabinets (a real trend in the 70's). Mostly apricot and cherry brandy. We drank cans of lager at the park, and on a big night out in Burnham-on-Crouch, we'd sink 2 aspirin in a large bottle of cider and drink it through straws to get drunk quicker. We got away with ½ pints of lager in the back bar of some pubs, and I remember being allowed to take part in a beer drinking competition at the local village hall - at the age of 16. I got completely smashed that night on whisky and I've never touched it since. I can't even stand the smell. Anyhow, the whole point of this is for you to see what I did with my identity crisis. I drank my way through it and anaesthetised myself. So now, at the grand old age of 57, I am working my way through it along with my mid-life one!

https://healthline.com/health/mental-health/identity-crisis#TOC_TITLE_HDR_1

Illicit/Illegal Substances - my mindset used to be; if it's illegal it's bad for you. Alcohol is legal so it must be OK and drugs are far worse. Whilst I'm not encouraging you to go and get hooked on drugs, I just wanted to clarify some facts. Alcohol is the most dangerous drug known to man, both to self and others, killing more people every year than all other drugs combined. Ketamine is now being prescribed for depression. Cannabis products (largely CBD) are being used legally for pain, anxiety and epilepsy and further research has been recommended in its use to treat cancer. Research trials are continuing in the use of:

MDMA (Ecstasy/Mandy) for Post-Traumatic Stress Disorder.

Psychedelic drugs such as LSD and Psilocybin (magic mushrooms) for:

- Anxiety and depression (especially in end-stage cancer)
- Anorexia
- Alcohol, Opioid and Crack Cocaine addiction

It is thought that these drugs could be prescribed within the next 5 years or so. Why have they not been available before now? Because just one trip can reset our brain. Now where is the money in that? But WAIT. Do not run out and buy yourself a trip, this can be very dangerous. Drugs are very addictive and kill thousands of people every year, and I've nursed people in wheelchairs who had jumped out of windows because they thought they could fly. And if you are on antidepressants or other medication, have high blood pressure, heart disease or other conditions, this could be extremely dangerous. Wait for the trials and for it all to become legal and supervised. The trials take so long, because it takes the doctors and clinics at least two years to get the go ahead to use these banned substances. For a great film about this from the World Science Festival, check out (122) Revealing the Mind: The Promise of Psychedelics - YouTube.

https://www.reuters.com/article/us-drugs-alcohol/drug-experts-say-alcohol-worse-than-crack-or-heroin-idUSTRE6A000O20101101

https://www.addictioncenter.com/community/why-alcohol-is-the-deadliest-drug/

Illusions - ever seen a monster in your room when it was just your dressing gown hanging on the back of your door, or seen a person on the side of the road that turned out to be a tree? Ever thought how amazing that magician was? They are all illusions. As are the wonderful, happy, amazing, glorified effects of alcohol. Do you want to be the puppet or the master?

Imposter Syndrome - that pesky self-doubt! The worry that we don't belong and don't deserve what we have, or where we are in life. The imposter syndrome is a fraudster. The first time I actually felt this was in my sobriety; I didn't deserve to feel so good. I couldn't understand where feeling so good came from. I couldn't remember ever feeling it before, my life was miserable and that is just life, right? WRONG! Life is wonderful and it is for loving, laughing and living. Our sober community can really help with this, they help us to fit in and belong and give us confidence to just be.

Inappropriate - oh the shame. Just think of the last time you were drunk and inappropriate. When you did something embarrassing, that you would not have done had you been sober. That situation that's played on your mind and filled you with regret and upset. From this moment on, do not beat yourself up about it, turn it around and put it in your **Tool Box**. Use it, whenever you need to, to help you to play it forwards, and keep you sober.

Incapacitated - means being unable to do things normally. Ever been ill or injured and unable to move around or do what you would usually do? On top of the pain and feeling ill that comes with this, a frustration usually emerges because we cannot freely do what we want to. When we get drunk, we are inflicting this upon ourselves. We are unable to talk, walk, or think straight. We are unable to make decisions and we become irrational. Things no longer make sense and we bring about our own frustration and make ourselves **Vulnerable**. We are trapped inside a body that does not function, with a brain and mind that cannot control it. If we keep on drinking, this will become permanent. If we stop, we can become free.

Indecision - it's horrible when we can't make our minds up, but it's better than making awful drunk decisions. I do get frustrated when I cannot decide and feel pressured when there's a time limit. Then I remind myself, at least I have the full **Capacity** to make one. It may not always be the wisest, and I make mistakes which I learn from, but at least they are not downright stupid and dangerous. I will take my time today. Decisions are important, and it's ok not to know the answer straight away, if at all. It helps to **Pause** and allow ourselves space and time.

Individual - is what we have the right to be and what we are. We all have our own ways, our own quirks, our own interests and our own wishes and dreams. No two people are the same, and that's what makes us interesting and **Unique**. For this very reason, what works for me may not work for you. It is important for us to respect each other's individualism and rights, especially in sobriety. We are all fighting a battle with a similar aim and goal. But we have to do it in our own way.

Inflammation - is bloody painful and can affect any part of our body, making it red, hot and swollen. But did you know, this is actually our body's defence to protect and heal damaged tissue? Alcohol irritates the stomach which inflames to protect us. This leads to increased stomach acid, nausea and vomiting. When we drink every day, this can make our stomach continually inflamed and change our gut bacteria, leading to chronic inflammation anywhere in the body. Gut inflammation can cause **Cancer**, bowel and liver disease and brain inflammation.

https://riahealth.com/blog/alcohol-and-inflammation/

Inner Child - we all have an inner child. Sometimes they sit silently, other times they are petulant and argumentative. Mostly, for me, little Corinna felt angry, rejected, unloved and sad. She was very scared and afraid and it was a horrible place to be. So, older Corinna drank to numb and silence her but she'd come out in all her glory when older Corinna had had enough and snapped with anger. Other times, the depression would hit, and the silence and anxiety would come. During my journey, I placed a photo of 2-year-old me on my fridge looking innocent, trusting and happy. Very slowly, I learnt to walk hand in hand with her again. With that came trust, faith and love. It now feels amazing. Your little you is in there, waiting patiently…

Insomnia - difficulty getting off to sleep, staying asleep, waking up early or sleeping at all. We all know it. **Sleep** is so important for growth and repair and poor sleep leads to all sorts of physical and mental health problems. Many of us drink alcohol to help us get off to sleep, but alcohol disturbs our REM sleep; our most restorative sleep stage. Just another reason why we wake up feeling like shite and still tired the next morning.

Inspiration - where do we get this from? Well firstly, from inside of us. Try listening to your heart instead of your head, look around and see what messages the universe is giving you. Who or what is out there inspiring you? Turn **Envy** and **Jealousy** into admiration, make a plan and go for it. When I first joined the **IAS**

community, I saw a picture of Chef56 standing under beautiful, tall, sunflowers which he had grown from seed. He was one year sober. I wondered how both things were possible, but could see that they were. I grew sunflowers from seed the next year, along with my sobriety. Never doubt what others see, the seeds you sow or the inspiration you grow in yourself and others. We are all an inspiration to someone.

Intestines - are part of our **Gut** and made up of our small and large bowel. They measure between 15 and 21 feet and run from our stomach to our anus. Our intestines are where most of our food is digested and where our nutrients are absorbed by our blood stream and waste products removed to form our poop. They make small muscular movements which move our food and poop along. Alcohol interrupts this muscle movement causing the diarrhoea many of us encounter after drinking. Alcohol also stops the absorption of all those wonderful nutrients, leading to damage to many parts of our body.

https://www.verywellhealth.com/enteric-nervous-system-5112820

https://pubs.niaaa.nih.gov/publications/arh21-1/76.pdf#

Intimacy - a feeling of closeness and connection to someone. This is something alcohol completely removes. How can we feel close or connected to someone if our physical being, emotions and senses are all numbed? How can we understand and have **Compassion** and **Connection** with others if we are struggling to make sense of what is in front of us? And it's not only affected when we are drinking. Regular, long-term drinking draws us away from others until we feel isolated and alone. The only intimacy we have left is with the bottle, and that is a horrible place to be. In recovery, **Connection** is key. And that my friend, is a wonderful place to be.

Iron (haemoglobin) - is found in our red blood cells and is vital to help carry oxygen around our body. Alcohol causes our red blood cells to die too quickly and reduces the amount that our bodies make. Low iron makes us feel very tired and look very pale. It can also cause dizziness, breathlessness and cold hands and feet. The good news is, it can be reversed by putting down the booze, getting a medical and eating healthily including meat, nuts, beans, spinach, cereals and bread.

https://pubs.niaaa.nih.gov/publications/arh21-1/42.pdf

J

Jealousy - is often due to our own insecurities. We feel jealous of others and what they have because we feel angry, frustrated, anxious and worried about ourselves and our own life. If we can stay in our **Hula Hoop**, and focus on ourselves, jealousy will disappear. Remember, the grass is not greener, everyone has their own issues and battles, no matter how wonderful their life may seem.

Jekyll and Hyde - when we drink even a small glass of alcohol our character changes and what may be OK one day, is not the next. We cannot be consistent, or give consistency, when we are anaesthetising ourselves. Alcohol makes us less tolerant and sends our minds wandering all over the place and our imagination running wild. Our ego cannot keep the other parts of our mind in line, and leads us on a merry dance into a fantasy world without rhyme or reason. One day we will be Snow White, the next the wicked stepmother. Now I'm not going to lie - the first few weeks/months of getting sober can be like this too, with our moods all over the place. But if we stick with it, eventually, we get to a place of calm and consistency which makes for a happier life for all involved.

Johari Window - sounds anciently oriental, doesn't it? It was actually formed by two American Psychologists in 1955; Joseph Luft and Harrington Ingham. This doesn't make it any less wonderful though. It is a model used to help us identify the parts of ourselves that we and others see, and helps with selfawareness:

- Open/ Free Area – the parts everyone can see
- Blind Area – the parts others can see but we can't – how do we really look from the back in real time? How did we really behave last time we were drunk?
- Hidden Area – the parts only we can see (all our hidden secrets)
- Unknown Area – unknown to ourselves and others (all the things we have locked tightly away and buried somewhere deep inside of us)

By telling others more about ourselves we gain trust, and by getting feedback from others we can learn more about ourselves and grow. In sobriety we can come out of hiding, and if we **Work It** we start to love ourselves a whole lot more. Getting sober is a voyage of discovery and eventually we become open and free.

https://www.selfawareness.org.uk/news/understanding-the-johari-window-model

JOMO - I love this phrase. The Joy of Missing Out. No more **FOMO** here. The thought of going to a noisy bar full of drunk people, battling my way through a 10 deep throng to get to a drink and getting covered in mine and other people's drinks actually makes me feel physically sick these days. I cannot think of anything worse. How times have changed. The old me couldn't understand why people went to coffee shops or cafés when there was a perfectly good pub next door that served alcohol at 11 am. Now I completely get it. I love me a little coffee or tea shop now. And as for a quaint little café ... the pubs can eat their hearts out.

Journal - a lot of people find it really helpful to journal. It's good to get it all out and it's also good to look back on and reflect. I didn't do a daily journal as in pen and paper, but I did post daily on the **IAS** app in the early days, and later blogged on Instagram and Wordpress. I do wish I had written or typed it all out in one place though. I listened to a sobertown podcast recently, with King13 and her gals, talking about the first two weeks of sobriety. I realised that I couldn't actually remember mine, only that I was done and I had a choice to live or die. I looked back on my IAS posts and was surprised to see that I had realised loneliness and boredom were triggers at just 2 weeks. Not the 2 months that I'd remembered. It can be really helpful to look back on our journey.

Journey - this is yours and yours alone. In sobriety we all have the same goal and aim. We will go through very similar things, but the journey itself is ours. It will be bumpy in parts and smooth at other times. It's important to remember we cannot expect others to join us on this journey or to understand it. After all, there will be parts that we don't even understand ourselves and that's OK. Like any journey, we will come across hindrances and help, but remember to keep hold of the wheel of your **Bus** and only let those on board that you want to.

Joy - I really didn't know that I could feel such depths of a wonderful emotion for so long. I was more used to holding onto depression and anxiety. With sobriety comes real joy and happiness and it is the best feeling in the world. It's there for the taking. Stop drinking. **Work It**. Feel it. Love it.

Judgement – is something we sit in constantly. We have our 'always already listening' way of being. We constantly listen to our **Ego** and **Monkey Mind**, and believe what they are telling us. But if we can just stop, and really look and listen, then we may allow ourselves time to see things differently. Most importantly, we catch how judgemental we really are. For today, try to come from a place of understanding instead of judgement. It's very refreshing.

Jump Right In - it's the easiest way to make change but it's best if you plan first. I didn't plan. I just did it, but I was lucky to find the **IAS** community. I've jumped right in several times before, following a "never again" experience, just to climb back into the pits a week later. **Plan and Prepare**, set a date and do it.

Junk Food - it's not just alcohol cravings we have when we quit, our body seems to want sugars and junk food. Maybe due to boredom, sugar replacement, reward or self-harm. I put on 7 kilos when I quit as I craved and ate things I don't usually even eat. Beware, forewarned is forearmed as they say. I would suggest making shopping for healthy snacks part of your planning and preparation, along with activities to distract yourself and use the 'Am I really hungry?' script which you can find at the end of the **Eating** section.

K

Karma - is not 'what goes around, comes around' in the way we use it. In Buddhism, it is not about punishment; it is about cause and effect. Any action we take today will lead to our tomorrow and anything we experience today is caused by something we did in this or other lives. If we plant sunflower seeds in our garden today, we would not expect tomatoes to grow. What we plant today will bloom in the future. What happens today, we planted in our past.

Kidney Disease - comes in two forms, acute and chronic. Alcohol, toxins and some prescribed medications can cause both. Drinking more than 14 **Units** of alcohol a week can double our risk of kidney disease. Drinking more than 14 units in one session, can cause acute kidney injury and hospital treatment which could include dialysis; a machine which filters our blood for us until our kidneys are working again, if at all. Damage to other organs and cells in our body from alcohol can also stop our kidneys from doing their job correctly, and this can all lead to chronic, long-term, kidney disease. Both acute and chronic kidney injury or disease can lead to death.

https://www.kidney.org/atoz/content/alcohol#

Kidneys - we have two of these powerful filtering machines. They remove toxins and waste products from our blood, and pass them out of our body in the form of pee. Most drugs and toxins exit our body in this way and therefore make our kidneys work harder. Our kidneys also keep the water balanced in our body which affects our blood pressure and hydration. When we drink alcohol, we dehydrate our body, altering the balance and putting extra pressure on our kidneys and this whole system.

Kindness - doesn't cost anything and can make us feel better about ourselves and the world we live in. It can enrich us and makes us far happier. If we are always criticising and judging, how can we possibly be happy? When we come from a place of **Understanding** and **Compassion** then we can be kind and **Happy**. Studies have shown an increase in **Serotonin** when a kind deed is done, for both the giver and the receiver. See under **Metta** for more on loving kindness.

https://www.psychologytoday.com/us/blog/in-the-face-adversity/201211/practicing-acts-kindness

Kintsugi - the Japanese art of mending broken pots and vases with gold and allowing them to proudly display their cracks, flaws and scars. Don't be afraid of yours. They are who you are, they make you whole. Embrace them.

Kiss and Make Up or Walk Away - so many times we 'forgive' others and let them back into our life only to keep raking up all the old stuff. Not only are we punishing them, but we are punishing ourselves too. If you cannot fully let it go, then let them go. It is kinder for all concerned.

Knowing - ours is inside of us. This is a term **Glennon Doyle** uses and I think it describes our **Gut Instinct**. Going with what our tummy and heart are telling us. Not what our mind, conforming and society wants us to believe. When you know, you know. Just go with it.

Knowledge - really is power. Many have gone before us. If we can read, listen and take it all in, it really does help. Become like a sponge, absorb it all, keep what you want and let the rest go.

Korsakoff's Syndrome - is a brain injury, similar to dementia, caused by poor nutrition and lack of Vitamin B1 (Thiamine) which can be caused by drinking alcohol. Low thiamine affects the parts of our brain (**Thalamus**, **Hypothalamus** and **Limbic System**) which help with our sleep, movement, sensation, nerves, circulation, thirst, hunger, perceptions, emotions and memory. It stands to reason, therefore, that a depletion of Thiamine will cause confusion, memory loss, poor co-ordination, visual problems and hallucinations. People with this condition often make up stories to fill in for the memory gaps, which they then believe to be true.

https://pubs.niaaa.nih.gov/publications/arh27-2/134-142.htm

https://www.alzheimers.org.uk/about-dementia/types-dementia/wernicke-korsakoff-syndrome

K Vitamin - is essential for the clotting of our blood and healthy bones. As we now know, alcohol affects our ability to absorb all vitamins and minerals and when we are drinking our diet is rarely a healthy one. Lack of vitamin K leads to bone weakness, bleeding and bruising. Foods high in vitamin K are green leafy vegetables and soybeans. It dissolves in fat so try and combine it with fats or a healthy olive oil.

https://pubmed.ncbi.nlm.nih.gov/3544923

L

Language - fascinates me! Have you ever sat back and thought about how we all communicate in different languages all over the world?   How can groups of us understand each other, whilst others cannot?   But did you know, only 7% of what we communicate is done with words?   Roughly 55% is through our body language; our movements, the way we stand or sit, the look on our face etc. and 38% through the tone of our voice.   Now, think about how all of this changes when we drink.   Both how we act and our understanding of others.   No wonder there are so many drunken brawls.   Sobriety truly is the language of love.

Language of Letting Go - by Melody Beattie.   A book of daily thoughts and meditations to help us through the day.   It is especially written for **Co-dependency** but a great daily reflection for us all.   I haven't personally read it but Pollya has shared some of the daily reflections with me which are wonderful.

https://melodybeattie.com

Laughter - really is the best medicine.   And there's a chemical reason for this.   When we laugh, we release **Endorphins**, our feel-good chemical and pain reliever.   Sober laughter is much more genuine and real and it comes so much easier.   For a good old belly laugh, put down the booze and go watch a comedy or spend fun time with friends.   If you like the theatre then I can thoroughly recommend The Book of Mormon.   Sober theatre at its best.

Learning - is key to our being. In sobriety I have learnt so much about alcohol. Learning is more than believing what we are told, or what we see or read. It is what we experience and what we think. It is about being open to questions and learning for ourselves. Life really is a self-directed study.

Lessons - are the important things we learn in life. But we have to be open to them. Many lessons will pass us by, whilst we are too busy being angry or frustrated with ourselves or others. Things really do happen for a reason, even the really bad stuff including the relapses and the resets. The important thing is to learn from them and make them count. Try to stay curious today, no matter what is thrown your way, and **Trust in the Process**.

Lies - are crippling. They put and keep us in a cage, and they increase our anxiety for fear of being caught out. It is so freeing to be honest and genuine instead of sneaking around. Even better, sober me is able to tell my own truth and realise all the lies I have been told and those I have told myself.

Life - you may believe we have more than one. You may not. Either way, we are in this one right now and it will end with our last breath. We never know when that will be, so live each day as if it is your last.

Life Force - is the energy that drives us. It's our pep, our vim, our mojo, our motivation, our get up and go. Alcohol wipes it out. If you want to get your **Mojo** back then you know what to do.

Light - really is at the end of the tunnel. The tunnel is different lengths and depths for us all, but the light is there even if we cannot always see or fathom it. Alcohol-fuelled life can be so dark, heavy and dreary. It affects the chemicals and the structure of our brain making life a lonely, sad, anxious, horrible place to be. The first step to seeing the light is to stop drinking alcohol, find a sober **Community** and get help. Eventually the light will become so dazzling that you will feel weightless in comparison.

Lighthouse - find yours, and hopefully you will become one too...

The Lighthouse Analogy

(From UK SMART Recovery website)

'Consider a lighthouse. It stands on the shore with its beckoning light, guiding ships safely into the harbour. The lighthouse can't uproot itself, wade out into the water, grab the ship by the stern and say, 'Listen you fool. If you stay on this path you will break up on the rocks.' No. The ship has some responsibility for its own destiny. It can choose to be guided by the light in the lighthouse. Or, it can go its own way. The lighthouse is not responsible for the ship's decisions. All it can do is be the best lighthouse it knows how to be. Randi Kreger and Paul T. Mason from *'Stop Walking on Eggshells'* 1998'

https://smartrecovery.org.uk/wp-content/uploads/The-Lighthouse-Analogy.pdf#

Limbic System – is made up off selected parts of the brain, including our fire alarm (**Amygdala**), librarian (**Hippocampus**), **Thalamus** and **Hypothalamus**. All these parts work together to help with our memory, motivation, emotions, feelings, sleep, heartbeat, hunger and understanding our senses – especially our smell (hence why smells can bring back so many memories). The limbic system is closely related to learning and our **Reward Pathway** including the stimulation of **Dopamine**. It influences our ability to choose and the realisation that sometimes we need to rewire our systems to make healthier choices!

https://www.sciencedirect.com/topics/neuroscience/limbic-system

www.albertpeia.com/generalpsychology/limbicsystem.html#

Liver - is our biggest organ and the only one with two blood supplies. Nutrients come into it from our intestines and oxygen comes into it from our heart. The liver is thought to carry out over 500 functions including, filtering the blood, storing nutrients, making and breaking down blood cells, helping digestion and absorbing nutrients, controlling disease, breaking down and changing food, drink and drugs. It is a vital machine that we need to keep oiled. Alcohol puts a huge pressure on our liver and can lead to inflammation, scarring, lesions, liver damage, **Cirrhosis** and liver failure. Fortunately, the liver can repair and regenerate itself so it is great if we can stop drinking before it is too late. Check out this YouTube video for a great overview into the liver: What does the liver do? - Emma Bryce - Bing video

Some people find bupleurum, turkey tail mushroom or milk thistle supplements helpful to cleanse and help repair the liver. https://www.medicalnewstoday.com/articles/305075

Living - *'Falling down is part of life, getting back up is living'* José N. Harris. If we don't fall down, how can we learn? After all, this is what taught us all to walk when we were toddlers. As

we get older, we are not quite so patient with ourselves and we are often looking for the next best thing and someone or something to make our lives wonderful. This often leads to disappointment, pain and addiction of some sort; we are all addicted to something. At first alcohol can make life seem more fun and even make life seem worth living. Eventually, it leads to just existing and darkness, and a slow, painful way out. If you are reading this then you are one of the lucky ones who has so far survived. Even luckier, is that you have realised something has to change. There really is more to life than death. We all need help and support, but it really is within our control to change. Take your life back from the clutches of alcohol, and start living in a way you never dreamed possible.
https://www.goodreads.com/author/show/4631437.Jos_N_Harris

Loneliness - we can feel lonely even when we are around others, but being alone can make us feel really sad. And bored! I didn't know this was a trigger for me until I stopped drinking, and after a long weekend alone the cravings started. One of the hardest things for me was to learn to just be with myself. There was no fancy stuff, I just sat and learned to feel comfortable alone, but it was the best lesson of all. I now like being with me and look forward to and love my alone time.

Lotions and Potions - well I don't know about you, but I've spent an absolute fortune on these over the years, trying to find the next best thing to resolve my **Skin** problems. Cleansers, creams and oils for my constantly changing skin; oily, dry, combination. Creams and balms to cover up and get rid of my red cheeks, **Rosacea**, spider veins and wrinkles. Latterly I was even buying organic and all natural products ffs! I still do buy natural and organic, but I'm no longer poisoning myself from the inside. Since getting sober, all I need is a bit of dermal face wash, a light natural moisturiser and a body oil which I spray on wet after the shower. The only red cheeks I have now is a rosy glow. And I have a much fatter wallet.

Lovable - that's you. That's all of us. Experience may well have taught us differently and whilst you may not agree with everything you have read so far, then believe this. You ARE lovable. Just for today, notice something wonderful about you. If you struggle then use the fact that you are reading this and considering or making changes to your life, you wonderful, lovable thing you.

Love - nearly all my relationships have been made with alcohol. I even had several drunk one-night stands trying to find love. I just wanted to be held and cared for. Of course, they just wanted a quick shag and farewell. So, in my quest for love, I actually left myself feeling used and even more bereft. We all need quality interactions, not just a sticking plaster to try and hold it all together. With sobriety real healing can begin. Even love for family and friends becomes more genuine. For the first time I can actually feel it. I mean really feel it. Yes I loved when I was drinking, but I never knew how wonderful love truly felt until now.

Lungs – two vital organs that are crucial to our existence as they enable us to breathe in oxygen and rid our body of carbon dioxide. They are connected to our nose and mouth by our air tubes (bronchial) and we now know that alcohol can change these overtime, including reducing our saliva and increasing our risk of lung disease, inflammation and infection. This includes pneumonia which is the leading cause of infection deaths worldwide. There is even a specific diagnosis of Alcohol Pneumonia. People who abuse alcohol are 10 times more likely to develop pneumonia and 4 times more likely to die from it than non-drinkers.

https://www.ncbi.nlm.nih.gov/pmc/articles/PMC5513688/

https://pubmed.ncbi.nlm.nih.gov/20150202

M

Magic - we have always had this. We often look around for a fairy godmother, a genie, or the ground to just open up and swallow us whole. We make wishes when we blow out our birthday candles, when we pull the wishbone or to overcome superstition. Catch yourself next time you think or say 'I wish ....' and ask yourself:

- What is it I really want?
- What part of that is within my control?
- What can I do to achieve this?

Look deep inside. Take back the reins. And, if it's time, make the drink disappear.

Maintenance Plans - these are great to keep us motivated and on track. I've been so busy focussing on my alcohol quit that I have let things slide a bit but am back on it today. This is my daily list which is on my fridge:

- Get out of bed by 9am
- Have a shower/bath today
- Pace and use **Mindfulness**
- Do my physio exercises/**Yoga**
- Get outside
- Eat healthily, sitting down and chewing well
- Avoid alcohol and drink plenty of water
- Take pain relief when needed

- Ask for **Help**
- Tackle something I've have been putting off
- Have an afternoon nap
- Stay curious
- Use **Acceptance**
- Live in the **Now**
- Bed by 9pm and lights out by 10

What are the things you need to do every day to stay well?

I also have a flare up plan which is basically: Make sure I'm doing all of the above, rest more, take extra pain relief and fill in the time with sitting down hobbies and catching up with friends and family on the phone. And remember, if you don't get it all done, do not give yourself grief, just aim for it again tomorrow.

Mantras - are sounds we repeat and chant over and over to help us relax, meditate or keep focussed on our goal. Mantras are sounds that connect us to nature and the universe, and get us in tune and harmony with both by connecting us to vibrations. We can chant them in our head, out loud, in a group or alone. They can really help us to keep focussed in meditation, yoga and breathing exercises. Here are a few examples, but you can completely make up your own if you prefer:
- A E I O U – hold each letter for a couple of seconds or more
- Buddho – rhymes with 'good oh'. This chant encourages the pure and natural part of us to arise
- Om – chanted as aum. It is said to be the sound of the universe
- Om Shaanti Shaanti Shaantihi – helps us to tap into our inner peace

There are many more out there, so if mantras appeal to you, have a little hunt around and find one or two that work for you.

https://yogasigns.com/difference-between-mantras-and-affirmations

Marketing - I've talked about advertising now let's talk about marketing – the promoting and selling of the **Poison**. Have you noticed how on every given occasion alcohol is introduced to the first aisle of the store? Easter, Mother's Day, Father's Day, Christmas, World Cup, Summer BBQ's. Hell, there was even a Spring Festival this year, just to promote alcohol. Many years ago, my partner worked for a superstore in the alcohol department. They would get a plan of how to market the booze, where it needed to be placed, how it was to be displayed along with pricing, special offers and banners. Just think of all the special offers that spring up around the store at the end of random aisles. I was in a store recently, with my son, looking at baby clothes and right next to them were random shelves of alcohol clearly designed to attract women. They looked like perfume bottles with their sparkles and fancy bottle tops. I mean WTAF?! Over the last couple of years, there has been strong marketing towards women and a complete rebranding of gin, previously 'mothers ruin', now the trendiest drink of our time.

Maslow's Hierarchy of Need - Abraham Maslow's theory covers 5 areas that he feels humans need for motivation. He sees our foundation as the physical things we need to actually survive; food, water, shelter, air, sleep, clothes, reproduction. Without these, we cannot achieve the other areas of safety, love and belonging, self-esteem and the desire to become the best we can. Now, just think about how alcohol affects our very basic needs. It dehydrates us, stops us absorbing nutrients, stops us eating well, impacts on our breathing of that precious air, disturbs our sleep, affects fertility and sexual performance and for many, it robs them of their homes. How on earth can we feel good about ourselves and life if we are robbing ourselves of our basic needs?

https://www.explorepsychology.com/maslows-hierachy-of-needs

Materialistic - it's the world we live in. Always looking for the next best thing and having things to show for all our hard work, almost like a badge of honour. If we have lots of things then it proves we have made it. But have we? It's just stuff at the end of the day. What I now have to show is my sobriety, and I wear that with pride. I have less things now than I have ever had in my life and I am the happiest I have ever been. **Happiness** cannot be found in things; it is found within. But if you really like your things, then quit drinking and you'll have lots more money to buy them!

Measures - are different all over the world. In the UK, one standard spirit measure is 25ml and is referred to as one unit. In the USA 1.5 ounces of 40% distilled spirits equals one unit. If you are wanting to stop, or just cut down your drinking, then I suggest you start by measuring and tracking your drinks. Any drink we pour at home is going to be far more than what we would purchase when we go out in the UK, so start by measuring. Read under **Units** for more information or get the **Drinkaware** app to help you keep track.

Medication - does not mix well with alcohol! Both are processed in the liver and affect hormones and chemicals in our body. When we drink alcohol, it can either heighten or reduce the effects of medication. When we stop drinking medication will work more effectively, but it may need to be monitored and adapted as a different dose may be needed. Be honest with your medical practitioner and work together on this. If you are drinking heavily and are physically dependent on alcohol (see

Dependency), then it is dangerous to just stop drinking. There is medication that can help with withdrawals and cravings. Again, see your medical practitioner and be honest – it could save your life.

Meditation - is a cleansing of our mind. It is quiet time spent with ourselves and our thoughts. It can be done sitting, lying, standing and walking whilst focussing on our breathing. It is observing our thoughts but not getting drawn into them. I used to find this really difficult, but a Buddhist relaxation retreat, **Acceptance** and daily practice has really made this easier. Start off with just 5 minutes a day. If all you get are a few seconds of peace then don't worry. It is not a competition. Just keep practising. You probably wouldn't go a week without an external wash, so why wait that long for an internal one?

Meditation Tricks - feel your connection to the ground and focus on your breath. Observe it going in and out:

- Meditate from the centre of your chest – not your head. Buddhists believe this is where our mind is. Gradually imagine your mind being pulled down to the centre of your chest until it sits comfortably there
- Think of your mind as a calm ocean, your thoughts and feelings as the waves. As the waves start to grow, you can either pull them back in and quieten them or give them energy to get bigger
- Imagine your thoughts as a toddler sitting on a blanket, each time it crawls off just gently bring it back
- Catch yourself with your wandering thoughts. Accept them, and come back to the breath
- Imagine you are a child at play and make finding your breath a game, like a child with a toy

- Imagine your mind as a clear blue sky, your thoughts as clouds forming, let them pass by and disperse

Melody Beattie - a teenage alcohol and drug user who turned her life around and has written many wonderful books about this and co-dependency, including:

'The Language of Letting Go',

'Journey to the heart'

'Codependents' Guide to the 12 Steps'

For her full list, and to read more about her, go to www.melodybeattie.com.

Memories - we add and take away from them all the time. Not just our experience of them, but the way our mind changes and distorts them over time. Add alcohol into the mix … drinking me only remembered the bad stuff. I would tell others I had an 'OK childhood' but deep down my memories were filled with bullying, pain and misery. When I got sober, I found happiness. And initially I declared "I have never felt like this in my life. I didn't know such happiness was possible". On reflection, it is more a case of not remembering. How could I? I was too fixed and focused on the anger and pain. Yes, my not so good memories arise, but I beat them away like my addict voice nowadays and gradually, far happier memories are taking their place. None of us will ever know the truth of any situation or occurrence, it is all of our mind's making.

Memory - we have short-term memory (in the here and now – our 'working' memory) and long term (ability to recall past information that our brain has 'filed'). Our memory is how we take in, translate and store information. Pretty hard to do that under the influence of an anaesthetic, whose main task is to make us forget. Getting sober does not only mean that I no longer have to reach for my phone with shame the next morning, but my memory is much clearer and sharper every day. I always say to mums with young children, "Enjoy knowing where they are, who they are with and what they are doing whilst you can". It is so nice to now enjoy this about myself.

Memory Loss - we have seen that our short-term memory can temporarily be affected by alcohol from the **Anaesthetic** effects and when we **Blackout**. Damage to our **Brain**, and especially our **Hippocampus**, and lack of Vitamin B1, caused by long term drinking can also lead to loss of our long-term memory. This can lead to **Dementia**, brain injury and **Wernicke-Korsakoff's Syndrome**. Heavy drinkers (that's 14 **Units** a week for women and 28 a week for men) have been shown to have 30% more memory problems than a non-drinker.

https://onlinelibrary.wiley.com/doi/10.1111/j.1530-0277.2003.tb04422.x

https://www.verywellmind.com/alcohol-damages-day-to-day-memory-function-62982

Mental Health - whenever we hear this term we tend to think of illness, but if we look at it in the same way we do physical health we start from a more positive place. This helps us to feel more in control and indicates that we can take action to keep ourselves mentally healthy. Eating healthily, exercise, fresh air, quitting drugs, drinking and smoking all go a long way in helping us to be mentally healthy.

Mental Illness - there are many, but be assured, alcohol can contribute to and can cause these. Not only does alcohol change our perceptions, it physically changes our brain size, chemicals and function. It is a mind-altering chemical; how can that be mentally healthy? Illnesses include depression, anxiety, schizophrenia, obsessional compulsive disorder and bi-polar disorder and may also be why some of us started drinking in the first place - to self-medicate. Another vicious circle, and another good reason to get ourselves medically checked. Especially if you have stopped alcohol and are worried about your mood.

Metabolism - is how our body changes our food and drink into energy. Alcohol affects our ability to metabolise nutrients leading to problems with our liver, kidneys, heart and circulatory system, digestive system and our brain.

Metta - is loving kindness and goes hand in hand with **Mindfulness**. A good place to start is by being kind to ourselves. Saying nice things about and to ourselves. It can be really hard, but we can start by just catching ourselves when we are being unkind. The other day I declared "I'm such a bloody idiot" and then I took a breath and said; "I'm not an idiot, I'm just frustrated with myself for making that choice. I cannot change it, I just have to accept it, learn from it and move on". All whilst breathing slowly! Try finishing your meditation with "May I be well; may I be happy and may I be safe from harm". Later you can extend this to others, even people you don't particularly like, as it is here that you will find peace, forgiveness and freedom!

Milestones - personally, I loved mine, but they are not for everyone, and that is completely OK. In AA circles we are only ever sober for 24 hours anyway - one day at a time. But for the first year I loved counting up my sober days. If you like your milestones, then **Celebrate** them and treat yourself. You can buy AA sobriety coins independent of attending AA. I have a couple and I also have my sobriety bracelet hanging on my drawer handle, to remind me of my journey and how I am one of the lucky ones. For a great personal and caring service check out the www.recoveringkindredspirits.co.uk. There are lots of other milestones to celebrate along the way; our first sober meal out, our first sober concert, theatre visit, club, anniversary, birthday etc.

Mind - this is our all-seeing and all-knowing. It is colourless and shapeless, it cannot be seen or touched, it has no beginning or end. It is completely separate from our body, but without it our body is nothing. Yes, our heart will beat, our body will move and our eyes will see, but it will all be meaningless. Our mind is what makes sense of everything. It gives us and life meaning. But beware, our mind is often distorted by our thoughts, feelings and experience, and this is what Buddhists call a delusion. Take a piece of chocolate cake for example: it can look delicious; we can crave it and think it will make us feel happy and maybe a slice or two does. But, imagine eating 50 slices of it. Will it still seem so appealing and wonderful then? If you've seen the film Matilda, you will know exactly what I mean.

Mindfulness - being and living in the **Moment**. I have used this to rewire my brain and neural pathways by repeating to myself every move. It helps with concentration, grounding, managing our thoughts and feelings and relaxing. It is a form of meditation that we can use anywhere, at any time. Here are some examples:

- Driving; you notice yourself getting closer and closer to the car in front, gripping the steering wheel and holding your breath. Catch yourself. Force a breath out and relax your breathing. Take your foot off the gas slightly, loosen your grip on the steering wheel, notice the weather, your surroundings and see the beauty all around
- Washing up; you notice yourself gripping everything tighter and scrubbing harder and harder. Maybe even slamming things down. Catch yourself. Feel your

feet on the floor, breath and relax your grip. Notice the bubbles in the sink, feel the water on your hands, notice any sounds or smells around you and slow everything down

- Out shopping; It's busy. You are getting frustrated and anxious. You think everyone is looking at you. You fear a panic attack. Force your breath out and focus on relaxing your breathing and feeling your feet on the floor. Face any shelf and look at it (a shelf slightly above your eyesight can sometimes work best but look where it is comfortable for you), focus on one thing on that shelf. Keep breathing and feeling your feet on the floor and pick up the product. How does it feel? Is it hot or cold, hard or soft? What colours are the packaging? What does it say on it? Stand there for as long as you need to and get back to the reality of the moment. Not what your mind is telling you

Mindset - is so important. If we tell ourselves we can't then we won't. If we tell ourselves we can, then we will. But how to shift it? Find your reason, your **Affirmations**, your **Motivation** and stick to it. Most importantly, remember you have a **Choice**. Only you can change this.

Miracles - we're all waiting for them to happen. Put down the drink and make them. You'll have better health, more money, happiness and love. What's more, you'll be awake and won't miss all the wondrous gifts the universe gives us. Miracles really do happen; the trick is not to sit around waiting for them.

Misery - initially many of us drink to boost confidence, make us happy, help us fit in and have fun. Then we find it useful to block pain and forget. Some of us may start drinking for this very reason. And, it does all these things at first. I'm not going to sit here and say that I never had fun with alcohol because that would be a lie, I've had some bloody good nights out on the stuff. And then I didn't because everything revolved around alcohol. What's the first thing you look at when you go out for a meal? I love not having to worry about food prices now. I buy the most expensive thing if I want it, because I'm not spending a fortune on booze. Eventually alcohol gets us in its grip and we end up waking up with regret, shame, anxiety and worry. We live in a world of lies and deceit and very often, end up drinking alone. It is a dark, sad, miserable world. There is a saying in addiction circles 'Sobriety delivers everything alcohol promised'.

Mistakes - are part of life. How would we ever learn without them? Ralph Steadman said *'There's no such thing as a mistake, really. It's just an opportunity to do something else'.* We cannot change what is done, but we can learn from it, change and grow. The trick is not to linger and beat ourselves up but to take the opportunity from it today.

Moan - go ahead and do it. It helps to have a good moan, just don't wallow in it. Get it all out, breathe a sigh of relief and move on. I call it verbal vomiting.

Moderation - when we first start thinking of quitting and take that step, many of us do so with the intention of seeing if we can stop for a while and then cut back and just drink every now and again. Nearly every single one of us discovers that we cannot. We give it several tries though! Moderation is not a thing for anyone who is addicted to something. Don't beat yourself up from being hooked, it is an addictive substance after all. Look at it this way; you are responding how you are supposed to. It's the people that don't get addicted that aren't!

Mojo - a supernatural charm, skill or magic that helps us achieve. Hopefully, by now, you are starting to see that you are your own good luck charm. I hope you find your mojo real soon.

Moment - is all we ever have. We only ever actually live in this moment. Our mind may tell us otherwise but **Now** is all we ever have. Many of us say 'one day at a time' when we are facing life's struggles, but sometimes it really is moment by moment. Breath by breath.

Money - isn't everything but, in this world, it helps and not spending it on alcohol gives us a whole lot more. Two years of not drinking has paid for my Bumblebee motorbike outright. What could you save for and buy with your alcohol money?

Monkey Mind - jabber jabber jabber! It can be non-stop at times, chattering away and even engaging us in conversation. The only thing I liked about face masks, was that others couldn't see me talking to myself as I walked around the shop! We can either resist our monkey mind and let it drive us bonkers or accept and make friends with it. It's there, it's part of us. But we can distract it by giving it something to do: focus on the breath or think of four things you can see, hear, feel. Three things you can see, hear, feel … my monkey mind mostly makes me smile now. I accept it for what it is and that it is all okay. **Meditation** and **Mindfulness** are the best ways to tame it.

Monkeys - I love the monkey analogy which I read many years ago in '*One Minute Manager*' by Ken Blanchard. This is what I remember of it:

> *Just imagine yourself as a manager, walking through the*

front door at work, towards your desk or office. On the way, you are stopped by several people asking you questions and instead of empowering them, you take their problem on. Visualise it as a monkey jumping on your back. By the time you get to your destination you are weighed down by several monkeys.

On second thoughts, scrap the office, just think of walking through the front door at home. Even if we live alone, we throw our own monkeys on our backs due to things we feel we need to do - the housework, correspondence, the garden ... no amount of drinking is going to get rid of our monkeys. They may feel lighter for a while, but they're still gonna be there, hanging on and feeling even heavier with a hangover, guilt and remorse. How can you get those monkeys off your back today? Or at the very least, stop yourself from taking any more on?

Moon - it has long been known that this controls the waves of the ocean and the pull of our gravity. It is also thought to affect our moods, sleep and wellbeing. Many of us in sobriety find that the moon phases have an even more powerful effect on us and we can become very emotional and tearful around the full moon. Is it because we are not numbing? Or could it be because we are made mostly of water and have much more of it now that we are not so dehydrated? Either way, be prepared to feel the feels even more with the moon.

https://www.thespiritscience.net/2016/06/21/the-connection-between-the-moom-cycles-and-your-mood

Motivation - we all need motivation to get started on anything and to keep going. I got sober 2 months before my grandson was born as I didn't want to be a smelly drunk grandmother. That propelled me, but I realised early on that I actually had to do it for me. Because I deserve to be a grandmother and I deserve to have a life. Others can motivate us and cheer us along, but we have to want to do it.

- What is your motivation?
- What motivated you to pick up and read this book?
- What can you do to keep the motivation going?

Multivitamins - are essential for us all in early-stage sobriety and even more so when we are drinking. You have read how alcohol affects our eating and absorption of nutrition. You will see the different vitamins as you read through this book and why they are so important. If you are considering sobriety (and even if you are not), or just starting out, then I would recommend getting yourself a good multivitamin today.

Muscle Memory - is where we repeat an action so often that it becomes part of our memory without us having to even think about it, such as swimming and riding a bike. When I went to test ride my automatic trike, I rode it much better than my partner who has been riding on two wheels for years. His muscle memory kept on looking for the clutch and the gears. Mine didn't, as I have no experience of riding a bike like that. He is however, much better at walking than me as I am still working on retraining my muscle memory to do this! **Habits** and addictions also become part of our muscle memory, that's why we have to retrain ourselves when we want to change.

Music - we have made this from the beginning of time. It can be happy, sad, uplifting and even motivational. Even animals appear to walk and run to a beat and just think of the beautiful birdsong. Nowadays, there is so much music to choose from, and for many this can make a huge difference in their sobriety. Music can connect us all and bring us together, but it can also help us to connect with ourselves. I remember, as do my parents, playing Michael Jackson's *'One Day in Your Life'* over and over again after my first love dumped me. It helped me cry it all out, and come out the other side feeling stronger. Another great break up one is of course Gloria Gaynor *'I will survive'* and we will. My motivational sobriety song was **'I Am Woman'** by Helen Reddy (great movie also). I would play it every morning and it really set me up for the day. Another personal favourite is Hazel O'Connor *'Driftwood'* - I saw the shoreline, I dived in, I swam with my sober community throwing me a lifeline at times, and now I really have come home this time.

N

Need - what is it you really need in life? What sort of life do you want? What small steps do you need to take to help you get there? Really give it some thought. Do not rely on others or the lottery to fulfil your needs, or allow them to stop you from achieving them. Take back the reins. Drive your own **Bus** today and be in control of your destination.

What sort of life do I want?
What do I need?
What do I need to do to achieve this?

Negativity - brings us and others down. Just think of someone you find draining; are they always moaning about the world and its wife? Now think of someone you enjoy being around; are they happy, fun and positive? We know a smile can be infectious, but so is yawning and moaning. A friend of mine (SJ333) uses red sticky dots to stick on people when they are being negative; with their permission of course! They usually end up with an armful by the end of the day. It's ok to have a moan and get it all out but don't stay in the land of negativity, because once we are there it is so difficult to climb back out. Alcohol can take and keep us there, until we find the strength and support to break the chains.

Neglect - is a form of abuse. When children are neglected, they might be left to fend for themselves and can be inappropriately dressed, dirty, underweight, overweight, pale and have physical and emotional problems. They are very **Vulnerable** and either unable to fend for themselves or extremely alert and can get into trouble with the police. Many will lie about what is happening, as they would rather be with their neglectful parents whom they love, than be living in a different world that they do not know. Alcohol is our abuser; it causes us to be neglectful of so much, especially ourselves. But with strength, help and support we can break free.

Negotiation - is something our **Addict Voice** loves to do. It encourages us to drink, we say "No because one will lead to another" and it will come back with a negotiation of some sort. It tries to convince us that we can moderate - that we can just have the one and stop, or that if we go without a drink on weekdays then it is OK to drink at the weekends. It even tells us it is OK to drink, that we don't have a problem like others do. Be prepared. Play the scenario forwards, tell your addict voice 'NO!'

and that it is not up for negotiation. Like a child wanting its own way, it will keep on. Remember your **Boundaries** and keep on practising the power that is **No**.

Neural Pathways - are formed by our neurons sending messages backwards and forwards between our body and our brain. If we touch something hot, our pathway of neurons sends this sensation to our brain that tells our body the object is hot and to pull our hand away. In a healthy or sober person this all happens in a split second. Whilst the majority of neural pathways work to keep us safe and healthy, they are also habit-forming. We are in pain - we have a drink - it numbs the pain. Next time we are in pain ... But the good news is, we can retrain our neural pathways. Firstly, we have to put down the drink and stop drinking our neurons and their pathways into oblivion and allow them to do their job.

https://www.greatmindsclinic.co.uk/blog/what-are-neural-pathways

Neurons - are part of our nervous system. They send and receive messages from each other through chemical and electrical energy. They are found throughout our body and we have around 86 billion of them in our brain and around 500 million in our gut alone! Alcohol stops our neurons communicating with each other and causes the slurred speech, poor memory and movement we encounter when we are drinking. It also stops us from listening to our **Gut Instinct**, which can lead to us making decisions that we may not have made had we been sober.

https://www.verywellmind.com/how-many-neurons-are-in-the-brain-2794889

New Brain - is the wrinkly outer layer of our brain also known as the neo cortex. It is the thinking part of our brain, helping us to question, imagine, analyse, plan, make sense of what is going on and remember things as it is where our librarian (**Hippocampus**) is situated. It is also the part that makes us overthink things and where our thoughts go round and round in our head. It is self-aware and comes into play when we take a deep breath and count to 10, stopping us from reacting instinctively to our emotions and feelings. It works alongside our **Old Brain** but can also trigger it with thoughts leading to **Anxiety** loops:

New Brain: *I'm not drinking, everyone is looking at me, I'm going to be boring*

Old Brain: *Sees danger and sets off our fire alarm (**Amygdala**) flooding our body with **Adrenaline**.*

New Brain: *I knew this would happen, I feel like I'm going to lose control, I need a drink*

Old Brain: *Reaches for that drink and gulps it down*

New brain: *That's better. Just keep drinking and everything will be fine.*

Our new brain will have a very different story the next morning though ...

News - is someone else's story of events. If, like me, you find it all depressing and upsetting, then just turn it off! I have not purposefully listened to the news for years. This does not mean that I do not care, I do and I send **Metta** and loving kindness out to the world every day. I have a general idea of what is going on as I catch it on the car radio, overhear people talking and some people tell me directly. At a recent retreat I was reminded that we are all connected, that what we experience together helps us to grow and find peace. I am work in progress, but for now I do not feel able to burden myself with things that are completely out of my control and cause me distress and upset. Sometimes I will even physically walk out of a room to avoid hearing things, and go hide in my **Hula Hoop**.

NLP (Neuro-Linguistic Programming) - a therapy that helps us to ground ourselves and so much more. I thought it might be useful to share a technique that you may find helpful in difficult or triggering situations. You can either read through this and then give it a go or ask someone else to read it out to you as you do it.

Identify an area on your body that is easy for you to apply firm but discreet pressure to but not routinely touched by others.

Think of a time when you were happy or calm and relaxed.

Close your eyes and think of your happy place and go there.

Where are you? What is happening? Who is there with you? What are they doing? What are you doing? What can you hear? What can you see? What can you smell? What can you taste? What are you thinking? What are you feeling?

When you feel really good, apply some pressure to the point you identified and stay in your happy place with the pressure on for 15 seconds, reliving every moment and taking in every detail.

Release the pressure, take a cleansing breath and open your eyes.

Think about something totally unrelated for a minute or two and then apply pressure to the area again. Do you feel anything? If not, or if it is only a weak reaction, then go back to your happy place again and repeat the process.

Keep doing this until you just have to apply the pressure to feel calm, happy or relaxed.

This is now your anchor point. Just press that point whenever you need to ground yourself.

No - is an option and the only one for our addict voice. Many of us are yes people and I am still working on my no. I am a people pleaser and I do not like to upset and offend others. In so doing, I have upset, overwhelmed and offended myself time after time. And then I'd drink to numb my frustration and anger with myself. I still get frustrated at times but I keep the anger at bay, avoid the drink and work on a better plan for next time.

Now - is all we ever have. We only have this moment. This moment will become the past, the next moment will become our now. Don't let it pass you by. Live for now. Live in the now.

Nurture - every living thing needs this, especially us. Plants need water and sunlight; children need love and guidance. As we get older, we still need these things but most of us still look to others to stroke our **Ego** and care for us. Others of us are determined we do not need anyone else's help and push people away. Neither are helpful, it's all about balance. When we learn to love and nurture ourselves and not rely on others to provide this, it all becomes easier. We can do this by putting our own needs first, learning to say no, practising **Self-Care**, accepting others for who they are, lowering our expectations and communicating our needs.

O

Objective - can be a goal or not bringing our own personal feelings into a situation. When I was drinking, my daily objective was to open a bottle of wine as soon as I could. This did not help me remain objective in any situation as my feelings would come into everything. I'd even create a situation with my words and actions. My daily objective now is to remain **Sober** and be non-judgemental and kind. It all takes work, but I am now conscious and present to my **Ego** voice and can catch myself and accept that we can all have a wicked and judgemental mind at times. What is your daily objective currently? Are you happy with this? If not, what would you like it to be and what do you need to do to make it happen?

Oblivion - not knowing what is going on, in or around us. I think we have probably all drunk to this. On many occasions, this has been my intent. To be completely numb and not feel anything. But then we have to wake up and deal with the consequences.

Observe - is all that we see, hear, think, feel, taste and smell. It is how we make sense of the world around us and inside us. As adults we are not particularly good at either, and even worse at the inside stuff. We often just glimpse over things, allowing our **Ego** and **Neurons** to make snap decisions and often making unhelpful assumptions. As children we have all the time in the world to take everything in, something that can really frustrate adults. Having learned the importance of living in the now, I absolutely love spending time with my grandson and watching him explore and find fascination in every little thing. I'm not as good at it as he is, but he is my **Mindfulness** Guru.

Obsessed – today one of my old drinking friends asked 'Are you still obsessed with being sober? Doing all those podcasts and stuff?' I thought it was a strange thing to ask at first, but on reflection I figure this is how it may seem to those still drinking. An obsession is something troubling that fills our mind and consumes us – for me that was drinking and definitely not sobriety. How can we be obsessed with something so fulfilling? We are working through a lifetime of stuff, getting ourselves better, supporting and sharing our ideas with others. Despite my **Ego** wanting to respond with 'Are you still obsessed with drinking?', I took a breath and simply said 'I am not obsessed, I'm just sober'. I write this here as it may be something you are asked - be prepared and remember to **Pause** before you respond to such questions.

Obstacles - can be physical or emotional, from others or of our own making. They are part of life; the important thing is not to let them stop us and to learn from them – seeing them as preparation for future events. I find it helpful to view them as a brick wall being thrown up in front of me; my job is to find my way round, over, under or through it. Sometimes it is just brick by brick, other times I can take a running leap. Most of us loved the obstacle race at school, so many challenges to overcome, it's just our adult **Mind** that makes them a problem.

Oestrogen - is a female hormone and part of our reproductive system. Alcohol is known to increase oestrogen levels and this can lead to breast cancer which is the leading cause of death in women. Regularly drinking 2 alcoholic drinks a day can increases our risk of breast cancer by 30 – 40% and just one drink a day post menopause.

https://www.ncbi.nlm.nih.gov/pmc/articles/PMC3318874/#

Old Brain – so called as it is the first part of the human brain to have developed in evolution. It is also known as our 'reptilian brain' and is our primitive response. It regulates our heartbeat, breathing, movement, hunger and thirst and is responsible for our survival. It is the oldest part of the human brain and is responsible for our feelings and emotions – but works in survival mode. It is also where our fire alarm (**Amygdala**) is based and brings on our fight/flight/freeze response (**Anxiety**). It helps keep us safe but can also cause us to **Panic** and react in a very primal way. When we take a deep breath and count to 10, it allows our automatic reactions to calm down and our **New Brain** to come into play.

https://open.lib.umn.edu/intropsyc/chapter/3-2-our-brains-control-our-thoughts-feelings-and-behavior/#

Omega 3 - is a good fatty acid. This is something that our body cannot make and we can only get from food or supplements. We get it from fish (who actually get it from seaweed), walnuts, dark leafy vegetables, seaweed and flax seeds. I took 3000mg when I quit, as guided by Craig Beck in '*Alcohol Lied to Me: The Intelligent Way to Escape Alcohol Addiction*'. He reports that mice studies show reduced interest and cravings for alcohol with high omega 3 in their body. He also claims that it will replace the fats we have killed off in our brain with alcohol. I have to say I really do think it helped me. Drinking aside, omega 3 is said to help arthritis, joint pain, depression and reduce the risk of heart disease.

Opinions - you are not right; I am not wrong. It's just a matter of opinion. Opinions can cause a lot of arguments and upset. I loved this **IAS** comment from trailgypsey:

> ''*What others think of you is none of your business*''

'There are different ways of saying this and different people who have quoted it. I didn't like this quote the first number of times that I heard it. I honestly could not let what others saw or thought of me go. I would obsess over it and mull over and over what someone 'may' have meant. I could spend hours drinking over someone else's opinion of me. I've had a few times recently where the old me would have been triggered and I felt myself spiralling out of sanity, but I repeated this quote and it really worked. I even said it out loud a few times to make others aware that it wasn't my business what they were saying about me. It shut them up too'.

Organic - is something natural and uncontaminated by chemicals. I have tried to eat healthily for a few years now and have really focussed on organic food. But I continued to pour poison down my neck. Even more ridiculously, I started buying organic wine! When I quit the booze, I continued with organic, but binged on junk food in between. I'm more balanced now. Just be mindful is all I'm saying. I can actually laugh about the irony of it all now.

Ostracised - we fear this when we stop drinking. That we are going to be left out, rejected or laughed at for not drinking. I didn't have this, as I owned and declared my sobriety and everyone accepted it. But I know of others who have experienced and felt this. If I'm brutally honest, I think this is down to ownership of our response and remembering we have no control over others. If we can just let others be and focus on our own feelings and reactions, then this will make it so much easier. In my experience, it is us who end up removing ourselves from the drinkers because we no longer relish a night spent with them. We honestly cannot keep up with the conversation. Sober people cannot understand drunk people and vice versa.

Overcompensating - we may need to make amends, but we do not need to make them unnecessarily excessive. This makes us more **Vulnerable** and could cause **Triggers**. It is good to own up and take responsibility for our mistakes, but we do not need to spend the rest of our lives grovelling because of them. We only need to take the responsibility that is ours, if others cannot accept this then that is their issue.

Overreacting - is something we become experts at when we are drinking. Even just one drink makes us see and react differently. How can it not, when it is making so many changes to our body, memory and mind? I can think of many times I overreacted, as I'm sure you can too. With sobriety comes a sense of peace and calm. A sense of understanding and realisation that we are the ones in control of all of our responses.

Overwhelmed - this is me right now. I'm trying to juggle writing this book, proofreading the first 3 chapters, sorting out social care and home support for relatives, supporting other sober warriors, looking after my beautiful grandson and taking care of my own health. And right now, I just want to scream and have a full on two-year-old tantrum! But instead, I'm going to take a deep breath and accept it all for what it is and wind everything back in. I'm going to save and close this programme and take a few minutes to focus on my breathing and be still. My latest affirmation is "Leave it to the universe".

Owning Our Sobriety - is something I found really helpful to keep me going. But it is very personal. I proudly tell everyone how long I have been sober for, but this is not for everyone. Many of us do not want to declare our sobriety to the world. I do not get a negative response to this, nor do I allow one. Some say "Really? I didn't know you had a problem" I don't take this as an insult, I just explain what I drank and how this affected me. I see this as a golden opportunity to get the truth of alcohol out there and shine like a **Lighthouse**.

Own It - all that we have done. The drunk texting, the arguments, the hurt and upset, the accidents and unrest that we have triggered and sometimes caused. Try not to blame it on the drink, that is just making an excuse. We are the ones who drank, we are the ones that acted in the way we did. We have to own it to free ourselves and let it go.

P

Pace - something us drinkers aren't great at doing. I'm not a pacer. I'm all or nothing, boom or bust. Not just with drinking, but with everything in my life. I used to be at 100mph or horizontal. I've been practising pacing over the last 10 years and I'm just about getting there. When I start to speed up, stress comes and so do accidents. The only thing I don't pace is my alcohol: not another drop, no matter what. As I type this, I commit to pace myself today. If I start to speed up, I will take a deep breath and get back in King13's cruising lane (see **Cars**). Hope to see you there. No overtaking!

Pain - is an uncomfortable feeling or sensation carried to the brain by our neurons. It is not one size fits all, it depends on the way we interpret and perceive it. For this reason, medical staff use pain scales to determine how bad our pain levels are to us. What is really painful for me, might not be so painful for you and vice versa. This can also change day by day. If we are tense and stressed then we will feel more pain, whereas if we are relaxed pain won't be as bad. When we feel pain, we automatically tense and hold our breath to protect the area but this actually makes pain worse. If we can learn to breathe into and relax the area, then pain will lessen. Here's a quick one: breathe in and tense every muscle in your body. Really squeeze. Breathe out and release everything. Feel the difference?

https://medical-dictionary.thefreedictionary.com/pain

Pancreas - is an organ just under our stomach and to the left of our **Spleen**. It produces insulin and glucagon (a hormone that raises blood sugars and fatty acids in the bloodstream and helps the liver metabolise sugars). The pancreas also helps with digestion by oozing proteins into our small bowel. Alcohol causes the pancreas to become inflamed and this is responsible for many alcohol related deaths. When our pancreas is inflamed, we also stand a higher risk of getting pancreatic cancer. Vomiting and stomach pain (which is relieved when leaning forwards), could be a sign of an inflamed pancreas. Acute inflammation can be treated quite easily but chronic treatment is more difficult. The main thing for both is to see your doctor and stop the alcohol.

https://pubs.niaaa.nih.gov/publications/arh21-1/13.pdf#

https://pancreaticccancer.org.uk/information/just-diagnosed-with-pancreatic-cancer/what-is-the-pancreas

Pandemic - is a worldwide infection or disease that causes death and destruction. Some think alcohol addiction is a disease, but no matter what our view on this, I believe we really are at pandemic levels with over 3 million deaths a year.

https://www.who.int/news-room/fact-sheets/detail/alcohol

Panic - this is a sudden attack of very intense anxiety or fear that can cause extreme physical symptoms of anxiety and our thoughts to run wild. It can leave us shaking, feeling completely out of control and as if we are going out of our mind. The important thing is to know our **Anxiety** warning signs and bring our breathing and **Anxiety Management** into play straight away. This can help us prevent a full-blown panic attack.

Paralytic - is a substance that paralyses us, such as alcohol. When we are paralytic (sometimes referred to as paraletic), we are so drunk that we cannot walk, talk, or move. Eventually we become unconscious, and for some, the heart and lungs will stop working. Writing this now, it saddens me to think back to the times my friends and I have laughed at ourselves or others for getting in this state.

Paranoid - that feeling that others are talking about us when there is no evidence that they are. The feeling that others do not like us, that they are looking at us or want to harm us. We may even feel that the whole room is plotting against us. Another great side effect of alcohol - let the arguing and fighting begin. And then we get sober and have the whole paranoid conversations with ourselves about what others will think and say...

Past - that's exactly where it is, leave it there. We cannot change it, only ourselves. We can learn from it, leave it behind, and grow. Eighteen months in, I realised that the memory I had held onto of my beloved Nan, was her passing. For 32 years I had held onto the ending, the guilt, the hurt and the regret. Not the fun times, the love, the understanding and adventures. I wrote her a letter, listing all the happy memories and vowing to do her love justice, to honour her by only holding onto the memories of the good times from now on. I cannot begin to tell you how wonderful and freeing that was.

Patience - really is a virtue. And eventually, we have loads of it for ourselves and everyone around us. But when we first start our sober journey, we can be a little agitated, impatient and snappy with everything and everyone. Part of this is physical withdrawal, but it's also that comfort blanket being whipped away. We have nowhere to hide and all that we've been covering is exposed. It comes and goes in waves and it helps if we can just learn to ride them. There will be a few duckings, but when we learn to ride the crest it is the best feeling in the world. We can get impatient with ourselves too, especially with the **Altered/ Unhelpful Thinking** chipping away at us - "I should be feeling better than this by now" - and the fact that we can't sleep also adds to all the frustration. If we read, write, connect, listen and work our butt off, it will all come together. There is no time limit on this, we have a lifetime of work to do, and it helps us to accept it as it is, not resist it and be kind to ourselves.

Patterns - are guidance and things that we duplicate and repeat. Imagine a sewing pattern, they guide us on the shapes to cut out of the material and how to sew them all together. If we don't follow this then the finished article will be different from the picture. In life we can have it all mapped and drawn out, but very often it will not go to plan and we develop patterns of behaviour that nobody intended. Addiction comes in all different shapes and sizes, but it is a pattern we can get stuck in and continually repeat. The only way out is to change the pattern, draw the outline of what we want and use all the resources we can to put it all together. Expect wonky seams, they are fine, just keep following the new pattern and eventually it will all come together.

Pause - before you respond or react. It's good to let our brain fully take everything in, to take a breath and get our thoughts in order. Feel the rest and freedom in that pause. And then proceed.

PAWS (Post-Acute Withdrawal Syndrome) - once we've been

through the acute withdrawal of alcohol, some of us can have continued symptoms affecting our mood, memory, thoughts and sleep. This can lead to bouts of **Depression**, **Anxiety** and **Panic** and make us quite irritable and moody. It can last up to a year after we stop drinking or taking drugs, including some prescribed medications such as antidepressants and other mental health medication. **Stress** can make these symptoms worse but you can help manage these with **Mindfulness, Meditation, Maintenance Plans, CBT** etc. If you are concerned, or feel you need extra support, then see your medical practitioner.

Paying it Forwards/Back - means helping people in the way others have helped us. Many people thank us for helping and supporting them. For me, sobriety and helping others was a full-time job in the first year or so but the truth is, it helped me in the same way that others from the **IAS** community had. It helps keep us sober, accountable and working our sobriety. And with every post, comment, podcast or book we are helping someone. Often, we are paying it back without even realising it as we all have something to offer. Aim to make a difference to someone's day today and see how good it feels. It could be as simple as giving them a **Smile**!

Peace - is freedom to just be. To be left alone and find any inner stillness and happiness. It can seem impossible in this crazy world, but we can all find peace if we allow ourselves to do so. It takes a lot of practice, especially as we have been finding it in oblivion. My peace plan is:

- Do not drink alcohol
- Do not purposefully listen to the news
- Stay in mu **Hula Hoop** and catch myself when I step outside of it
- Accept that everything that arises must cease

- Meditate and use **Mindfulness** daily
- Come from a place of **Compassion**, **Understanding** and **Kindness**
- Send **Metta** to others as well as myself; even if I do not know the full ins and outs of everything that is happening in the world, it does not stop me from wishing everyone well and safe
- Live in the **Now**
- Breathe and say the **Serenity Prayer**
- **Forgive** myself for anything that I do not achieve today

How would your peace plan look?

My Peace Plan

A.

B.

C.

D.

E.

F.

G.

H.

I.

Pema Chodron - is a Buddhist Nun who has helped my journey enormously. Born in New York in 1936, she has two children and 3 grandchildren and worked as a teacher before becoming a novice nun in 1974. She has many YouTube videos that are great listening and has written several books including; *'Three Steps to Courage'* and *'No Time to Lose'*.

https://pemachodronfoundation.org/about/pema-chodron

Perception - this is what our brain makes of everything we hear, see, feel, taste and smell. This includes our past learnings and interpretations. Perceptions help us form opinions and vice versa. I see the colour red for example, because I have been taught from an early age that the colour I see is red. But is it the same as the red that you see? I know how an apple looks, tastes and smells to me, but is the colour taste and smell the same as yours? For more on this and perceptions check out the World Science Festival on YouTube: (122) The Reality of Reality: A Tale of Five Senses - YouTube.

Perhaps also look at the picture on the back of this book. What do you see? How do you think I got up there to strike the 'Ryker Pose'? Well, it took two grown men, some step ladders, determination and a hell of a lot of **Mindfulness**!

Perfection - is something we continually strive for but can never actually achieve because it's different for everyone. What's perfect for me is not necessarily so for you. Perfection just makes us chase our tail. It can really help to purposefully do something imperfect and live with it. Don't forget to breathe and live a perfectly imperfect life with me today.

Perplexing - is how you may find this book, confusing you and filling you with doubt. After all, everything we had been led to believe about alcohol is proved wrong when we start to dig deeper. Drinking and sobriety in themselves can feel very confusing, and we often don't know what to do for the best. Hopefully this is becoming clearer for you now. Stopping drinking can feel complex and complicated and, as you've seen, it is more than simply putting down the drink. But if we **Plan and Prepare**, and use our **Resources** and the tools in our **Tool Box**, then it does not have to be as perplexing as it first seems.

Personality - is what we show to the world and how life has shaped and moulded us. With modern technology we now know that the experiences we encounter in life can actually change the functioning of our brain. Our personality is unique to us and is how we think, feel, act and behave. Some of us have many different sides and personalities. Society tells us we should behave in certain ways to be accepted. If we don't, then we are given titles and disorders. Alcohol blocks and stops us from feeling and thinking and changes the way we act and behave. When we stop drinking, we begin to discover who we really are. It can be bumpy at times, but eventually we get to walk hand in hand with all parts of us and discover how wonderful we truly are.

Personal Space - ever felt uncomfortable when people get too close? It's because they are invading your personal space, uninvited. It's that area inside our **Hula Hoop** or arm span and it's all ours. If we cannot control anything outside of it, then no-one else should be able to control inside of it and it is our right to tell them so.

Pink Cloud – everyone's searching and waiting for that pink cloud moment and, when it comes, it does feel great. But this can also fill us with a false sense of security. Thinking that we've 'got it', that we are sorted and that maybe, just maybe, we can now moderate ... As the old proverb goes, 'Forewarned is forearmed'.

Plan and Prepare – your sobriety journey, as like with most things in life, this really does help. I admit I didn't plan, I just did it, but I was fortunate to find the **IAS** app where there was so much great support and advice that I didn't have to white knuckle it and fumble my way through. I was lucky, but the advice I would give myself now is:

- *Look at my **Choices** and **Motivation***
- *Write a **Care Plan***
- *Set a date*
- *Get rid of all the alcohol in the house*
- *Tell everyone what I am doing*
- *Identify my sober **Community***
- *Start reading/listening to **Quit Lit***
- *Get diversions and activities in place; even a Netflix series lined up*
- *Book time off of work*
- *Get plenty of soft drinks and healthy snacks in*
- *Do it, post and connect with my community straight away*
- *Blog, **Write** and **Journal***
- *Write a **WRAP** plan*

What could you do to plan and prepare?

1.

2.

3.

4.

5.

6.

7.

8.

Plans - how many have you cancelled due to being drunk or hungover? I can think of several. I have not cancelled any plans since being sober. Covid may have, but I haven't. And that feels so good. **Plans (direction)** - I used to want to know where I was heading in life. If I didn't know, or things went wrong (as they naturally do) then I felt really unsettled. I know that we rarely go from A – B directly and that we are diverted along the way, but I just had to know where I was aiming and each day had to go my way. Now I absolutely relish waking up to the unknown, accepting the day for what it brings, and trusting in the universe when I start to freak out.

Playing it Forwards - this is my absolute key tool in my **Tool Box**. Whenever I'm tempted by that nasty liquid and start fantasising about that first sip, I play the tape forwards in my brain. That sip will become a glass, will become a bottle, will become two and I'll be right back in it. I love that one of my sober friends *Rebirth* has a cassette tape tattooed on her wrist to remind her of this.

Pleasure - is the opposite of **Pain**. In the same way that **Happiness** is the opposite of **Suffering**. I'm sitting here trying to think of any pleasure or happiness I had when drinking. I had fun times, but did alcohol itself give me the pleasure that the adverts and marketing suggest? Maybe opening the bottle and the first sip did initially, but what about after that? Reflecting now, the only thing alcohol truly brought me was pain and suffering. Pleasure and happiness were long gone, not even on the horizon. Look at it this way: think of something you absolutely love or loved doing. Something that brings/brought you real pleasure and happiness. Has alcohol ever truly made you feel this way? For many of us, alcohol replaces all those fun things but sobriety brings them all back.

Podcasts - are wonderful support tools. I would recommend listening to them whenever you can. There are so many out there and there are many platforms now to make your own; Podbean, Spotify, YouTube, Apple … But of course, I have to recommend my community www.**sobertown**podcast.com. It is an amazing place to start! Here are some more recommendations from my sober friends:

- The To 50 and Beyond podcast with Lori Massicot (For sober women)
- Sober Awkward with sober mums Vic and Lucy
- F***ing Sober – the first 90 days – an 8-part series
- Soberful with Veronica Valli and Chip Somers
- Recovery Rocks with Lisa Smith and Tawny Lara
- Sober Squad by Nazhike
- Seltzer Squad with Jes Valentine and Kate Zander
- Sober Sisters Society with Nicole and Tammie (formerly Social Sisters Social Club)
- Tell Me Something True with Laura McKowen
- Home Podcast with Laura McKowen and Holly Whitaker
- Recovery Elevator with Paul Churchill and others
- This Naked Mind with Annie Grace
- Alcohol Free Life with Janey Lee Grace
- How I Quit Alcohol with Danni Carr
- The Alcohol Recovery Show with Antonia Ryan
- Sobriety Unleashed with Ellen Woods and Simon Chapple

Poison - is a substance that can kill us; or at the very least, make us extremely unwell. If we swallow poison, we are likely to feel and be sick, have diarrhoea, head and stomach ache, feel weak and tired, become dehydrated and have problems with seeing and speaking. You know how we hate vomiting when we are drunk? It is actually the best thing that can happen. It's our body getting rid of poison. But try to remember to lay on your side whenever you have been drinking, and encourage others who have been drinking to do this also. Choking on our vomit is a big cause of alcohol related deaths. If I see someone lying on their back in the street, I gently encourage them to lay on their side – if I feel it is safe to do so.

Positive - is the best state of mind to have. Easier said than done I hear you say? But is it? Just think of all the energy and pain we cause ourselves, and others, when we are constantly feeling negative about everything and everyone. All the energy we waste in continually moaning about others and getting angry about things that we have absolutely no control over. Take road rage for instance; we think the person in front is driving like an idiot. That's actually just a matter of opinion. Getting wound up about it is only going to affect and ruin everyone's day, especially our own. It really helps if we can accept that we only have the right to drive our own car (or **Bus**), nobody else's, breathe, get back in our **Hula Hoop** and let it go. Being positive is just a state of **Mind**. There is only one person preventing it - you!

Power - we all love power and control. Even if we deny it, our **Ego** will be wanting at least some of it. The problem is, we spend most of our lives trying to wield it in the wrong direction. Then when we don't get our own way, we don't like it and turn to things such as alcohol to make it all feel better. The only power and control we ever have is over ourselves. But this does not mean we have to give up the fight. If we can redirect our energy into fighting that **Addict Voice**, we can take back control and know the true meaning of a powerful life.

Powerless - is not having control over anything. The only person that can give up our control is us. Only we can make ourselves powerless. In some addiction programmes people are asked to admit that they are powerless over alcohol. If this works for you then fine. But it doesn't work for me (probably because I'm a bit of a control freak). We always have some power, if we can just overcome our ego and addict voice.

Power of Positive Thought - so let's just combine the last 3 headings. Especially as your ego is probably now in overdrive and flexing its muscles at me! As we have already discovered, if we hear something often enough then we start to believe it. It is the same for what we tell ourselves. Positive thought is powerful and freeing, and often it's just a matter of turning things around:

We are worried about our health or the future and are continually asking ourselves "What if X happens?"

This makes us feel worried, anxious, sad, depressed, nervous and fearful

Next time this happens, ask yourself "What if it doesn't?"

You have taken the power back from your thoughts and gained feelings of freedom, peace, and happiness

Practice - one of the best ways to achieve is to practice again and again - until it becomes part of our **Muscle Memory**. Try to remember those old sayings: 'If at first you don't succeed, try, try again' and 'Practice makes perfect'. Whatever perfect is!

Pregnancy - it is well known that we should not drink when we are pregnant. In fact, at the time of writing, this is the only warning on alcohol containers in the UK. But, if you are planning a pregnancy, both parties should actually stop drinking before getting pregnant. Not only will this increase fertility and pregnancy chances, but also the health of your baby. We need our body to be fully functioning, ready and able to nurture our new creation. How can we do that if we are depleting ourselves with alcohol?

https://www.yourfertility.org.au/everyone/drugs-chemicals/

alcohol#

Prelapse - is what happens before relapse. Belle Robertson talks about this in her *podcast 'Tired of Thinking about Drinking'* (book also available by the same name). Know your signs of heading for a relapse and scale it from 0 -10. Catch it before you get higher. If you find yourself at a 1 or 2 then take action. If you're overwhelmed take a step back and a breath, tap into and recognise what you are feeling. Use **HALT** – are you hungry, angry, lonely or tired?

https://www.tiredofthinkingaboutdrinking.com

Pressure - many of us are pressured to quit drinking by loved ones or the courts and it's not a great place to start. Pressure brings our **Id** out to play and dig its heels in, "I don't want to and you can't make me" whilst our **Ego** and **Superego** are trying to keep us on the right track without losing face! Maybe take a **Pause** and listen to what others are saying. And if we can remember to accept our areas of **Control**, we can come from a different place and agree to do it for a better **Life**.

Pride - in some sobriety and religious circles, pride and feeling proud is discouraged and seen as a sin. I guess this is due to a sense of an over-inflated ego (big-headed) and using pride to cover for how we are actually feeling inside (poor **Self-Esteem**). In recovery, we need to get in touch with our real feelings and emotions and not put on a show to cover up. Personally, I feel we have a right to be proud of ourselves and others providing we are coming from a place of dignity, respect and contentment. So go blow your own trumpet if you want to. Just not too loud and not in the wrong place. Let it be music to everyone's ears.

Priorities - are the most important things! Mine are now my **Values**: family, friends, love, compassion, support and being a **Lighthouse**. I like to think that these have always been my priorities, but in reality, for many years, drinking was top of my list. I remember the times I would pick my son up from somewhere and greet him with a miserable and moody face. Why? Because my drinking had been delayed. I can't change that. All I can do now is put the biggest smile on my face when I see him and greet him with the love and respect he deserves.

Process - is a chain of events. Steps we need to go through to achieve something. Things do not always go smoothly, but it's all part of the process. **Everything Happens for a Reason** and from every breakdown there is a breakthrough. It is a voyage of discovery and learning. Trust in it.

Procrastination - you may have noticed that one of the things on my **Maintenance list** is 'do something you have been putting off' because delaying is something I am great at! I will find anything and everything to do just to avoid starting or finishing a particular task. The result is, my **Anxiety** builds and I start to put pressure on myself to get the task done and lead my **Id** and egos on a merry old dance. We can even do it when trying to set a date to quit drinking. We find lots of excuses to delay; that wedding, that birthday, that party, that theatre trip ... You have to do it at the right time for you, but just be aware that the longer you put it off the more pressure and anxiety you are putting on yourself.

Psychodynamic - is the understanding that all our experiences form who we are, even if we are not fully aware of them. Things that happen in childhood can affect us for all of our life, even if we are not consciously aware of it. They are stored and come from the biggest part of our mind, the unconscious. This is where our **Id** and **Superego** are, whilst our **Ego** is more in our here and now mind, our conscious. Battle stations everyone!

https://www.simplypsychology.org/psychodynamic.html

Psychotherapy - is a broad term for many talking therapies that can help us manage our mental health. They can be used alone, or alongside medication, and can treat many issues such as depression, anxiety and trauma. Some studies have shown talking therapy can make changes in our brain in the same way medication does.

https://www.psychiatry.org/patients-families/psychotherapy

PTSD (Post Traumatic Stress Disorder) - after any traumatic event it is perfectly normal for us to spend a few weeks feeling upset and anxious, having problems with sleep, reliving the situation and picking it apart. This is our mind's way of processing what has happened and storing our memories in sequence. Sometimes we can get very stuck in the experience which could be a one-off event or repeated trauma that we have endured over a number of years. The most common symptom of this is **Flashbacks** which can be triggered by anything at any time and will take us right back to the event as if we were reliving it. Other symptoms can be: poor sleep, anxiety, depression, avoidance, anger and feeling numb. **Psychotherapy** and medication can help. At the time of writing the most effective therapy is thought to be **EMDR**.

Punishment - is mostly what we give ourselves and comes from **Shame**, **Frustration** and regrets. We continue to blame, hold onto and beat ourselves up for things we have done. Things we cannot change or do anything about. This makes us unhappy and miserable and, in so doing, can make for an uncomfortable life for both ourselves and those around us. We are indirectly punishing others for things they know absolutely nothing about or things they have long forgotten. We cannot undo what is done, but we can let it go. By so doing, we set everyone free.

Q

Qi - also known as Chi and Ki, is the Chinese belief of the life force energy that flows through our body. Translated it means 'breath' or 'air'. There are said to be different levels of Qi, which change and grow throughout our life. It is the **Yin** and **Yang**. When Qi becomes blocked or stagnant it leads to poor health, and vice versa. Ways to restore this are thought to be with reflexology, acupuncture, tai chi and qigong.

https://www.learnreligions.com/what-is-qi-chi-3183052

Qigong - breathing, meditation and body posture to help with the flow and embracing of Qi. I found this wonderful introduction on YouTube whilst researching: Qigong for Beginners - Bing video by Yogi Yoga and Qigong.

Quench - can be to satisfy something or to extinguish it. I love this word. It has just made me take a big slurp of water and triggered a recent memory. My partner Andy and I were at a hotel for afternoon tea and, as we sat outside, we saw a wedding party come out of the building opposite. Many were wandering around with glasses of bubbly, and I had a sudden craving for ice-cold prosecco with my afternoon tea. I voiced this out loud to Andy, telling him all the reasons why I would not be ordering this, and we shared a pot of tea instead. Afterwards we asked for a bottle of water. It came with two glasses filled with ice and a slice of fresh lemon. As I took the first mouthful, I felt a wonderful sense of pleasure and relaxation. What I had actually been wanting was an ice-cold drink to quench my thirst. This experience has given me another tool for my **Tool Box**, drink water to quench a craving.

Quiet - there was a time that I was only quiet when I was sneaking an extra drink! And I would drink to quieten my mind, my emotions and everything life was throwing at me. I felt uncomfortable sitting quietly without distraction, because that would give my **Monkey Mind** licence to jabber on and on. Now, I love to just sit quietly listening to everything around me and inside of me. It is calming and soothing. If sounds annoy us, we can either tune in or tune out to them. I actually love an MRI scan now. Probably the noisiest and most enclosed medical procedure we can undertake. But instead of resisting the bangs and loud noise I tune into them, breath along and relax into them. And there, I can find quietness and peace.

Quit Lit - is the term used to describe books that are not part of a recognised recovery programme, such as AA, but can help us quit alcohol. You are reading one right now and hopefully it has given you ideas of other books that could also help you in your journey. Here are the favourites of some of my sober buddies:

'*Alcohol Lied to Me: The Intelligent Way to Escape Alcohol Addiction*' by Craig Beck

'*Drinking: A Love Story*' by Caroline Knapp

'*Everything You Ever Taught Me: If you've got a lot on your mind, go for a walk...*' by Person Irresponsible

'*The Miracle Morning: The 6 Habits That Will Transform Your Life Before 8AM*' by Hal Elrod

'*Drink? The New Science of Alcohol and Your Health*' by Professor David Nutt

'*Sobering; Lessons Learnt the Hard Way on Drinking, Thinking and Quitting*' by Melissa Rice

'*Sunshine Warm Sober: The unexpected joy of being sober - forever*' by Catherine Gray

'*The Recovering: Intoxication and its Aftermath*' by Leslie Jamison

'*Love Yourself Sober: A Self Care Guide to Alcohol-Free Living for Busy Mothers*' by Kate Baily and Mandy Manners

'The *Body Keeps the Score: Mind, Brain and Body in the Transformation of Trauma*' by Bessel van der Kolk

'*Your Second Life Begins When You Realize You Only Have One*' by Raphaelle Giordano

'*The Four Agreements: Practical Guide to Personal Freedom*' by Don Miguel Ruiz

'*The Sober Diaries*: *How one woman stopped drinking and started living*' by Clare Pooley

'*Walking Back To Happiness: The Secret To Alcohol-Free Living & Well-Being*' by Nigel Jones

'*The Sober Girl Society Handbook: Why drinking less means living more*' by Millie Gooch

'*The Unexpected Joy of Being Sober*' by Catherine Gray

'*This Naked Mind: Control Alcohol. Find Freedom, DiscoverHappiness & Change Your Life*' by Annie Grace

'*The Alcohol Experiment: 30 days to take control, cut down or give up for good*' by Annie Grace

'*Rewired: A Bold New Approach to Addiction and Recovery*' by Erica Spiegelman

'*Alcohol Explained*' by William Porter

'*The Sober Lush: A Hedonist's Guide to Living a Decadent, Adventurous, Soulful Life – Alcohol Free*' by Amanda Eyre Ward and Jardine Libaire

'*The Gifts of Imperfection: Let Go of Who You Think You're Supposed to Be and Embrace Who You Are*' by Brené Brown

'*Warrior Goddess Training: Become the Woman You Are Meant to Be*' by Heatherash Amara

'*The Daily Stoic: 366 Meditations on Wisdom, Perseverance, and the Art of Living*' by Ryan Holiday and Stephen Hanselman

'*Recovery: Freedom From Our Addictions*' by Russel Brand

'*In the Realm of Hungry Ghosts: Close Encounters with Addiction*' by Dr Gabor Maté

'*Mindfulness for Alcohol Recovery*' by Lewis David and Antonia Ryan

'*Overloaded: How Every Aspect of your Life is Influenced by your Brain Chemicals*' by Ginny Smith

'*The Biology of Desire: Why Addiction Is Not A Disease*' by Marc Lewis

'*A Course in Miracles*' by Helen Schucman

'*We are the Luckiest: The Surprising Magic of a Sober Life*' Laura McKowen

Quotes - there are quite a few in this book, but here are a few more from me and my sober buddies:

'*Don't quit before the miracle happens.*' Fannie Flag from her book '*I Still Dream About You*'.

'*Everyone you meet is fighting a battle you know nothing about. Be kind always.*' Robin Williams.

'*Have no fear of perfection, you'll never reach it.*' Salvador Dali.

'*Recovery is about progression and not perfection.*' Alcoholics Anonymous.

'*You can't go back and change the beginning, but you can start where you are and change the ending.*' C. S. Lewis.

'*Difficult Roads lead to beautiful destinations. The best is yet to come.*' Zig Ziglar.

'*The only person you should try to be better than is the person you were yesterday.*' Matty Mullins and Tony Robbins have both been credited with this quote.

'*The devil whispered in my ear, "You're not strong enough to withstand the storm" I whispered back: "I am the storm."*' There are many variations of this but its origins are unclear.

'*Do not speak badly of yourself. For the warrior within hears your words and is lessened by them.*' David Gemmell.

'*If you are going through hell, keep going.*' Winston Churchill.

'*Everywhere you go, there you are.*' Jon Kabat Zinn.

'*It is what it is.*' Earliest known writing J. E. Lawrence.

'*Sobriety delivers what alcohol promised.*' Book by Justine Whitchurch.

'*This too shall pass.*' Abraham Lincoln.

'*Sobriety is not an anchor. It's a pair of wings.*' Unknown. But it is a guided sobriety journal.

'*What others think of you is none of your business.*' Possibly adapted from Martha Graham "*What other people in the world think of you is really none of your business*'.

'*You can't take stuff with you, only your story, so you might as well make it a good one.*'

This is what I have been saying for years following watching the film Australia (screenplay by Baz Luhrmann, Stuart Beattie, with Ronald Harwood and Richard Flanagan). But the actual quote is:

'*Most people like to own things. You know, land, luggage, other people. Makes them feel secure. But all that can be taken away. And, in the end, the only thing you really own is your story. Just try and live a good one*'.

Just another testimony to how our individual minds interpret, adapt and remember things! On the plus side – I've made my own quote!

R

Reading - thank you for choosing to read this book. I truly hope that it has helped you to be more curious, ask more questions and inspired you to make changes to your life. But don't stop here, keep on reading, there is so much out there to learn and choose from. You will find a bibliography and reference list at the end of this book for ideas and inspiration.

Ready - are you? The most important thing about quitting alcohol is to do it when you are ready. This may take several trial runs and that is perfectly OK. Very few of us manage to quit on our first attempt. Mostly because it is a rebound from one of those 'never again' moments. But if we have the right **Mindset** and **Plan and Prepare**, then our time will come. But it has to be our time. When we are ready. If we are not, then we are just setting ourselves up to fail time and time again.

Reassurance - others can help to take away our fears and our doubts, but we have to be willing to listen and accept the support being offered. Life is a learning curve. It is a journey with a beginning and an end. We can either choose to sit alone on an island or be protected by a herd. Whilst others cannot tell us what to do on our journey, they can offer support, help, encourage us and be our cheerleaders. The best people to do this are those walking by our side in the journey of sobriety. Our **Community**, **Podcasts**, books and if you are lucky, family and friends.

Receive - is accepting something that is offered or given to us. We have no control over what others offer, but for the most part (physical attacks and illnesses aside) only we can accept it and take it in. This includes love, anger, friendship, hatred, support etc. Others can try to give us their anger or hatred, but if we do not accept it, then it stays with them. In the same way that love can feel wonderful when it is accepted and returned, but awful when it is not.

Recovery - does not mean getting back to our old selves or being fully well. It is about living the best we can in our current situation and circumstances. It means pacing, setting achievable goals, accepting and **Being**. Recovery does not happen overnight; it is a process in which we learn new ways to live and take back or keep control of our lives. We have a diagnosis, we have a doctor, therapist, family and friends, we have a treatment plan. But, most importantly, what are we bringing to it all? What can YOU do today to aid YOUR recovery? Because it is yours. Nobody else's.

https://www.mentalhealth.org.uk/explore-mental-health/a-z-topics/recovery

https://www.ncbi.nlm.nih.gov/pmc/articles/PMC4418239

Recovery Dharma - is a Buddhist based recovery support network. Most of their meetings are via Zoom and you can therefore join in from anywhere in the world. Meetings contain social time, readings, meditation and sharing.

https://recoverydharma.online

Reduce Gradually - if you are drinking every day, then it is advisable to gradually reduce your alcohol intake before you stop completely. Start by making a note of what you are actually drinking, work out your daily **Units** (you could use the **Drinkaware** app to help with this) and gradually reduce this down by 10% each day. You can do this by either lowering the amount you drink or the strength of what you are drinking. According to the article referenced below, when you have had a week of drinking 10 units or less a day it should be safe for you to stop drinking. But again, I would encourage you to speak to a medical practitioner for support with this.

https://www.wearewithyou.org.uk/help-and-advice/advice-you/how-safely-detox-alcohol-home/

Relapse - is a setback. It is when we have stopped drinking and start to do so again. But for me, this is when we give up trying to quit. It's a big bender or binge, not just one or two drinks. They are just little **Slips**. I am forever in awe of the people that get up time and time again following a relapse, having learnt from that experience and then getting back onto the sober path.

Try, Try Again

by William Edward Hickson 1836

"Tis a lesson you should heed,
Try, try again;
If at first you don't succeed,
Try, try again;
Then your courage should appear,
For, if you will persevere,
You will conquer, never fear;
Try, try again.

Once or twice, though you should fail,
Try, try again;

If you would at last prevail,
Try, try again;
If we strive, 'tis no disgrace
Though we do not win the race;
What should you do in the case?
Try, try again.

If you find your task is hard,
Try, try again;
Time will bring you your reward,
Try, try again;
All that other folks can do,
Why, with patience, should not you?
Only keep this rule in view:
Try, try again.'

https://discoverpoetry.com/poems/william-edward-hickson/try-again

Relationships - change naturally with time and even more so with alcohol and sobriety. Especially if they were formed and/or based on or around drinking. Relationships are about connection and for some, alcohol was the connection. With this in mind, you can see how scary it can be for others, as well as ourselves, when we are considering quitting. It is going to shake the foundations that some of our relationships were built on. **Understanding** this, may help you to accept their behaviour towards you and your sobriety goal. It's back to our choices – the relationship can stay as it is, it can continue with change, or it has to end. Most importantly, do whatever is best to protect your sobriety.

Relax - easier said than done when we mostly live our life on the defensive, with expectation and trying to achieve the next best thing! Many of us feel we 'don't have time to relax' but it is only us stopping ourselves. **Meditation**, **Exercise** and **Visualisation** are great ways to relax but we need to make time for them. This is what I particularly like about **Mindfulness**; I can use it wherever I am and whatever I'm doing at that moment. In your busy day, try to find moments to relax. Instead of eating lunch at your desk or in the car, make time to move away and eat elsewhere. Set a timer and take a few minutes out of every hour to stretch your legs, arms and back. When you're stuck in a meeting, take time just to feel your feet on the floor, the seat supporting you, and take some mindful breaths...

Relief - Buddhists believe that everything we do is to give us relief from our previous activity (and I really like reflecting on this concept from time to time). We sit down to rest our legs, we stand up to get rid of our numb bum/fanny, we breathe in, we breathe out, we sleep to relieve tiredness, we wake up to survive, we eat to feed our hunger, we burp when we are full, we drink alcohol to forget, we vomit to get rid of the **Poison**, we drink alcohol to numb the pain, we get sober to feel again ...

Repetitive - you may have noticed that about this book at times, it's intentional - the more we are told something, the more we believe it. I mean, how did we ever get to feel we were so rubbish and undeserving? How did we ever get to believe alcohol was the answer to everything? Keep on repeating **Boundaries** with yourself and others. Tell yourself over and over that you are doing a good job at this thing called life, that you are just fine the way you are, and that alcohol really is poison and not worthy of your time. You are enough. I am enough. We are enough.

Rescuer - is that what you are? I know I am. I have ended up in many relationships with my inflated **Ego** thinking I can be the one to make it all OK. But we can't. The only person who can, is the person themselves. I don't know what it is that makes me run in like a caped crusader, but I do know that I am now learning not to and to realise when 'helping' is not actually helping anyone! It's great when we accept that it really is OK for others to feel emotions and deal with their own stuff. How are they going to learn otherwise? Obviously others still sit back and expect me to rush in, but I am gradually becoming fluent in the language of '**No**'.

Research - I have done some for this book and I hope it has inspired you to do some of your own. It is so much easier nowadays with the internet, but don't believe everything you read! Hopefully, you are now realising how tainted and flawed articles about alcohol can be. Even educational and medical research can be biased. The trick is to check who is conducting it. Very often it is big pharma or others who have a vested interest in the outcomes. As with this book, try not to take what you read as gospel, but instead approach it with curiosity and let it open up ideas from within.

Resets - can be numerous and disheartening. Just remember 'Falling down is part of life, getting back up is living' José N. Harris. And when you do get back up, you should be very proud of yourself. Learn from it and move on. See more under **Slips** and **Relapse.**

Resistance - I resisted for far too long. I knew I had a problem with alcohol, that I was drinking too much. I tried to cut down, slow down, moderate and just stop. I convinced myself that it was OK really as lots of people drink a bottle of wine a night, reminding myself that it is legal so it cannot be that bad. Then when I realised enough was enough, and I declared out loud that maybe I needed to go to AA, I was met with resistance from others. Did I shake in the morning? No? Then I was obviously fine and just feeling emotional from a hangover. But the best resistance I have ever done is to listen to myself, not others, and take my first steps into sobriety and resist my cravings. I did this by accepting that my **Addict Voice** and my drinking companions did not have my best interests at heart. And I flipped the resistance of quitting drinking to one of not giving up on sobriety. It kept me drinking for many years so it can damn well keep me sober too.

Resources - are anything that can help us get to where we want to be. Books, films, podcasts, communities, support groups, affirmations, HALT, ACT, and many other things I have written about in this book. Collect what works for you and put them in your **Tool Box**.

Responsibility - only we are responsible for our actions, our drinking and our sobriety. Whatever we decide is not down to others, it is down to us. If we accept we have choices and **Capacity**, we realise we have **Control**. And with control, comes responsibility. Whilst we are wholly responsible for our own actions, we are not 100% responsible for interactions with others, especially arguments. It takes two to tango so don't ever take 100% of the blame - even if others try to make you! Life really is too short to figure out who 'started it'. So ner ner ner ner ner!

Rest - is so important. We are so busy that we often forget to rest until we fall into bed at the end of each day (or night shift).

Rest isn't just about sleeping, it's also about stopping and stilling our body and mind and allowing them to recover from what has gone before and prepare for what is coming next. And the best way to do this, is to be in the moment. Just stop, close your eyes, take a few focussed slow breaths and notice how good it feels. Next time you have a cuppa just sit and drink it. Just you and your brew (and your monkey mind of course!). No computer, no phone, no conversation, no distraction. Just rest.

Retreats - are wonderful places to go to rest, learn, physically and emotionally reset and there are some wonderful places out there. Have a little search and see what's right for you. My go to is the Nagarjuna Kadampa Centre at Thornby Hall in Northampton. Yes they cost money, but maybe work out how much you spend or spent on alcohol a month and treat yourself. If that's not possible then you do not have to miss out. Retreat means to withdraw for a while. We can do this in many ways – a night without the kids, watching a movie, turning off our phone, going on a picnic or a walk alone, meditation or just sitting and being.

https://meditateinnorthants.com

Reward Pathway - when we experience something rewarding, such as sex, food, chocolate, alcohol or drugs, we release **Dopamine** in our brain. This affects our **Amygdala** making us feel calm and happy. Our librarian (**Hippocampus**) remembers it all and we want to keep on repeating it to get more and more. The problem is, over time, we need more and more of the pleasurable activity to give us the same feeling and reward. Cue addiction.

https://www.simplypschology.org/brain-reward-system.html#

Rewired: A Bold New Approach to Addiction and Recovery -

a book, community and resource by Erica Spiegelman. Learn new ways to rewire your thoughts and help you get physically, emotionally, mentally and spiritually sober.

https://www.ericaspiegelman.com/rewired-program

Rocket Man - a great movie based on Elton John's life and battle with addiction. I watched it when I was drinking and it was OK. I watched it again during my sobriety journey and OMGoodness! I could resonate so much. The end just had me howling. Especially as I had just reached that point myself. No spoiler alerts here.

Rollercoaster - buckle up and strap yourself in. Sobriety is a bumpy ride. There are the uphill climbs, the downward spirals, the wobbly and bumpy tracks, not knowing what is around the next corner and sometimes you will feel as if you are going to loop the loop. But remember, everything that goes up must come down and sobriety promises to provide you with all the fun of the fair. The thrills and the spills. The adrenaline, dopamine and endorphin rushes. Not that you'd ever catch me on an actual rollercoaster!

Rosacea - is a reddening of the skin mostly on the cheeks but it can also appear on the chin, forehead and nose. It comes and goes, can affect both men and women, and can be quite painful. Mine used to get really hot and sting and get worse with wine … so I just spent a fortune on skin care products to try and reduce and cover it. I was even prescribed an antibiotic cream on a couple of occasions. Alcohol is known to trigger it, as are spicy foods, hot drinks, caffeine and high energy exercise. For some reason mine has now completely gone…

https://www.nhs.uk/conditions/rosacea

Rose Elliot - vegetarian chef and author of *'I Met a Monk. 8 weeks to Happiness, Freedom and Peace'*. Rose writes about her journey into mindfulness with a group of people and a visiting monk. I took a lot away from this but the most enlightening thing for me, was to remove the word I from a feeling or emotion and replace it with There is. It is so freeing:

I am suffering	*There is suffering*
I am angry	*There is anger*
I am lonely	*There is loneliness*
I am sad	*There is sadness*
I am in pain	*There is pain*

Rules - there is a lot of guidance for sobriety, but no hard and fast rules. How can there be with us all being such wonderfully unique individuals? You have the choice of how you want to live today and your journey is down to you. But maybe just consider enjoying the times of peace, calm, acceptance, clarity, love and happiness when they arise.

Running – go actually do it if you want. You're certainly going to have more energy. But one thing you will no longer be doing in sobriety, is running away. It feels so much easier to no longer feel the need to run and hide. Here I am, hula hooping away and nailing my ego back to the floor from time to time!

S

Sabotage - is when someone deliberately tries to stop others from succeeding and is something we are all capable of – we even do it to ourselves. Hello again **Ego.** When it comes to our old drinking partners their sabotage can come out in full force. Remember we cannot control others or their actions, just our own reactions. It is difficult when we have the **Addict Voice** tempting us to drink, but when 'friends' jump on board too it can make it even harder to resist. The only people that will try to sabotage our sobriety journey, are those who have an invested interest in us still drinking! True friends will cheer us on and be proud of us. If someone encourages you to drink today, ask yourself what it is they have to gain from you doing so and what it is you have to lose. If you give in you will be sabotaging your own **Recovery**.

Sadness - is a normal emotion. It is OK to feel sad in the same way it is to feel happy, anxious, joyful and angry. For many of us, we do not like to feel the more painful emotions and so we numb and ignore them as much as we can. Sadness is often caused by feelings of hopelessness, loss of control, grief and disappointment. But remember, there is sadness. And this too shall pass.

Safety - the majority of us take our personal safety very seriously, becoming frightened when life gets a bit risky. We may tell others where we are going, who we are with and let them know when we are safely back home. We take self-defence classes, carry mace and attack alarms and avoid walking down dark alleys alone. We take calculated risks and weigh up the safety in this. Personally, I'd prefer not board a plane unless I had a parachute strapped firmly to my back - but I have to look at the risk calculations and accept it is the safest form of travel and away I go. Having said that, I have yet to fly sober! Previously, I figured that if the plane was going to fall out of the sky, I didn't want to know anything about it. I would take anxiety medication, sleeping tablets and drink lots of alcohol to block it all out ... and put myself more at risk. We can take all the measures we want, but when we drink alcohol safety goes out of the window. We are numb, we lose **Capacity**, become **Vulnerable** and put ourselves and others at risk.

Scared - you may have felt this at times whilst reading this book. Dealing with our emotions and other people can be really frightening. But it is only us putting the fear there. Others can try to bully and coerce us and try to make us feel this way, but it is us that allows this to happen. Others will try to stop us in life, and brick walls (**Obstacles**) will be continuous, but remember it is up to us to find a safe way over, under, through or around them. Fear and anxiety are OK. Take strength from them, but pace and cruise (**Cars**). This is not a race. We cannot do all of this in one day, we are all work in progress. And we will always have a scared little person inside of us. But when we can embrace ourselves and walk hand in hand, it gives us the strength to face the world.

Scars - are marks that are left on us from the many wounds we get in life. I have a few physical ones, some from drunken antics but many from childhood sober times. Physical scars are evidence of our wounds having healed, but we have a tendency to leave emotional wounds gaping. We keep sticking plasters on them by blocking, diverting and numbing, but this does not allow us to heal. When we rip off the plasters it can be really painful but, like a physical scar, full exposure and some tender loving care will enable our wounds to gradually heal.

Secondary Trauma - is when we are emotionally affected by listening to someone else tell us of their own trauma. Looking back on this, I think this is another big reason for cracking open the wine as soon as I got in from work every night. Listening to people recount their trauma, abuse and difficulties day after day, for so many years, took its toll. As professionals we are trained to reflect, debrief, talk about our feelings and the effects this has on us and channel this into meaningful activities; but we are all human and there is only so much channelling we can do. This, along with direct trauma, is why many health care and front-line workers' drink. To block it all out. Not everyone of course, but I would hazard a guess at the majority.

Self - our **Ego** is the view we have of ourselves and what we build around us to make us feel safe. We become who we and life has made us, not who we truly are. So, who are we? Some believe we find our true essence of self in the gap and silence of meditation.

Self-Care - is imperative to our wellbeing and survival. We can do really nice things for ourselves such as getting a massage, having a candlelit bath or spending time with friends. But we have to remember the really basic things too. At the end of my nursing career, I would start each day with *"today I am going to eat when I am hungry, drink when I am thirsty, wee and poo when I need to and rest when I am tired"*. This is basic self-care, but we miss it when we get wrapped up in life. Today, listen to your body and respond to its needs. Take a break, **Rest** and have some time out for you. Check your **Maintenance Plan** if you have one and aim to follow it.

Self-Centred - in this busy world of serving others, being self-centred can be seen as a bad thing. But it is not, it is very different from being **Selfish**, and it is what we truly need to be in order to succeed with sobriety. If we can look inward and put ourselves and our sobriety first, then everything else will follow. If the staff aren't happy then neither are the customers. Help others today by looking after yourself first.

Self-Esteem - is how we feel and value ourselves. Many of us have low opinions of ourselves and this leads to lack of confidence and low self-esteem. We are not born with this way of thinking. This is shaped by life events, other people's **Opinions** and how society views the so-called 'norms'. Things such as bullying, **Abuse**, **Addiction**, **Trauma** and even struggles with money, housing and study can lead to low self-esteem. We may have once been confident but someone called us 'big-headed' and this can turn it all around in an instant. This can lead to us feeling worthless, worrying about how others see us, being anxious or depressed, blaming ourselves for everything and being very unhappy.

Self-Esteem Boosters -
- Stop drinking alcohol
- Find someone to talk to – a good friend, community, therapist etc
- **Meditation** and **Mindfulness**
- **Acceptance**
- **Self-Care**
- Do something for you every day – put 30 minutes aside, even if it's in 5-minute sessions
- **Exercise** and get out in the fresh air
- Try to come from a place of **Kindness**, **Compassion**

and **Understanding**
- Learn to forgive – especially yourself

https://www.psychologytoday.com/us/blog/nurturing-self-compassion/201703/8-steps-improving-your-self-esteem

Self-Harm - is any action we carry out that causes physical or emotional harm. I refer you once again, to Gabor Matés' take on **Addiction.** Self-harm is not necessarily cutting, burning or hitting ourselves (but it can be). It can be about punishment, but mostly it is diverting an emotional pain into a physical one as we seem to find this easier to deal with. My take on self-harm is probably very different from the general population, including many of my old medical colleagues. Many see it as a 'learnt behaviour' whereas I see it as a natural response to an uncomfortable feeling. Just think of a toddler, especially in the so-called 'terrible twos' when it really must be terrible for them too. How do they respond to their frustration? To their not being able to communicate clearly, being heard or understood? They head bang, stamp their feet, bite their hands and bash their arms on the floor. This is the only way they know how to communicate that they are not feeling comfortable inside. Take it back even further – what do WE do when our babies are teething? We use teething rings and pacifiers. As adults when we have a dental procedure for example, we can find ourselves gripping the arms of the chair. How often do we squeeze the hand of another to divert our pain or bite our own lip? These are natural instincts and show another reason why addiction can be a hard habit to break. We drink to block our pain, we make ourselves ill, we say 'never again' … we drink to block the pain … and we hurt ourselves time and time again.

Selfish - is thinking of ourselves and only ourselves, with disregard to everyone else. When we are being selfish, we do not think of others and this is actually OK from time to time as long as we don't make this our daily base! Deep down, I believe that we are all fundamentally a little selfish in that we do not do something for nothing. We always get something out of it – even the reward of happiness when we are being kind. It's what motivates us. The difference here is that we are also thinking of others and coming from a different place from intense selfishness, whereby we act only to fulfil our own needs. When drinking buddies encourage us to drink, they are the ones being selfish.

Self-Love - is the best love. Some of us spend our whole lives looking for the love of others to make us feel whole and worthy, but I don't think we can truly love back unless we love ourselves. Self-love is about **Acceptance**, **Forgiveness**, being authentic and putting ourselves first. And it starts with **Self-Care**.

https://www.bbrfoundation.org/blog/self-love-and-what-it-means

Senses - generally we refer to our 5 senses of smell, taste, touch, hearing and sight. Although some scientists now say we have a sixth sense - balance. No matter how many, alcohol affects them all. When we drink our world becomes grey and dark. When we sober up, life becomes technicolour again. Don't believe me? Then just try it for yourself. Everything is numbed and dampened down when we drink. Now I can hear the dawn chorus, see the green grass (which is definitely better on my side), feel the sun make my skin tingle, smell the coffee and as for food... who knew it could taste so good?

Serenity Prayer - another great tool that gets me through each day and reminds me to stay in my **Hula Hoop**. It is adapted from a much longer prayer, written around 1932 by religious scholar Reinhold Niebuhr, and commonly goes like this:

'God grant me the serenity
To accept the things I cannot change;
Courage to change the things I can;
And the wisdom to know the difference'.

https://.verywellmind.com/the-serenity-prayer-62614

Serotonin - is our happy, feel-good chemical. It helps with sleep, mood and appetite. 90% of this is in our gut and only 10% in our brain. That is why our head and stomach are so well connected and affect each other (along with our **Vagus Nerve**). The butterflies in the stomach when we are nervous, the nausea and vomiting when we are anxious, the diarrhoea when we are scared. Serotonin helps our nerves carry messages to one another, the more availability of this in the gap between our **Neurons** the better the message sending. Alcohol reduces the amount of available serotonin and is therefore known as a depressant:

 Imagine driving along in the rain – our vision is disrupted by the raindrops hitting the windscreen and we cannot see clearly. Our windscreen wipers will clear it momentarily but then the raindrops keep on coming. The gap between our **Neurons** is our windscreen allowing clear messages to be sent backwards and forwards all over our body, the windscreen wipers are our serotonin levels allowing the messages to be sent effectively and alcohol is the rain – washing it all away and making everything slow and blurry.

Sex - very rare are the occasions that I have had sex without alcohol. A confidence booster it may be, but it also removes us from the scene. My sober buddy Shickey talked about his sex life in one of our **Sobertown** podcasts:

'Two years before I gave up drinking there were a few times where I'd wake up wondering if we 'did it' the night before. One morning I made the fatal mistake of asking my wife if we'd had sex the night before. It didn't go down well. For all I know she could have put in her best performance ever and I couldn't remember. I never made that mistake again. It was becoming more and more frequent that I couldn't remember. I was waking up and thinking "For f*** sake, it's the best part of the week and I can't remember it!" In the end I got a little plan together. I'd go to bed in just my boxer shorts and in the morning, I'd wake up and look under the duvet. If I had my boxer shorts on that meant 'no action' but if I had no boxer shorts on it meant 'Bingo! We'd seen action'. It's terrible. The only way a 45-year-old man knew if he had a sex life was by checking his pants in the morning. At least now when I wake up, I know exactly where my boxer shorts are – on the chandelier where I left them! Bedroom exercise is so much better sober. I'm like an Olympic champion now, whereas before I couldn't even finish the race, let alone make it to the podium'

And then there's the old brewer's droop. Alcohol reduces the blood supply to a man's penis and dampens down his desires. This can be temporary or lead to long term problems. Research shows that alcohol can ruin relationships, lead to adultery and 30% of people committing sexual assault have alcohol in their system.

https://www.healthline.com/health/alcohol-and-erectile-dysfunction

https://www.alcoholproblemsandsolutions.org/drinking-and-sexual-assualt-the-connection/#

Shame - can lead us to drink and drinking can lead us to feel shame. Another vicious circle. Shame is felt when we are embarrassed about something we have done or regret our actions, and unfortunately, it is the culture we live in and part of our conditioning from a very early age. It is not a helpful emotion as it can lead us to hide from others, lie about what we have done and maybe blame others. Many of us start to use substances to numb and block it all out, leading to addiction, and we can be really unkind to ourselves. We cannot change the past but we can block our future by hanging onto shame and **Guilt**. Or we can let it go and live in the now …

https://mentalhealthathome.org/2021/04/30/what-is-the-shame-compass

Share - your stories, your fears and your dreams. Telling our story really helps us to go through and process our memories. The feelings and emotions I had about my story when I shared it over a year ago are far different than they are today. A great way to get started is with *'The Compassionate Mind Workbook: A step-by-step Guide to developing your compassionate self'* by Chris Irons and Dr Elaine Beaumont. It really helped me to start at the beginning, tell my story as I saw it then, and get me to where I am today. We all have stories that we need to tell and others want to hear. In telling our stories, fears and dreams, we free ourselves and others, and create our today.

Side Effects - are the effects of a drug or substance, other than what it is being used for. Every drug has a side effect, even paracetamol - the intent is to block pain, but in so doing it can also cause skin rashes, bruising, feeling sick and liver problems. The actual effect of ethanol/alcohol is as an antiseptic, fuel and to dissolve other substances. For most, we initially drink it to have a good time. The side effects are **Anxiety**, **Depression**, nausea, **Vomiting**, headache and that's just the short term …

Silence - if you are lucky enough to have found silence between your breaths in meditation, then this is where Buddhists think we find ourselves. Have you ever been up into the mountains or somewhere so quiet that you could 'hear a pin drop'? Just thinking about such a time now has made my shoulders, face and **Solar Plexus** relax. Lately I have found myself driving without listening to the radio or podcasts and just being with me, myself and I. In that silence, my mind has processed so much, I have had many realisations. Even if my actual intent was just to drive my car from A to B.

Singing - is a wonderful way to express ourselves, even if the cat covers its ears when it walks in the room. I love to sing. There is such a sense of freedom in it. Until others tell us otherwise and try to constrain us. Unless you are lucky enough to be a good singer of course. I'm tone deaf but I love nothing more than singing out loud. Luckily for me, my 18-month-old grandson loves it! Take the shackles off today, turn up the music and let your lungs and voice box run free.

Singing Bowls - were originally made of metal and go back thousands of years. They make music through vibrations when we hit the rim with a soft mallet and then circle it around the rim (just like my dad used to do with water on the edge of the glass when I was a kid). Singing bowls are thought to help with **Meditation**, aligning our **Chakras** and **Healing**. Nowadays you can buy them in crystal as well as metal and you can buy chakra singing bowls in colours and notes pertaining to the area we want to balance and heal. Mine is yellow and tuned to E for my solar plexus. It really helps me just to take some time out of my day. You can find the colours and notes under **Chakras**.

Skin - is our biggest organ and measures around 20 square feet. It is the protective covering for our body, keeping things both in and out. Many things can damage our skin such as chemicals, trauma, sunlight and of course alcohol. We've talked about **Acne** which settles down and gets a whole lot better without alcohol. As does **Rosacea**, the red and purple nose and those damn spider veins. I was forever getting prescription cream for my rosacea and spending a fortune on lotions and potions to soothe and hide it. All I had to do was put down the booze and drink plenty of water to keep hydrated to look and feel a whole lot better.

Sleep - is so good for us. When we sleep our bodies grow, heal and repair and, as you can see under **Dreams**, our memories get sorted and filed. Whilst alcohol can help get us off to sleep it does not help with a good night's sleep. It affects our **Circadian Rhythms**, body chemicals and sleep stages. Typically, our sleep cycles change every 60 – 90 minutes and we therefore go through several cycles each night. These are divided into REM (Rapid Eye Movement) and non-REM sleep.

Non-REM sleep is the first phase and has 3 stages:
- Stage one is when we are dropping off to sleep and only lasts a few minutes.
- Stage two is thought to be our longest stage, a light sleep from which we can be woken
- Stage 3 is our deepest sleep state and when all our healing and repairing is done

REM Sleep has two phases – one when rapid eye movement occurs and one when it does not. It is when we are dreaming and our mind is at its most active, processing all our memories and making way for new ones.

Alcohol (even just one glass) makes us sleep heavier for the first half of the night but lighter once the sedating effects of it wear off. This interferes with our sleep cycles, especially the deep state (stage 3) and REM sleep which is when the most important functions are performed by our body. It really is hard to get a good night's sleep when we are drinking. When we quit, many of us struggle with sleep at first, finding it especially hard to get off to sleep. The stress of this can make sleep even worse. The fact is, although our sleeping hours may be less when we initially quit drinking, sober sleep is much more restorative than drunken sleep. It really is a case of quality over quantity.

https://thesleepdoctor.com/alcohol-and-sleep#

https://www.healthline.com/health/healthy-sleep/stages-of-sleep#

Sleep Apnoea - is when our airway narrows or closes during sleep, stopping our breathing and usually waking us up. This interrupts our sleep and can lead to tiredness and other illnesses. Drinking alcohol relaxes our muscles and makes us more prone to this and the less dangerous, but extremely irritating for others, act of snoring. If you naturally suffer from sleep apnoea then alcohol can make this far more dangerous, as it increases the time between stopping breathing and waking up. https://www.ncbi.nlm.nih.gov/pmc/articles/PMC5840512

Sleep Hygiene - do you remember having a bedtime routine as a kid? No matter how old, we need a good bedtime routine to get a good night's sleep. Here are some ideas to help you:

- Set a bedtime and waking up time for each day. Do not be tempted to lie in, even if you have had a rough night
- Ensure your bedroom environment is the right temperature for you, is comfortable and quiet. If your mattress is uncomfortable then save your alcohol money for a new one. Get black out blinds for the window or wear an eye mask. You want the room as dark as possible. Turn off all lights and

ban all electronic devices, such as your phone, iPad, computers etc from the bedroom. Use ear plugs, if need be, or sleep in a separate room if you have a snoring partner

- Avoid caffeine, alcohol, and nicotine for six hours before bedtime. These are all stimulants and will keep you awake. Whilst people think the alcohol helps them get off to sleep, it does not actually induce a healthy, full sleep cycle
- Avoid a heavy meal and exercise for four hours before bedtime. A healthy diet and exercise during the day can aid sleep at night. If you are hungry before bed then have a light snack, or a hot chocolate with nutmeg or a banana milkshake as these will aid sleep
- Avoid all electrical devices, including the television, for two hours before bedtime. When the sun goes down our bodies release melatonin which helps make us sleepy. Electrical devices trick our bodies into thinking the sun is still out
- Have a wind down bedtime routine. Take a warm bath, read a book, knit, meditate and/or have a cup of bedtime tea. Find what is right for you
- Teach yourself a body scan or relaxation technique to help get you to sleep. Look on **YouTube** during the day for ideas. My one is (91) MINDFULNESS by Corinna Alderton (to aid sleep and manage anxiety, worrying thoughts and pain) - YouTube
- If you wake up, avoid clock watching. Looking at the time will just put more pressure on you to get back to sleep.
- If you wake up and can't get back to sleep then have a cuppa (not caffeine), read a book or try a body scan or relaxation again. **Acceptance** is key. Resistance will just make you stressed and upset and make it harder for you to get back to sleep.
- Many sleep hygiene tips will advise you to avoid napping during the day but for many of us with health conditions, this is actually vital. I recently heard on

the radio that research shows the optimum nap time is 90 minutes, between 1 and 3 pm. Time for a siesta!

If you really are struggling, I have read research in the past showing that a couple of nights camping can reset the body clock. No electronics or tech mind. Go to bed and get up with the sun.

Slips - we all have them, but if we get straight back on the sober path then it's not a **Relapse**. It's just a little stumble. Just a bump in the road. Let it go. Don't beat yourself up. That will only lead to drinking more. Don't focus on the bump, focus on your **Recovery**.

SMART Recovery (Life Beyond Addiction) - has meetings throughout the UK and uses a 4-point programme:
- Building and Maintaining Motivation
- Coping with urges
- Managing thoughts, feelings and behaviour
- Living a balanced life

For more information and to find your local meeting go to Self-Help Addiction Recovery | UK Smart Recovery or https://smartrecovery.org.uk.

Smell - this is the sense most associated with memory. Ever walk into a room or building and smell polish, bleach, alcohol, flowers and been transported back to another time? This is due to our olfactory (nasal) nerve going directly to the area of the brain responsible for memory. I wear perfume to remind me of good times. One I particularly like is Happy by Clinique. The first time I smelt this, I was pregnant and in a physically and emotionally abusive relationship. It was an awful time. I didn't feel emotionally or physically safe at home. Work was my haven. One morning, a staff member breezed in with the biggest smile on her face, saying "Good morning" and she was smelling gawjus! It made my day and completely turned it around. When I asked her what the perfume was, she advised it was Happy. This summed up her personality, the situation and the smell perfectly. It's always on my Christmas list and on my wrists and neck when I need a little pick me up. What's your scent? If you don't have one yet then just look out for it to come to you at the right moment. I never take perfume on holiday with me. I buy a new one at the duty free on my way out, wear it all holiday and every time I wear it in the future it reminds me of my trip.

Smile - never underestimate the power of a smile. It brightens even the dullest day for both the giver and the receiver. I once walked to work, smiling and saying good morning to everyone I met. I got some strange looks but I felt great by the time I got there. I used to work in a school who had, in my opinion, the most miserable receptionists you have ever met in your life. They had the smile poem on their door. The irony made me laugh!

'Smiling is infectious
You catch it like the flu.
When someone smiled at me today
I started smiling too.

I walked around the corner
and someone saw me grin.
When he smiled, I realised
I had passed it on to him.

I thought about my smile and then

I realised its worth.

A single smile like mine

Could travel right around the earth.

So, if you feel a smile begin

don't leave it undetected,

Let's start an epidemic

And get the world infected.'

Jez Alborough 1991 (often quoted by
and credited to Spike Milligan)

https://www.onlygoodnewsdaily.com/post/smiling-is-
infectious#

Snacks - stock up on lots of healthy snack options because quitting alcohol makes us crave sugar and makes us want to feed our **Reward Pathway**. You can do the latter with exercise, laughter, caffeine and sex but lots of fruit, nuts and seeds will help with the sugar cravings.

Sober - is to be clear-headed and free from alcohol, or serious and solemn! Being sober, our heads are certainly clearer: we can think straight, be more thoughtful and sensible. But we are far from solemn and I'm far less serious than I ever was when I was drinking. I laugh now until my sides hurt and the tears run down my face. Even better, I can actually remember what the laughter was all about. Interesting that the word they have given non-drinkers makes us think our life would be miserable without the alcohol!

Sobertown Podcast - this amazing resource was started by my

IAS pal Drifter, and you can hear many amazing people telling their drinking and sober stories, sharing helpful information on recovery and there is an amazing **Tool Box** of resources by Todd Crafter. You can also hear me chatting about many of the subject headings from this book in Positive Recovery with Corinna and Two 4 One with Polly and Corinna. There are before and after photos, sobriety tattoos, book suggestions and so much more. The website is growing and developing day by day so, if you haven't already, go check it out at www.sobertownpodcast.com.

Sobriety - is to be **Sober**, in either sense! But to avoid being solemn and miserable then don't just put the drink down. I can imagine this term would relate well to a **Dry Drunk** so if you want to be happy, work, work, **Work It**.

Social Media - can be a great thing, but it can also be our own worst enemy. It is an ego feeder or deflator and an addiction all of its very own. I mean who doesn't want likes? I know surgeons who feel that thumb transplants will be replacing those of the hip and knee in the future. That aside, it can be a really helpful form of support. There are lots of great sober warriors on Instagram, Tumbler, Twitter, **YouTube** and Facebook etc. You can find me and link to my sober followers @canamgirluk.

Solar Plexus - is in the pit of our stomach, in the area where our ribs divide. Many of us feel so much here and there is a very good reason for this – it is full of nerves (including our **Vagus Nerve**) and triggers us to run, fight or hide when our fire alarm goes off (**Anxiety**). Our solar plexus also helps with the functioning of our stomach, liver, kidneys and adrenal glands (little glands situated on top of our kidneys that release **Adrenaline** and its counterpart noradrenaline).

https://www.healthline.com/health/solar-plexus-pain

Solitude - is wonderful. Yes, it is about being alone but it is very different from loneliness. It is not easy at first, and I still struggle at times, but when we get to the point of being with ourselves and hearing the silence it is wonderful. We can learn so much from solitude and it can bring us so much peace. It takes practice to just be, so don't give in. Open up your mind to all that comes in and just allow it to be. Because, in this moment, it simply is.

Soul - is said to be the essence of who we are – our feelings, our mind and our will. It is also sometimes referred to as our spirit although some see these as two completely different things. In a nutshell – it is the part of us that is not physical and which we can develop more spiritually if we wish to do so. There is a great movie called '*Soul*' by Pixar, about a man who gets a second chance at life. It really is the chance sobriety gives us. It's a great watch.

Spirals - in one of her books (I don't know which as I heard it on a podcast) **Stephanie Covington** talks about spirals pulling us down and pushing us back up again. I imagine this as an eddy or whirlpool spinning me round and round, sucking me under and drowning me in my drinking days. In sobriety it is bringing me up to the surface, letting me breath and be free again.

Spirit - another word with completely different meanings. It can be the inside part of us, the part some refer to as our soul or our mood such as 'in high spirits'. For us drinkers, the first meaning that usually comes to mind is a strong alcoholic drink (liquor). Crazy that this spirit can rob us of our inner one and bring our mood crashing down.

Spiritual - many people in sobriety start to find a more spiritual path. Even those that were really anti it before. Not because this is what we are told or taught, but because we start to notice things that we didn't before. Messages and signs that have probably always been there, but we just didn't see. **Sober**, clear headed and thoughtful makes us more observant and curious and we start to question everything, exploring ourselves, our beliefs and the world we live in.

Spleen - is an organ just behind our stomach, on the upper left side of our tummy, tucked under our ribs. It is part of our immune systems and makes white blood cells, destroys damaged red blood cells and helps to prevent infection. If our liver becomes enlarged then so can our spleen, especially in disease such as liver **Cirrhosis**, which is often associated with alcohol. An enlarged spleen can affect its function and lead to pain, infection, low red blood cells and iron (anaemia) and bruising.

https://www.msdmanuals.com/home/liver-and-gallbladder-disorders/alcohol-related-liver-disease/alcohol-related-liver-disease

Sponsors - we all need support in our life and never more than when we quit the drink. Groups such as **AA** use sponsors (usually someone with 1 – 2 years of sobriety) to help support another through **The Twelve Steps** and in their sobriety journey. Anyone can have a sponsor whether in a group or not. I have a multitude, but groups and communities are not for everyone. If an individual sponsor is more for you then find someone with lived experience of addiction and sobriety. They are everywhere, and pop up in the most surprising of places! Just look and listen out, or join a community with the purpose of connecting with someone who can offer you more responsive and individual support.

Spots - well, if you haven't got spots from drinking, you're more than likely going to get them when you quit. Just think of it as all those nasty toxins finding any which way out of your body, and your hormones resetting to where they should be. If you started drinking in your teenage years then welcome back to your youth. Eventually though your skin will be hydrated, clear and radiant.

Statistics - the grisly facts about alcohol:
- It is the third biggest preventable cause of death in the USA
- It causes over 3 million deaths a year worldwide (5.3%)
- It is a contributing factor to over 200 illnesses and injuries
- It causes death and injury early on in life – 13.5% of deaths of 20 – 39-year-olds
- Its misuse is 7th in the world for causing premature death and disability
- It is the most harmful drug overall (health, society, economy) – nearly 3 times more than cocaine and tobacco
- The World Health Organisation recommended an action plan for 2013 -2020 to reduce harmful use of alcohol and the burden of this. It would appear it has been largely ignored. See **WHO** for more information.

https://www.niaaa.nih.gov/publications/brochures-and-fact-sheets/alcohol-facts-and-statistics

https://www.who.int/news-room/fact-sheets/detail/alcohol

Stephanie Covington - an absolute icon for women in addiction.

Stephanie is a counsellor, author and recovering addict. She works tirelessly to promote the understanding of gender specific support and works all over the world spreading the word and supporting women. She has written many books, some gender specific for both men and women, covering trauma, anger and addiction, including '*A Woman's way through The Twelve Steps*'.

https://stephaniecovington.com/books/bookstore/a-womans-way-through-the-twelve-steps

STOPP - this is something I do when I am feeling stressed, overwhelmed or anxious:

- **S**top what I am doing and stand still, feeling my feet on the floor
- **T**ake a breath or do an emergency blow out (see **Anxiety**) and steady my breathing
- **O**bserve what is happening around me and inside of me and understand it
- **P**rocess what I am feeling and thinking and what I need to do to calm everything down
- **P**roceed with what I need to do, or with what I was doing, once I am able

Stopping - if you want to stop drinking then work out when is the right time for you. Maybe write a list of reasons to continue drinking and reasons to stop and see what is best for you in the here and now. If you choose not to stop today then just keep revisiting your lists. If you choose to stop then keep looking at it. This can be a great motivator to keep you heading in the right direction. You can write your reasons down, and add photos, on the **IAS** app. Only you will see these unless you choose to share them.

Stress - a little bit of stress is good for us and motivates us to get out of bed in the morning and get things done. Life can be stressful though and there are many events that are out of our control that can pile the pressure on. We are also good at pressurising ourselves and letting others do so, leading to us feeling very stressed. It can seem as though we are juggling our way through life whilst trying to meet the demands and deadlines of others. And holding our breath on the way. If we don't learn to manage our stress then it can lead to health problems such as high blood pressure and strokes, anxiety and depression.

https://www.mind.org.uk/information-support/types-of-mental-health-problems/stress/what-is-stress

Stress Bucket - imagine a bucket filling with water. Each drop is a different size and shape. Eventually it will overfill and it could be the tiniest drop that makes this happen. This is exactly what happens with stress dripping into our body - if we don't do something with it, then we become completely overwhelmed. If we drill holes in our bucket, we gradually let the water out. For many years I did this with alcohol. Now I know that whilst this was a relief because it was numbing the stress, it was also causing bigger dops to go back in! And so commenced the daily cycle. Now I am sober, I have healthy holes in my bucket and my stress is much reduced. For me it's **Mindfulness, Acceptance**, my **Hula Hoop**, saying **No**, setting **Boundaries** and sticking to them, reading, knitting, podcasting and riding Bumblebee. We need to replace old **Habits** with new ones. Make them healthy. What holes can you put in place to relieve stress?

Stuck - is something we all feel from time to time and it can happen in many areas of our life. We can feel stuck in a routine, in unhelpful patterns and in a rut. Sometimes, we can feel so stuck that we really do not know what to do or where to turn, and that is a horrible place to be. It actually makes others around us feel stuck too. If you are feeling stuck with your drinking, or any area of your life, perhaps look at the **Choice** section again.

Suffering - is something that happens to us all in our pursuit of **Happiness**, although we are often looking in the wrong places and expecting people and things to make us happy. This can lead to disappointment and upset, time and time again. If we are not suffering then we are happy, if we are happy then we are not suffering. But how to change all this? For me it's firstly remembering that **Everything Happens for a Reason** which I learnt at the age of 9 – although I didn't heed the lesson until much more recent years. I was due to go on a school trip to the Tower of London. I was really excited and I imagine you can relate to my disappointment, when on the day the trip, the bus we were taking broke down and we were unable to go. Later that day, a bomb exploded in the White Tower killing one person and injuring 41 others – many of them children. I am crying as I write this, with gratitude for myself and compassion for all of those affected. There is suffering. If we can accept what is, stay in our **Hula Hoop**, and try and see it all as training for the future (whilst remembering there will be a breakthrough) then we can stop some of our own suffering. Buddhists work on a principle that there are no problems 'out there', what happens simply happens. The problem is what our mind makes of it all.

Sugar - we ingest so much sugar when we drink alcohol that our body craves replacement when we stop. It's our choice whether to ride it out in the same way as alcohol or to succumb. Sugar is not good for us and is linked to obesity, heart disease, diabetes and poor energy levels. Beware the sweeteners though as many have been linked to far worse conditions. Stevia plant appears to be the most popular currently but ensure it is 100% pure. Sugar triggers our **Reward Pathway** stimulating our **Dopamine** and **Endorphins**. We therefore get cravings and withdrawals when we stop. These include:

- Headache
- Sleep problems
- Depression
- Poor concentration
- Anxiety
- Restlessness
- Feeling sick
- Dizziness
- Lack of energy or feeling tired
- Muscle cramps

Every day I remind myself that I have a choice to eat sugar and feel ill, or abstain and feel so much better in myself.

https://www.healthline.com/health/sugar-detox-symptoms#

https://www.verywellmind.com/sugar-withdrawal-symptoms-timeline-and-treatment-4176257

Suicide - by the time you finish reading this section, somewhere in the world another two people would have taken their own life. And a further person every 40 seconds after that. Between 2001 and 2018 suicide was the leading cause of death for 20 -34-year-olds in the UK. It remains the leading cause of death for men under the age of 45 in the UK. Alcohol is present in 1/3 of all suicide cases. Alcohol may take the edge off of suicidal thoughts, but it can also numb our **Superego** and makes us less rational. Suicidal thoughts come to many of us during our life but the important thing is to reach out, talk about them and keep ourselves safe until they pass. Writing a safety plan (example below) can really help, or having a safety box with photos, happy memories and self-soothing items in. 'Stay Alive' is also a great app for your phone. Remember that every thought and feeling will pass, our job is to keep ourselves safe until it does. There is a short podcast on this on my **YouTube** channel (76) Suicide

Support - YouTube.

My Safety Plan (example)
When I feel I cannot keep myself safe I will:
Talk to: *Mum 01234 – 567890*
Angela 01234 – 567891
Samaritans – 116 123
Get help from:
Mum and Sarah next door
Go to my safe place: *My bedroom*
Calm myself by:
Listening to music, lighting candles and stroking my furry cushion or cuddle a teddy
Other ideas for keeping myself safe:
Have a bath
Ask friends or mum to come round
Visit friends

If you have suicidal thoughts then consider writing your own safety plan now.

My Safety Plan
When I feel I cannot keep myself safe I will:

Talk to:

Get help from:

Go to my safe place:

Calm myself by:

Other ideas to keep myself safe:

Sunlight - is good for us. We all feel better and brighter when the sun is shining and there is evidence that it really does increase our **Serotonin** levels. On a physical level, when sunlight hits our skin, our bodies make it into vitamin D strengthening our bones and reducing pain. Yes, we have to be careful of skin cancer, and I fully support all sun care safety advice, but personally I still get 30 minutes of unfiltered sun each day – just not in the midday sun (unlike drinking me, who would sit out in it all day getting dehydrated and sunburnt!)

The Five S's of Sun Safety

(Widely Used but original source unknown)

- Slip on a T-Shirt
- Slop on the sunscreen (at least factor 30)
- Slap on a hat
- Slide on sunglasses
- Shade from the sun

https://www.skcin.org/sunSafetyAndPrevention/theFiveSsOfSunSafety.htm#

Superego - another of Freud's theories of the mind 'Uber Ich' – the Over I. The critical and moral side of us. Working with our **Id** and our **Ego**. You know that conversation in our heads? When our id wants a drink now, our ego wants to be with the 'in crowd' and our superego is reminding us of our commitment and what we want to achieve. The good, the bad and the ugly, all having a rumble in the jungle. And the next morning, it's our superego that will be filing us with regret if we have succumbed or filling us with joy if it won.

Supplements - I used **Craig Beck**'s advice on supplements for alcohol withdrawal and I'm convinced it really helped me:

- **Omega 3** – take lots of it. He recommends 3000mg of fish oil. I took this for 3 months and then reduced down to my usual 1000mg a day. There is no upper limit that I could find. I have now cut out the middleman and gone straight to the vegan source – seaweed. You can also get this from flaxseed. Omega 3 is thought to rebuild fats in the brain and, in mice studies has proved to lower alcohol cravings
- A good multivitamin
- Vitamin B complex. We especially need vitamin B6 as this supports the nervous system, and B12 as this helps us to absorb nutrients. We destroy B12 when we drink (**B Vitamin**)
- 1000mg of vitamin C - best taken in two doses of 500mg at separate times of the day. Do not take more than 1000mg a day as you can overdose on this (**C Vitamin**)

Surrender - many of us do not like this term as it is often equated to powerlessness. But try seeing it as **Acceptance**; of our past and of the here and now. Acceptance of what is. This morning I listened to a voice message from my amazing friend and beautiful sober sister, and it summed up the essence of surrender to me:

> 'I have finally found sober solace, meaning peace in this process. I think the very hardest part of trying to get sober is the whole word 'trying'. It's like you are trying so hard but you are also fighting against yourself, because your self doesn't really want to be sober. You are seriously doing the worst kind of internal battle and the stakes couldn't be higher. It doesn't finally click until you can just surrender and release into the peace of it. There has to come that point, where you are no longer even battling it. It's just like "Ok. There's only one choice, one outcome, and that has to be not drinking". Once the brain can agree with that, and stop fighting against it, it becomes so much easier than the times when you are climbing the walls wanting to have a drink. When the rational part of you is saying "No you can't" and the other part of you is screaming like the nastiest, crabbiest baby that just wants its drink. Once the baby can just be put to sleep, or grow up enough to figure out that it doesn't actually need drink anymore, then it can stop harassing the part of your brain that really does want to be well and really does want to stop ruining its life.'

Mermaid Must Not Drown - 14th February 2022 - 6 weks sober.

Survivor - if you are reading this, then this is you. Not only have you managed to negotiate your way through life to this point, but you have also managed to avoid the fatal effects of alcohol. Many of us have also experienced trauma in our life, but whilst it may feel as if we are barely holding it together at times, the fact is we are still here in the flesh. Emotionally **Trauma** affects us all differently but, one thing is guaranteed, using alcohol to cope will just remove us further from ourselves.

Survivor's Guilt - is something felt by people who have survived an event in which others have died. It can also affect people who have survived an illness from which others die – such as cancer. The symptoms are the same as **PTSD** and can be part of this, or completely separate. The important thing is to allow yourself to grieve, learn **Forgiveness**, remember you are not alone and get help through support groups, **Psychotherapy** or medication.

https://www.verywellmind.com/survivors-guilt-4688743

T

Talk - get it all out. Often our friends and family can be our best therapists, other times we may need someone independent to talk to, but talking is the important part. Very often, by just saying something out loud, it eases the burden and helps us. Even as a nurse, some of my best therapy sessions were done over a cuppa or when taking a stroll together along the beach. And the best support for my sobriety journey has been from strangers in **IAS** who very quickly became good friends.

Taste - it is said that the taste of pure alcohol is disgusting – that's why flavours are added but, in one study, scientists have found that our genes for bitter tastes affect how we all perceive this. It is thought that people who find the taste of alcohol less bitter are probably more likely to drink and become addicted. Another study showed that having more than 4 drinks of alcohol a day can impair our taste, possibly due to damage in our nerve fibres and cells from the alcohol. In this same study alcohol was not found to affect our smell (which is usually associated with taste) and light drinkers were actually found to have a better sense of smell than non-drinkers! Taste problems can also be related to heart disease, cancer, age, ethnicity and low vitamin B1. Alcohol can cause 3 of these. Two years in, my smell is actually still rubbish but food tastes so good now.

https://www.livescience.com/47970-alcohol-taste-perception-genetics.html

https://www.pennmedicine.org/news/news-blog/2017/april/

effects-of-smoking-and-alcohol-on-smell-and-taste

Thalamus - is the part of our brain through which all our sensory nerves travel. It helps us to feel, see, hear, smell, and taste. It also helps with our co-ordination, movement and **Circadian Rhythms** and is thought to form part of our **Limbic System** regulating memory, emotion, motivation and pain. And of course, alcohol changes all of this.

https://human-memory.net/thalamus

https://brainmadesimple.com/thalamus

Thankfulness - is our practical response to our feeling of **Gratitude**. We can show we are thankful from time to time, whilst feeling continually grateful. I will be forever grateful to my sober community for helping me in my journey but I only thank them from time to time.

The Boy, **the Mole, the Fox and the Horse** - this book by **Charlie Mackesy** made a huge difference to my life and my sobriety journey. It taught me that it is OK to ask for help and to show my weaknesses. Another great resource that completely turned my life around. I have bought a copy for many a friend and I read it to my little grandson regularly. It is a book for life that I think all kids and adults should have.

The Twelve Steps - are the principles of recovery in the AA programme (as well as Narcotics Anonymous and Overeaters Anonymous). These are worked through in order and help us to face our addiction. They are listed here as found on The Twelve Steps | Alcoholics Anonymous (aa.org):

1. *We admitted we were powerless over alcohol — that our lives had become unmanageable.*

2. *Came to believe that a Power greater than ourselves could restore us to sanity.*

3. *Made a decision to turn our will and our lives over to the care of God as we understood Him.*

4. *Made a searching and fearless moral inventory of ourselves.*

5. *Admitted to God, to ourselves, and to another human being the exact nature of our wrongs.*

6. *Were entirely ready to have God remove all these defects of character.*

7. *Humbly asked Him to remove our shortcomings.*

8. *Made a list of all persons we had harmed, and became willing to make amends to them all.*

9. *Made direct amends to such people wherever possible, except when to do so would injure them or others.*

10. *Continued to take personal inventory and when we were wrong promptly admitted it.*

11. *Sought through prayer and meditation to improve our conscious contact with God as we understood Him, praying only for knowledge of His will for us and the power to carry that out.*

12. *Having had a spiritual awakening as the result of these Steps, we tried to carry this message to alcoholics, and to practice these principles in all our affairs.'*

This is not something I have followed in my journey, and I'm very aware that my **Ego** wants to run a mile whenever I see it (something to reflect on and ask myself what that is about), but it helps many people every day such as my beautiful sober sister SJ333:

'The 12 steps are like a jigsaw puzzle that fits together perfectly, it's a programme of hope, strength and unity and courage. We learn that we are suffering with a disease that affects our mind and body and if we put

any mind-altering substances in our body we disconnect with our higher power. The 12 steps are magical in so many ways, and for me steps 4 and 5 changed everything. Understanding resentments and putting myself in the other person's place helps me let go of what I've been holding onto for years and also see my part in it: Step 9 - doing amends to people I have harmed and sweeping my side of the street clean. Also, by finishing the steps I can then pass on freely what was given freely to me and help other people which is a gift. Doing the 12 steps is the best thing I've ever done, I've grown spiritually, and am present for everyone who comes in my path, my tool box is full of things that will help me be the best version of myself until I leave this earth. Also, the obsession to drink or do drugs has been completely removed. I'll be forever grateful to the founders of AA as the programme has completely changed my life'. June 25th, 2022 – 290 plus days sober.

Thich Nhat Hanh - was a Buddhist monk to whom many famous sayings and quotes have been attributed. Here are a few to wet your whistle:

> *'To be beautiful means to be yourself. You don't need to be accepted by others. You need to accept yourself.'*
> *'Walk as if you are kissing the Earth with your feet.'*
> *'Hope is important because it can make the present moment less difficult to bear. If we believe that tomorrow will be better, we can bear a hardship today.'*

He wrote many books in his life and I love my little pocket book simply called *'The Pocket Thich Nhat Hanh'*, a selection of some of his published works, collated by Melvin McLeod and covering most Buddhist themes.
https://www.hitc.com/en-gb/2022/01/22/thich-nhat-hanh-quotes

Think - we do not need to know the answer or make a decision straight away. We all need a little space and thinking time. Have you ever found yourself being pressured into making a decision and soon afterwards regretting it? I know I have. Salespeople are the worst (or best) at this and know how to put the pressure on. They are not there to think about us - they are 'in it to win it'. Typing this, my **Addict Voice** comes to mind - the pressure, negotiating and tempting deals. Sober we can all think much more clearly, **Pause**, think and say 'no deal'! Even if we are naturally impulsive, in the absence of alcohol our thinking is far straighter and more rational than it is with it.

This Naked Mind: Control Alcohol. Find Freedom, Discover Happiness & Change Your Life - written by **Annie Grace**. This book was a real games changer for me and many others I know. Easy to read and a complete myth buster and eye opener to the truth of alcohol.

Thoughts - form our ideas and opinions, which can also form other thoughts. Our thoughts can be constant, altered, relentless and all over the place. Many of us drink to get some peace and quiet from them, but they will always come back - often louder and stronger. We cannot escape our thoughts; they will always be there and can often seem to come out of nowhere – like little people standing at the back of our mind firing arrows of thoughts into our consciousness! But if we can accept and acknowledge them, even welcome them like an old friend, then we can get them into a more logical order and have better control over them. **Meditation, Mindfulness, CBT, NLP** and **ACT** can help with this. As can stopping alcohol.

Time - many of us wonder what we are going to do with all that time if we stop drinking, but it is a needless worry. If we put as much time into our sobriety as we do/did into drinking, it becomes a wonderful life filled with doing all the things we love. Things we didn't even know we wanted to do or would enjoy. In sobriety we find so many things we love to do, which we didn't have a clue about when we were drinking, and wonder how we ever actually had time to drink!

Time Out - is not just for children or for punishment, it is for creating space and clearing our head, mind and body and then carrying on from a place of clarity. Whenever I see or hear this phrase, I instantly see Timon from the Lion King shouting '*Time out. Time Out. Let me get this straight. You know her. She knows you. But she wants to eat you. And everybody's okay with this? DID I MISS SOMETHING?*' This always makes me smile, and on proof reading this today, I can liken it to my relationship with alcohol. We can take time out in moments of stress but we all need general time out every now and again - from our thoughts, others, routine, gadgets and just life in general. Thirty minutes 'me time' a day is great for our physical and mental health but it doesn't need to be taken in one go.

Timing - for our sobriety is so important, it really does have to be the right time for us. Often, we think that there is no right time for anything, and will even find reasons not to act, but we have to be in the right **Mindset**. If we stop drinking purely for others then we will not be sober, we will just stop drinking. And that is such a miserable place to be. Very few people stop and succeed at their first attempt. The majority of us have several warm up laps before we really get in the race and that is okay, there is no rush (unless we are very ill from drinking or have a court order). To succeed we have to give ourselves time to commit to sobriety and recognise that there are seven stages to change:

1. Precontemplation – you feel the need to change but aren't quite ready
2. Contemplation – you start to consider what you need

THE A- Z OF ALCOHOL AND SOBRIETY

to make the change
3. Preparation – you **Plan and Prepare**
4. Action – you do it!
5. Maintenance – you **Work It**
6. Termination – this has become the new you and part of your **Muscle Memory**
7. Recycling – **Slips and Relapses**, recognise it, learn from it and start where you need to on the seven stages of change

If you keep resetting but learn with each drink then it's OK. If you keep resetting and getting anxious, frustrated and angry then perhaps it is not your time just yet? I'm not saying this is fact. I'm just suggesting you question your motives and look again at your **Choice**s and **Motivation**.

https://www.prevention.com/life/a20429391/seven-stages-of-change

Tolerance - our brain and body get used to repeated actions. This includes alcohol. It numbs and dampens down our nervous system and our body adapts to it to compensate. Over time (and not as much time as you'd think) our brain and body get used to the amount we are drinking and we need more and more to have the numbing effect we desire. This causes **Withdrawal** when we stop drinking. On the plus side, we have lots more tolerance for everything and everyone once we get sober – even ourselves! We realise that patience really is a virtue.

Tongue - oh wicked organ. How many times have you bitten it or wished you could just stop it from wagging or take everything back that you said? Although in this techno world it's more like wicked thumbs. My nan had two sayings that whirl around in my brain "Least said soonest mended" and "If you can't say anything nice then don't say anything at all". It's so much easier in sobriety. We are actually able to engage our brain before our tongues.

Tool Box - this is our box of tricks to beat off our **Cravings**, **Triggers**, **Altered/Unhelpful Thinking** and **Addict Voice**. Every job needs tools for the work to succeed, sobriety is no different. One size does not fit all and we need lots of tools to help us through. What works for us one day, may not work the next. We need a good selection. Hopefully, reading this book, you have now got some really good ideas and **Resources** but that does not make your tool box full. We can really learn from ourselves - from each craving, milestone, challenge and reset. Stay curious and don't be the poor work person who always blames their tools!

Torture - is being punished or receiving pain. Addiction is torture. We can make alcohol our torturer if we like, but we have to realise that only we have the power to break free. In the end, it is us that is repeatedly punishing ourselves.

Toxic Relationship - is any relationship that is not helpful to us. If others make us feel uncomfortable, do not hear us, continually berate us and put us down, or try to stop us from achieving our goals then they do not deserve a place in our life. It does not matter who these people are – our boss or our parents – if they repeatedly make us feel worthless and fill us with fear and anxiety, then it's time to let the relationship go. Often, we stay in these relationships because we think we 'should' or 'ought to do the right thing' but who for? For them? Because of who they are? Because society expects it? To save face? What about us? We deserve to be happy and alive. We can only try so much, we cannot make others change the way they are (nor should we), we can only change our response. We are going to get so fit with all this hula hooping!

Trauma - can be physical or emotional and both can cause physical and emotional pain. A physical trauma is an injury to our body which in turn can be very frightening and distressing and lead to long term upset. We can also have an emotionally traumatic experience which, in itself, is stressful and terrifying and can lead to physical pain such as headaches, stomach ache and body pain. Both situations can lead to **Anxiety, Depression, PTSD,** other **Mental illness** and more serious physical health conditions. **Talking** helps with trauma as can **Psychotherapy**.

https://www.psychologytoday.com/us/blog/think-act-be/201609/21-common-reactions-trauma

https://www.ming.org.uk/information-support/types-of-mental-health-problems/trauma/about-trauma

Triggers - many of us are aware that we are drinking to numb, others of us not so. For some it has just become a habit, a **Dopamine** addiction that we have needed more and more of to fulfil us. I found unknown triggers on my sober journey but if we can go with it, and let it be a voyage of discovery, then we are onto a winner. There are certain situations that we know will trigger us, and I would encourage you to avoid them for the first few months. Make your excuses and just do not go to that bar, that wedding, that birthday party. Feign illness if you have to. OK so that's kinda drinking behaviour deceit, but it really is for the greater good this time round. Anticipate expected triggers and avoid exposing yourself to them until you feel strong enough. Forget **FOMO** and remember **JOMO**. Some triggers will be unavoidable and will come suddenly out of habitual response. Anger, stress, pain, hurt, upset; you feel the need to numb. Be prepared for these. Have a diversion list, take a deep breath and distract yourself until you calm down. Then think it all through, remembering your area of **Control** and having **Acceptance** at the centre of all things. Other triggers will come out of nowhere. Boom! Where the f*** did that come from? Take a breath, note the situation: who are you with? what's happening? what happened just before? what you are feeling? what you are thinking?Use **ACT**, **HALT** or **STOPP** or anything else in your **Tool Box**. Just do not pick up that drink or press the **F*** It Button**.

Trust - for many of us this is a really hard thing to do. Our trust may have been broken just once, or time after time, to make us defensive and not let others in. Often, our expectations of others are so low that we actually look for evidence to prove ourselves right. I did this for years thinking 'you cannot trust men' and I'd scurry around in every relationship trying to 'prove' that they were cheating. Some were and some weren't, but they'd all get tired of my searching for clues in the end. In sobriety I have learned to trust in the **Moment** and that **Everything Happens for a Reason**. I have my area of **Control**, I cannot second guess. I may have my **Gut Instinct** but that too can be wrong when my **Ego** interferes , so talking and naming the elephant in the room is what I now put my faith in. And I trust in myself to have the **Capacity** to make a decision and take the **Pressure** off of myself.

Trust in the Process - have faith and trust that it will all work out OK. Essentially this is about accepting our areas of **Control** and letting go! What will be, will be. If we can do this then we become calmer, more patient, happier, able to recover more quickly, less stressed and more accepting of change and our areas of control. When I'm struggling and don't have the answer I now simply 'leave it to the universe'. One of my favourite film quotes is from The Best Marigold Hotel: *'Everything will all be alright in the end so if it's not alright, it's not the end.'*

https://www.minimalismmadesimple.com/home/trust-the-process#

Truth - sets us free. But we have to listen to our own truth, to what it is that we really want and need. When we break away from the lies and **Deceit** and start to live an authentic life then we can find freedom and happiness. When we tell the truth our suffering ends, but we need to be careful that in so doing we do not cause others to suffer. Check your motive. Some things really are best left unsaid.

U

Uncertainty - there are some things in life I am certain of, such as I would never jump out of a plane with a small canopy attached to me just for the sheer hell of it. But even for the more daring amongst us, there would probably a moment of doubt. Especially when standing at the aircraft door, seeing the target below with lots of wide open, unknown space in between. Will I hit my head as I jump? How is it going to feel? What if my chute doesn't open? How am I going to land? The unknown fills us with uncertainty. It is often easier if we have someone by our side, someone who has got our back (or our parachute), such as our sober **Community**. Sometimes we just have to feel the fear and do it anyway. But I'm still not jumping out of an actual plane unless I absolutely have to!

Understanding - is to literally stand under everything. Only by letting everything pour over us can we fully understand ourselves. By letting the pain and suffering rain down, accepting it and allowing it to just be. We will never fully understand others, as our **Perception**s are all different. All we can do is our best and show **Compassion** and **Kindness**.

Unexpected Joy of Being Sober (The) - a great quit lit book from **Catherine Gray**. A light-hearted but eye-opening read. She discusses situations to which many of us can relate with some great strategies for getting and staying sober.

THE A- Z OF ALCOHOL AND SOBRIETY

Unilateral - this journey is not. It is not one size fits all. Sometimes we have to try on many different coats, to find the one that fits, on that given day. It's fine. This is your journey. You have to do it your way.

Unique - in case it hasn't already sunk in, this is you. Completely individual, unique, a one off. Even identical twins are different in some way. They really did break the mould when they made you and that is what makes you so special. Priceless in fact. Now, would you drive along with a million-pound vase rolling around in your car? Of course not! So don't take risks with yourself.

Units - obviously I recommend that you do not drink any alcohol, but the current guidelines recommend we do not drink more than 14 units a week. This should be spread over 2 – 3 sessions as more than 8 units in one session is viewed as a binge. But what are units? Many of us think that one spirit is 1 unit and a pint of beer, stout or cider 2. But what size and strength is the spirit you've poured and how strong is your pint? And what about all the different wine strengths and sizes? If you are wanting to cut back and monitor your alcohol, then I encourage you to start measuring your drinks and recording them (the **Drinkaware** app will help you to do this). Here is a rough guide to UK units:

25ml spirit (40%) = 1 unit

175ml wine (12%) = 2.1 units

568 ml (pint) lager/ale/cider (5%) = 2.8 units

An easy way to calculate this is to multiply the millimetres by the strength and divide it by 1000.

E.g.   A 700ml bottle of wine at 12% - 700 x 12 = 8400 divide by 1000 = 8.4 units

Even easier still then just try these alcohol converters. The top one is for grams and the bottom one converts grams and ounces:

https://alcoholchange.org.uk/alcohol-facts/interactive-tools/check-your-drinking/alcohol-units

https://www.nutritionheart.com/alcohol-drinks-grams-of-alcohol

Universe - science and religion continue to battle out how this came to be, but I don't really get involved in all of the particulars. I just know that when I'm struggling, I acknowledge that 'there is suffering' and I leave it to the universe. Because I'm sure it has a plan …

Untamed - I absolutely loved the first half of this book by **Glennon Doyle**. I was completely engrossed and learnt so much, especially how to listen to my '**Knowing**'. The book starts, describing an event at a zoo with a cheetah. It performed the tricks as trained, but Glennon's daughter noticed that it looked sad. The keepers tried to reassure her that it was fine as it was raised in captivity, but Glennon could see it looking out of the cage at its wild. She likens this to humans. Trained with expectations on how we act and perform from a very young age. And in my view our conditioning continues later with false advertising and lies. After all, how can we possibly go on holiday, watch a sporting event or go to a party without alcohol? Hopefully, you now know the truth and I really hope that you are starting to break free.

Unwelten - a wonderful German word (pronounced oonvelten). This is a theory that every species and organism experience its environment and surroundings differently. It suggests that we are inseparable from the world, because it is our interpretation of it. Our sober view of the world is very different from our drunk one. The world really does not owe us anything, but we owe everything to it.

V

Vagus Nerve - is the biggest nerve in our body and carries messages to and from our brain, heart, tummy and near enough every organ in our body. It plays a major role in keeping our body running including steadying our heart rate and blood pressure and helps us to talk, swallow and digest our food. It is also responsible for our gag reflex, our **Gut instinct** and telling our body that it needs to vomit. It is thought that by stimulating our Vagus nerve with things such as humming, meditation and yoga, we can reduce inflammation and our risk of diabetes and heart disease, stress and anxiety.

https/www.verywellhealth.com/vagus-nerve-anatomy-1746123

https://www.getsensate.com/blogs/news/everything-vagus-nerve?

Values - What truly matters to you in life? What is the most important? Do you get enough of it? And what can you do to get more of it?

Example

> *My biggest value is my family but I only spend about 10% of my time with them.*
> *Work is fairly important to me but it's fairly low in what I value but I spend about 80% of my time doing this.*
> *I really value going out to the theatre and cinema but only go about 3 times a year.*

> *I really value my friends but I only speak to some of them once a year.*
> *I do not value drinking alcohol but I spend at least 3 hours a day doing this.*

What are your values? Maybe look at these headings and see how much they matter to you and how much time you actually give to them. Give each heading a number 1 – 9 with 1 being the most important and 9 being the least. Then give a rough percentage of the time you spend doing that activity each day.

If nothing else, it gives us a great guide on what we can do with all that spare **Time**!

Activity	Value	Time
Work		
Money		
Health		
Family and Friends		
Romance		
Personal Growth		
Leisure Time		
Your home		
Drinking		

Victim - we have all been this at times in our life whether through abuse, accident, crime or intent. When horrible things happen to us, which are out of our control, it can be very upsetting. It is an invasion of our physical and emotional **Personal Space**. We sense a loss of power and helplessness at the time, and rightly so. How we feel, is how we feel and that is OK. But it is unhelpful to unpack and stay there or numb and block it, as this can cause us to become **Stuck**. Even if we experience **Trauma** from the event, we can take back our area of control by getting help and support. Staying a victim allows our perpetrator to keep control and drive our **Bus**.

Village - the old proverb 'it takes a village to raise a child' originates from Africa. When we have lots of role models and different types of help and support it helps us to learn, grow and thrive. We do not have to do anything alone in life unless we choose to do so. There is always someone willing to guide or show us the way. But they don't come looking for us, we have to reach out and ask for help!

Virtual Reality - I felt compelled to write about this today whilst I sat in a subway carriage with about twenty other people. A slightly older man was reading a newspaper and a woman a magazine. Approximately 80% of travellers were sitting looking at their phones with earbuds in. Half the women had false lips, nails, hair or eyelashes. I am not judging – I used to be exactly the same, but a sense of sadness overcame me as I realised that so many of us are trying to escape reality in any way that we can. Choosing to live in a false and virtual world rather than the one we are actually living in. The only evidence of any human writing was the word HATE daubed graffiti style across one of the doors. There is actually so much to love in this world if we just stopped running and trying to escape from it. As the train filled up, a much younger woman got on and sat opposite us and started reading a book. As she read, she pulled faces that I perceived to be of surprise, took out a pencil from her bag and then an actual real-life notebook and made notes in it. That filled me with hope. I then got out my phone and wrote some notes on it to jog my memory when I came to type this (Doh emoji).

Visualisation - is a great way of relaxing and calming our body and mind and beating our **Addict Voice**. It is very different from **Mindfulness**, and being in the here and now, but who doesn't like a little fantasy every now and again? We can just close our eyes and take ourselves to a happy place (memory or made up) and relax in the moment. Sometimes I'm floating on a fluffy cloud and feeling weightless, other times I'm sitting by a log fire and feeling warm and cosy or laying on a tropical beach listening to the waves. Afterwards I always take a moment to be grateful for something in my here and now too – the sun shining and making me happy or the rain falling and watering my garden. A less relaxing but very necessary visualisation is when we are **Playing it Forwards**. It helps me to actually see in my mind what would happen as well as thinking about it. The sip becoming a glass, a glass becoming a bottle or two … the drunk texting, falling asleep on the bathroom floor instead of my nice comfortable bed, waking up with a hangover and writing off yet another day or two.

Vitamins - are essential for our health and wellbeing. We get these from the foods we eat, our own body and the sun. Alcohol affects the absorption and production of these and it is therefore helpful to take supplements. I have written about the individual vitamins under the relevant headings in this book. e.g., Vitamin A is under A, and B under B etc.

https://healthfully.com/vitamins-depleted-by-alcohol-6843537.html

https://livestrong.com/article/375909-what-are-the-effects-of-alcohol-in-vitamins-minerals

Voice - we all have one and it can help or hinder others. When we use it positively, with kindness and generosity, then it can be wonderful. We all have the right to our own **Opinions**, thoughts and ideas, and often these can be really helpful to others, so use your voice and share your successes and your struggles. Verbally or written – whatever we say will always help someone else in their journey. Don't forget to always be Kind, ask for **Help** and keep practising saying **No**. This section helped Lisa as she was proofreading:

> *'You've really got me thinking tonight! In a good way (for me). My thoughts have gone to the place where I learned to own my past, my mistakes, the less positive parts of myself and when I did start voicing these things they no longer had a hold over me and it was as if others knew they couldn't hold these things against me with any power because I was owning them. Wow - you're giving me therapy as well.'*

Vomiting - is the body's way of getting rid of **Poison**, toxins, bugs and all things nasty. Thank goodness for our clever bodies. Without this gut reaction we'd probably be long dead, but when we've been drinking, or feel sick, we should always lay on our side to reduce the risk of choking on our own vomit. The really stupid thing is, I absolutely hate vomiting. It is the pits. Yet I'd inflict it on myself time after time, to the groans of "Never again" ... and repeat ...

Vulnerable - drunk we are completely exposed. Even if we are just a little bit tipsy, we will do things we would not usually do. Our defences and senses are down. We drink away our **Capacity** for understanding, remembering, communicating and running. Remember the **Anaesthetic** effect. We drink ourselves into **Oblivion** and complete and utter helplessness. And that is one hell of a scary thought right there.

W

Waiting - what are you waiting for? There will never be a good time, but it has to be the right time for you. **Plan and Prepare** and set a quit date. Otherwise, you will just be sitting and waiting ...

Waking Up Refreshed - Oh the wonders. I never knew it was possible. I was the pyjama girl with 'I hate mornings' and 'Wake me up at lunchtime' emblazoned across them. I had to be in bed for at least 12 hours to get anywhere near a resemblance of 6 hours sleep and literally peel myself out of bed the next morning. Day after day I'd wake up knackered, hungover or drunk and asking myself "Why do I wake up feeling so shit?" As if it wasn't obvious. But no one wants to blame their addiction. Their **Comfort Blanket**. Now I know drinking ruins sleep, our bodies and our minds, and I'm wide awake in so many ways. Nowadays I'm usually up by 7 am, refreshed and loving my quiet time with the dawn and ready for the day. In fact think I need to invest in some new pyjamas!

Walking - many people rediscover walking in their sobriety. It is good to get out in the fresh air and into the sunlight (even on dull dreary days). The daylight is good for our **Serotonin** levels and mood and the exercise itself releases **Endorphins**. Some people walk miles every day but I have a daily baseline of about 200 yards. If I can do more then that's great, but just achieving my baseline is good enough. If you are unable to walk then try and get out onto the doorstep each day or sit by an open window. And if it's too cold, just sit in front of a window with the daylight on your face.

Walking With Others - I may not be able to physically walk far, but over the past 2 years I have walked many miles with others. They have held my hand and I have held theirs. Always walking side by side, never in front, never behind, just together. This is the biggest comfort of all. This is another benefit of finding a sober **Community**. It really is wonderful to share our journey with others and get the support we both need and deserve.

Warrior - we are all brave in acknowledging our addiction, facing and preparing to go into battle with it. Fortunately, there are many experienced sober warriors out there whose lead we can follow. Whilst we walk side by side on this journey, there is no pecking order, it is good to acknowledge the value of the experience of those who have gone before us and give their time to support and help us. A successful warrior is prepared, works with others and uses all the weapons and skills available. You too can be a warrior, if you choose to be so.

Water - really is the elixir of life. Our adult bodies are 50 – 60% water dependent on our hydration levels. Alcohol makes us pee more than any other drink and dehydrates us, so it's my guess that we do not have all the water we need inside of us. Water lubricates our joints, helps us get rid of toxins, takes oxygen and nutrients to our cells, keeps our body temperature level, helps us digest and break down foods and nutrients, and protects our organs, brain and spinal cord. No wonder we feel so rough the morning after the night before! If you are still drinking, then at least try and have a glass of water in-between drinks.

https://www.thoughtco.com/how-much-of-your-body-is-

water-609406

Weakness - I never used to allow myself to show my weaknesses. My experiences in earlier years made me feel that asking for help was not a good thing as it could lead to rejection, a feeling that I struggled to tolerate. Even when I started my sober journey, my posts were all upbeat and positive, regardless of how I was actually feeling inside. And then I read *'The Boy, the Mole, the Fox and the Horse'* and it completely turned my world around. I realised that it is OK to show my weakness, that this is actually my strength, and that asking for help is a brave thing to do. So, I learnt to be strong and brave, to reach out, and that it is OK to show others our true feelings. And that actually, in so doing, this helps so many.

We Are the Luckiest. The Surprising Magic of a Sober Life - a **Quit lit** book by Laura McKowen. As a result of this the Luckiest Memoir support group was formed, with more than 30 Zoom meetings a week. The majority are large groups with between 150 - 300 people, but quite a few leave their cameras off. Attendees are mostly from the USA, but it is international, and 90% female. There are also some smaller focused Zoom meetings and related resources such as a book club and short courses led by Laura and others. There is a small monthly fee of around £11.50/$14USD. My thanks to Chef56 for this information.

Welcome Everything - even the horrible stuff. If we resist it makes everything a whole lot worse. It is what it is. We cannot change or control it, but we can accept it and just let it be. There is suffering but there is happiness too. Stay curious and welcome the breakthrough with open arms.

Wernicke's Encephalopathy - a brain injury caused by lack of Vitamin B1 and poor nutrition often caused by alcohol and eating disorders (but not exclusively). It can happen very suddenly and causes confusion and difficulty with our walking and sight. It can be treated with high doses of Vitamin B1 (Thiamine) and other B vitamins given by injection. If we do not get treatment then it can lead to more permanent damage and **Korsakoff Syndrome** which 80 – 90% of people addicted to alcohol will go on to develop.

https://pubs.niaaa.nih.gov/publications/arh27-2/134-142.htm

Wernicke-Korsakoff's Syndrome - sometimes referred to as **Wet Brain Syndrome** – is a term often used to refer to **Korsakoff's Syndrome** and **Wernicke's Encephalopathy**, although they are actually two different conditions and can occur completely independently of each other.

https://Korsakoffs.org/home/what-is-wernicke-korsakoffs-syndrome

Wet Brain Syndrome - sometimes referred to as **Wernicke-Korsakoff's Syndrome**, is due to alcohol stopping us absorbing **Vitamin B1** leading to **Wernicke's Encephalopathy** and **Korsakoff's Syndrome**.

https://www.rehabclinic.org.uk/fundamentals-about-wet-brain-syndrome

What Do You Want? - this is such an important question. What do you want from life, yourself and sobriety? Try asking yourself this - If you could wake up tomorrow to your perfect day how would it look? How would it feel? What would you be doing? Who would you be doing it with? It's not all going to be possible but it is a great guide. Be careful about asking what you want of others. We cannot change people and they will not always be everything we want. It is up to us to accept that none of us are perfect and we cannot get everything we want from one person. That's why we have different people in our life. Relate wisely to them and to your hopes.

My Perfect Day

I would wake up at (place and time):

I would be with:

What would be happening:

I would feel:

I would get up and:

Next, I would:

Then I would:

It would feel:

Continue writing in your workbook for the rest of your day, step by step, until bed time.

What, When, Where and Who - back to our **Care Plan**. Once we've got our what, we need to look realistically at the when, where and with who. It might just be with yourself; in fact, a lot of this journey is. But getting to know yourself is wonderful as is doing things for and with yourself. We truly are worth it. When I need a kick up the "I can't be bothered" butt, I say to myself "You'd do it for X, so go do it for yourself". At times this could be as simple as making myself a cuppa or something to eat. **Plan**

and Prepare, set a date, think about where you want to be when you quit and get a list of people that you can get on board to help you when you need it.

WHO (World Health Organisation) – is an agency under the United Nations responsible for public health. In 2010 it set out a strategy to reduce the harm of alcohol worldwide and included this in its 2013 – 2020 for prevention of non-transferable diseases. This included increasing taxes on alcohol, restricting the availability of alcohol and advertising across all platforms. Instead, this appears to have been ignored and become more available. WHO recognises the following:

'Health, safety and socioeconomic problems attributable to alcohol can be reduced when governments formulate and implement appropriate policies.

Policy-makers are encouraged to take action on strategies that have shown to be effective and cost-effective. These include:

- *Regulating the marketing of alcoholic beverages (in particular to younger people);*
- *Regulating and restricting the availability of alcohol;*
- *Enacting appropriate drink-driving policies;*
- *Reducing demand through taxation and pricing mechanisms;*
- *Raising awareness of the health and social problems for individuals and society at large caused by the harmful use of alcohol;*
- *Ensuring support for effective alcohol policies;*
- *Providing accessible and affordable treatment for people with alcohol-use disorders; and*
- *Implementing screening and brief intervention programmes in health services for hazardous and harmful drinking'.*

WHO aims to reduce the harm of alcohol by 2030, but recognises that this relies on countries, governments and stakeholders to work together on this. I'm not holding my breath, but we can hope and I have my petition to support this Petition · Alcohol Truth to be Declared · Change.org.

https://www.who.int/news-room/fact-sheets/detail/alcohol#

Why - is a question to which we hardly ever find or know the answer to and it can drive us bonkers trying. For this very reason, it is virtually banished from my vocabulary. For example: Teacher asks 5-year-old Jack "Why did you throw that book across the room?" He is likely to respond with "I don't know Miss" because he really doesn't know why! It just seemed like a good idea at the time. Instead of why try asking yourself:

What drove me to my addiction?

What relief does it give me?

What are my thoughts about giving up?

Where can I get support in giving up?

What is my action plan?

When can I do it?

Willing - whilst others can encourage and support us to change our lives for the better, we have to be willing to do so. If we are not, then it is doomed to fail because we will not put in the work that we need to make and embrace that change. **Pressure** can make us dig our heels in, resist change and participate even more in addictive behaviours. I am so happy that you have taken the step to pick up and read this book and I hope that it has made you more curious about your life and what you want for yourself. If you want to get sober then that's even better, but you have to be willing to do it. And when you do, and discover how amazing it is, just remember that we cannot force it on others, we can just be a **Lighthouse** until they themselves are willing to change.

Willpower - it takes so much more than this to beat any addiction. In essence, it is about having the ability to resist an urge to satisfy ourselves. As we've seen, our behaviours, habits and addictions are so much more than something we can simply resist. For many of us, they have become what our life revolves around. Willpower alone will make us into a **Dry Drunk**, it will not get us sober. But we can use the intention of willpower to make us more determined to reach our goal, so it might be worth adding to your **Tool Box**.

Wisdom - comes from experience, and who better to give us this than those who have lived through it and walked their own path? The first time we get sober we do not have any wisdom on this as we have never experienced it. Yes, there was the time before we started drinking, but that really was a lifetime ago. This is why it is so important to listen to the wise words of others, until we find our own.

Wise - is what we get with experience. Being wise isn't what we learn from books, it's what we learn from our experiences, from our **Breakdowns** and breakthroughs. That's why each event, occurrence and experience is so important - no matter how painful. We become wise by staying curious, working through, assessing and **Understanding** it all. Only then can we make a wise and sound judgement. Hopefully this book has helped you learn a lot about alcohol and sobriety, but only you can become wise to it all.

Withdrawal - whenever we take something away that we have become used too, we will go through a period of physical and emotional withdrawal. When we stop drinking alcohol we can expect to have some of the following, so buckle up your seatbelts:

- Headaches
- Sweats
- Sugar cravings
- Shakes
- Joint aches
- Anxiety
- Low mood
- Mood swings
- Anger
- Hallucinations
- Illusions
- Paranoia

Beware that if you stop drinking suddenly it can cause epileptic fits, vomit in your breathing tube and lungs and severe **Hallucinations**. If you are a very heavy drinker then please seek medical advice as you may need a medical detox. If you really feel unable to do this, then at the very least, **Reduce Gradually** the amount you drink day by day.

Words - are only a small percentage of what we communicate. Most is down to our body language and the tone of our voice. In this world of technology and gadgets it's not often that we actually talk over the phone or face-to-face nowadays. Therefore, lots can get lost in translation and very often, messages can be misread and misheard. I am always mindful of this whenever I am sending a text or email (now that I'm sober anyway!) as I am aware that our words can be read or heard differently from our intention and cause upset and arguments. And if I'm annoyed or angry, I try and **Pause** and remember my nan saying to me 'Least said, soonest mended.'

Work It - sobriety is so much more than stopping drinking. If we just put the drink down we will be white knuckling it, climbing the walls and more likely to **Relapse**. It's what many refer to as a **Dry Drunk**. We have to work our sobriety:

- Read **Quit Lit**, listen to **Podcasts**, join a sober **Community** and post, read, reach out, connect.
- Join **Zoom** meetings, **AA**, or other support groups.
- Learn to identify our emotions and work through them. Get help to do so; books, podcasts, online courses, therapists.
- Use our **Tool Box**

We don't have to do all of this, and certainly not all at once, but the more we do, the more sense it will make and the easier it will be. If we put as much effort into our sobriety as we put into our drinking, then we are far more likely to succeed.

Worry - there's no point me telling you not to worry because it's what we do. If we tell ourselves not to do something then we do it even more: if I tell you not to think about a pink elephant then what are you now thinking about? Worrying can be made worse by our **Altered/Unhelpful Thinking** and can lead to **Stress**. Anchor points (see **NLP**) and **CBT** techniques can help to lessen worry, as may asking yourself:

- What are the facts?
- What is in my area of control?
- Have I done everything I can?

Relaxation, **Mindfulness**, **Meditation**, **Exercise** and increasing our **Dopamine** levels can help reduce worry. But not alcohol. That will just make everything a whole lot worse. You may also find the Living Life to The Full website www.llttf.com helpful.

WRAP (Wellness Recovery Action Plan) - this is a fantastic tool, helping us to look at our **Maintenance Plans**, personal **Triggers**, early warning signs and recognising when things start going wrong. It also reminds us what we can to do to get ourselves back on track as well as what to do in a crisis. This tool was devised by mental health professional and author Mary Ellen Copeland and helps us to take a more authentic approach to our **Mental Health** and **Recovery**. I feel it can also be used to help us manage our physical health and addiction. A free download of the workbook can be found at North Staffordshire Combined Healthcare Wellness Recovery Action Plans (WRAP).

https://www.combined.nhs.uk/person-centredness-framework/wellness-recovery-action-plans-wrap

Write - in a journal, in a blog, in this book, in a sober community, in a notebook. Just let it all pour out. It is so powerful to write our thoughts and memories down and get them out of our head, where they have a habit of going round and round:

- If your thoughts stop you sleeping at night then write them all out.
- Have 'to do' lists and write everything down. And then forget about it until you have time or motivation to deal with it all.
- Review your pending lists. Have you done everything you can do? Is it now reliant on others doing their bit? If so, let it go. You can do no more for now. Put a note in your diary to revisit it in a few weeks.
- Get your feelings and emotions out on paper and let them go. Burn them, bin them or keep them for later reflection.
- **Journal**s are great to look back on and remind ourselves of how far we've come

Wrong - there is no wrong way, there is only the way that is right for us – and that might actually be to keep on drinking – the **Choice** is ours! Right and wrong are just **Opinions**. Yes, I know there is the law, and the rules of society, and I'm not encouraging you to go out there and break them. Although we are far less likely to do so sober! This may have stirred you up but just remember – statistically alcohol is the most dangerous drug known to man but it's legal. So go figure.

https://www.addictioncenter.com/community/why-alcohol-is-the-deadliest-drug/

X

X - just a random thought – you know the big X and buzzer sound they sometimes have on game shows when the contestant gives the wrong answer?   Maybe we could play that in our head when our **Addict Voice** comes calling or as we walk past the drink aisle at the shop? If you don't know what I mean, have a little search on the internet. I just have and the noise is enough to put anyone off!

Xoanon - is derived from the Greek word for "carve" and it's time to do this for your future. Be authentic. Be the author of your own life and the driver of your own **Bus**. Get carving. Get loving. Get living. It truly is a good life and it's yours for the taking...

X-Ray – there are lots of body imaging and scans being done, especially on the brain, to help us view and understand the devastating effects of alcohol, but what of actual X-rays? Well, they can be used to detect breaks, enlarged organs and tumours which could be associated with cancer – all of which can be caused by alcohol. Long term use of alcohol can actually lead to a thinning of our bones and make us more prone to fractures.

https://pubs.niaaa.nih.gov/publications/arh22-3/190.pdf#

On a more imaginative note, I love this from my beautiful sober sister Mermaid Must Not Drown:

'*Often as drinkers we can completely ignore and avoid what drinking does to our insides because we can't see them. If we were able to x-ray ourselves whilst drinking, or after consuming too much over a period of time, we could compare these with how they should look - a healthy x-ray versus a poisoned one. And what if we could get an x-ray vision of what it does to our emotions and to our soul? If we could x-ray our actual souls when we are partaking in poison, to see unequivocally what is happening as we are doing it to ourselves, maybe our souls would cry out to us through those x-rays and plead with us to stop. Same as our organs*'.

Soul x-ray
What do you see?
What hides within
That intense mystery?
See it take shape
Like a shadow at play
Here on an overcast
Rain stormy day...
Is it alive with the will of a dove?
Is it in need of enchanted true love?
Does it dance bubbling, frothy with joy?
Does it contain itself, playing it coy?
If you can, wave at it, so it can know
You are its shepherd wherever you go
And inside your temple it's sacredly shrined
'Til clock stops tick tock on your humankind mind
Then wonderment whooshes the moment you meet
A light so much brighter than mortals can see
And soul that inhabited body and bone
Leaps into ether to happily roam
From loved one to loved one to comfort and hold
Hearts with the answers our ancestors know
People will come and yes people will go

But on everlasting lives each precious soul…'

'Your soul is reaching for you, yearning to connect with optimum, whole-body health. Synchronise yourself through sobriety'.

Mermaid Must Not Drown. 19th June 2022 – 5 months sober.

Y

Yang - a Chinese concept of energy and light force which is masculine, positive and light. We can stimulate it with exercise, group activities and by getting physically creative. Its opposite is **Yin**.

Yes - if like me you are a 'yes' person then you will know how exhausting this can be. With sobriety comes change, and the word **No** becomes key. This enables us to stick to our **Boundaries** and make time for ourselves and our sobriety. It does become easier with practice, and then when we do say "Yes!" it's much more appreciated and valued.

Yin - is a Chinese concept of energy and light force which is female, dark and negative. We can stimulate it with acupuncture, massage, self-care and sleep. Its opposite is **Yang**.

Yin and Yang - they go together like "Rama lama lama ka dinga da dinga dong" (couldn't resist). They are the opposing life forces that attract to make things whole. Opposing energies of light and dark, hot and cold, back and front, activity and rest, positive and negative of all beings. It seems that opposites really do attract.

https://subtle.energy/whats-the-difference-between-yin-yang-qi-energy

Yoga - originated in India but is now practised the world over. There are many different types, but in western world practice, it mostly aims to improve our physical and mental health and calm our body and mind through gentle exercise, stretches, breathing and relaxation, without religious content. This gentle calming exercise can help with the stress and anxiety of addiction and definitely helped me at times with my cravings. Like sobriety, yoga is not a competition, we can go at our own pace and to our own level. There are videos on YouTube and there are generally in person classes around – just have a little search.

You Can Do This - as others have proved it can be done. Others, who like you, were worried about their drinking or addicted to alcohol. They have been where you are now, with the confusion, fear and anxiety. Take heart that thousands of people start their sober journey every day and I suspect there are millions of sober people out there. Take hope and inspiration from them, follow their shining light, until you too become a **Lighthouse** to others. It takes work and commitment to get sober, but it takes even more to continue drinking.

Your Journey - remember this is yours and yours alone - no one else's. Others are not responsible for your success, in the same way that you are not responsible for theirs. It really is none of our business what others do or think. If friends and relations still want to drink and encourage us to do so, then that is up to them. Our response is up to us. There is lots of support out there and we can choose to use it or not. But we have to do this our way.

Yourself - is who you have to put first now. In so doing, you are more likely to get and stay sober and then you'll be there for others. It isn't always easy, focusing on ourselves - no longer numbing and hiding what we really feel and having to deal with all the shite that led to us feeling that way in the first place. But once we can sit and learn to be with ourselves, discovering who we really are and want to be, then we can embrace every part of our being and walk hand in hand with ourselves again.

YouTube - to listen to me talking about many of the headings on here, head over to my YouTube Channel: _Positive Recovery with Corinna. It's just a girl talking into her phone, in the hopes that you can imagine us sitting together and chatting over a cuppa. You can also hear these and many more of my podcasts at **Sobertown Podcast**.

Z

Zealous - I hope that reading this has made you as passionate about sobriety as I now am. I love it so much that I get very excited when others start their journey and then find all the joy, peace and wonder that **Sobriety** brings. It stirs the fire in our soul and makes us a very zealous lot. Boring and solemn we are not!

Zen - a calmness that comes from inside of us, from our inner **Understanding**. This is something we aim for in **Meditation** and the word actually originates from a Japanese form of Buddhism with this very goal in mind. It's so lovely now to tune in instead of drowning it all out with booze.

Zoom - is a wonderful thing in this busy world, and was a great resource to many during lockdown (and continues to be so). Many communities have Zoom meetings and you can usually find one somewhere in the world at a time to suit you. **AA** have one every day of the week, as do the **IAS** community, Luckiest Memoirs (**We Are the Luckiest**) and **Recovery Dharma**.

ZZZZZ - if you still aren't sure what to do, don't worry, just sleep on it. See what comes up in your **Dreams** tonight and look over your notes again tomorrow. Recap, **Plan and Prepare** and jump in when you are ready, knowing that I am right there with you, walking by your side and cheering you on. And if you need to contact me, you can email me: alcoholandsobriety@gmail.com.

Take Care. No luck needed – you have all the **Magic**
and **Gold** you need, right there, inside of you.

Chin Chin ♥

ACKNOWLEDGEMENT

Massive thanks and gratitude to Lisa Martin and Joy Burns for all their hard work and input in helping me to transform my written ramblings into a published book. In this process, I've discovered that writing is the easy bit – getting it all edited and sorted is where the hard work begins. Your support and belief in me and my book have kept me going and given me hope, even during my times of doubt. Thank you to my sober communities at I Am Sober, Instagram, sobertownpodcast.com and Telegram support groups for all your love, support and guidance, for giving me inspiration and hope and helping me get to where I am in my sobriety today. There are far too many of you to mention but I will be forever grateful to you. An extra special thank you to those of you who contributed to this book with your written and spoken words and advice: alexdagreat, Bay24, Bryant S, Carmello, Chef56, countrygirl81, creative-ly, Drifter, Elius Veturius, er(Eileen)1961, everything is brilliant, Houndlessgirl, jock, kdw06244, King13, KollyD, Lauralei, LovelyLila, Macca247-365, MamaQ, Mermaid Must Not Drown, Mike.B1, Newbeginnings20, PDX2019, perfectlyimperfect, pollya, Rach1, Rebecky19, rebirth, Redeemed, shickey, SJ333, Small Steps, sober_suz, Spicey Currey, Sunny Days, trailgypsey and Virginia. Thanks also to natqc and the I Am Sober book club for approaching me to use this book in their club – your belief in me has inspired me to keep going. Thank you to my partner Andy for sticking with me through my sober journey and tolerating the fact that I spent more time on my phone than I did talking to him for the first year... and then on my laptop in the second one! Thank you also for sorting out my ABC. Looking forward to touring and having more quality time together again now. Last but by no means least, thank you to my wonderful son Jack for all the times you looked after me, carried me home and kept me safe, for your encouragement to stop continually punishing myself by blocking and numbing with alcohol. Just for being you and giving me the two most precious gifts of all – yourself and my beautiful grandson. My life is now complete. Love you to the moon and back.

REFERENCES AND RESOURCES

AA: Alcoholics Anonymous. https://www.alcoholics-anonymous.org.uk/About-AA/Historical-Data. 20th October 2021.

Abuse:

Mankind. https://www.mankind.org.uk. 20th June 2022.

Refuge. https://www.nationalhelpline.org.uk. 16th July 2022.

Refuge. https://www.refuge.org.uk. 16th July2022.

Women's Aid. https://www.womensaid.org.uk/ 16th July 2022.

Women's Aid. https://www.womensaid.org.uk/womens-aid-directory. 16th July 2022.

National Domestic Violence Hotline. https://www.thehotline.org. 16th July 2022.

Acetaldehyde: Delta. https://www.deltanutra.com/pages/where-does-it-come-from. 16th July 2022.

Acne: Manage Your Life Now. https://www.manageyourlifenow.com/does-alcohol-cause-acne. 22nd July 2022.

ACT: Good Therapy. https://www.goodtherapy.org/learn-about-therapy/types/acceptance-commitment-therapy. 16th July 2022.

Adrenaline: Berit, Brogaard. https://healthfully.com/adrenaline-cortisol-4594433.html. 16th July 2022.

Affirmations: Yoga Signs. https://yogasigns.com/difference-between-mantras-and-affirmations. 21st July 2022.

Alcohol: World Health Organisation. https://www.who.int/news-room/fact-sheets/detail/alcohol. 16th July 2022.

Alcohol Abuse: Gov. Uk. https://www.gov.uk/government/publications/alcohol-use-screening-tests. 31st July 2022.

Anger: Good Reads. https;//www.goodreads.com/quotes/9921515-anger-is-the-punishment-we-give-ourselves-for-someone-elses-mistakes. 16th July 2022.

Annie Grace:

This Naked Mind. Control Alcohol. https://thisnakedmind.com/blog-the-alcohol-experiment/ 16th July 2022.

Grace, Annie. This Naked Mind. Control Alcohol, Find Freedom, Discover Happiness & Change Your Life. London. HarperCollins *Publishers* Ltd., 2018.

Arsenic:

Jade, Clara. https://justwineapp.com/article/what-is-arsenic-should-consumers-be-concerned-about-arsenic-levels-in-wine. 16th July 2022.

The National Environmental Professional. https://nationalenvironmentalpro.com/arsenic-in-wine. 16th July 2022.

Autopsy: Leigh at Whereapy. https;//www.whereapy.com/downloads/human-body-alcohol-effects-organs. 16th July 2022.
Vitamin A: NHS. https://www.nhs.uk/conditions/vitamins-and-minerals/vitamin-a/ 16th July 2022.

BAL: Sheahan, Kyra. https://healthfully.com/effects-alcohol-oxygen-absorption-8017604.html. 16th July 2022.

Beriberi Disease: BYJU's. https://byjus.com/biology/beriberi/ 16th July 2022.

Blackout: White. Aaron M. Ph.D. https://pubs.niaaa.nih.gov/publications/arh27-2/186-196.htm. 16th July 2022.

Bloating:

Health Jade. https://healthjade.net/enlarged-liver/#what_is_a_spleen. 16th July 2022.

Wedro. Benjamin. https://www.emedicinehealth.com/ascites/article_em.htm. 16th July 2022.

Blood: Ballard, Harold S. https://pubs.niaaa.nih.gov/publications/arh21-1/42.pdf. 16th July 2022.

Brain:

Soniak, Matt. https://www.mentalfloss.com/article/49024/does-drinking-alcohol-kill-brain-cells. 16th July 2022.

Crafter, Todd. https://www.sobertownpodcast.com/sober-podcast-episodes/episode-60-fires-together-wires-together.

17th July, 2022.

Breathing Issues: Sheahan, Kyra. https://healthfully.com/effects-alcohol-oxygen-absorption-8017604.html. 17th July, 2022.

B Vitamins:

Martin, Peter R et Al. https://pubs.niaaa.nih.gov/publications/arh27-2/134-142.htm. 17th July 2022.

Perkin, Daya Dr. https://healthfully.com/thiamine-alcoholism-5987452.html. 17th July 2022.

BYJU'S. https://byjus.com/biology/vitamin-b/ 17th July 2022.

Cancer:

Hassen, Al-Sader et Al. https://www.ncbi.nlm.nih.gov/pmc/articles/PMC3318874/# 17th July 2022.

Roumeliotis, Ioanna & Witmer, Brenda. https://www.cbc.ca/news/health/alcohol-warning-labels-cancer-1.6304816. 17th July 2022.

Jones, Brandi. https://www.verywellhealth.com/types-of-cancer-caused-by-drinking-alcohol-513626. 17th July 2022.

Capacity: Medical Protection. https://www.medicalprotection.org/uk/articles/assessing-capacity. 17th July 2022.

Capillaries: Taylor, Tim. https://www.innerbody.com/image_lymp01/card66.html. 7th July 2022.

Catherine Gray:

You Magazine. https://www.you.co.uk/catherine-gray-how-a-sunset-saved-my-life/ 17th July 2022.

Gray, Catherine. The Unexpected Joy of being sober. London. Octopus Publishing Group Ltd., 2017.

CBT: Living life to the full. https://llttf.com. 17th July 2022.

Chakras:

(117) Chakra Meditation for Balancing and Clearing, Healing Guided Sleep Meditation - YouTube

Alchemy Crystal Bowls. https://www.alchemycrystalbowls.co.uk/chakras_notes_singing_bowls/ 17th July 2022.

7 Chakra Colors. https://www.7chakracolors.com. 17th July 2022.

Charlie Mackesy:

Mackesy, Charlie. The Boy, the Mole, the Fox and the Horse. London. Ebury Press, 2019.

Mackesy. Charlie. https://www.charliemackesy.com. 23rd July 2022.

Circadian Rhythms:

National Institute of General Medical Sciences. https://nigms.nih.gov/education/fact-sheets/Pages/Circadian-Rhythms.aspx. 19th July 2022.

Suni, Eric. https://www.sleepfoundation.org/circadian-rhythm. 19th July 2022.

Cirrhosis: British Liver Trust. https://britishlivertrust.org.uk/information-and-support/living-with-a-liver-condition/liver-conditions/cirrhosis/ 19th July 2022.

Co-Dependency: Mental Health America. https://www.mhanational.org/co-dependency. 19th July 2022.

Compassion: Cherry, Kendra. https://www.verywellmind.com/what-is-compassion-5207366. 19th July 2022.

Conforming: Doyle. Glennon. Untamed. London. Vermilion, and imprint of Ebury Publishing, 2020.

Cortisol: Berit, Brogaard. https://healthfully.com/adrenaline-cortisol-4594433.html. 19th July 2022.

Craig Beck: Beck, Craig. Alcohol Lied to Me: The Intelligent Way to Escape Alcohol Addiction. Wroclaw. Amazon Fulfilment, 2019.

Cross-addiction:

Gaba, Sherry. https://www.psychologytoday.com/us/blog/addiction-and-recovery/201904/the-challenge-cross-addiction. 19th July 2022.

Every day Health. https://www.everydayhealth.com/drugs/ascorbic-acid# 19th July 2022.

Death:

The National Academies. https://needtoknow.nas.edu/id/threats/global-killers. 9th July 2022.

Office for National Statistics. https://www.ons.gov.uk/peoplepopulationandcommunity/healthandsocialcare/

causesofdeath/articles/leadingcausesofdeathuk/2001to2018. 22nd July 2022.

World Health Organisation. https://www.who.int/news-room/fact-sheets/detail/the-top-10-causes-of-death. 19th July 2022.

Debt: Step Change Debt Charity. https://www.stepchange.org/?channel=ppc&gclid. 19th July 2022.

Delirium Tremens: Miller, Leah. https://americanaddictioncenters.org/alcoholism-treatment/delirium-tremens-symptoms-and-treatment. 19th July 2022.

Dementia:

Alzheimer's Society. https://www.alzheimers.org.uk/about-dementia/risk-factors-and-prevention/alcohol. 19th July 2022.

Ayaga, Vince. https://www.addictiongroup.org/alcohol/effects/dementia. 19th July 2022.

Depression: NHS. https://www.nhs.uk/mental-health/conditions/clinical-depression/symptoms. 19th July 2022.

Diabetes:

WebMD. https://www.webmd.com/diabetes/drinking-alcohol# 19th July 2022.

Pietrangelo, Ann. https://www.healthline.com/health/diabetes-and-pancreas. 19th July 2022.

Dopamine: Keller, Amy. https://www.drugrehab.com/addiction/alcohol/alcoholism/alcohol-and-dopamine. 19th July 2022.

Drink Aware: Drinkaware. https://www.drinkaware.co.uk. 19th July 2022.

Driving:

Gov. Uk. https://www.gov.uk/drink-drive-limit. 6th August 2022.

Gov.UK. https://www.gov.uk/government/statistics/reported-road-casualties-in-great-britain-final-estimates-involving-illegal-alcohol-levels-2019. 6th August 2022.

Drunk: How It Works. https://www.howitworksdaily.com/why-do-we-get-drunk. 19th July 2022.

D Vitamin:

NHS. https://www.nhs.uk/conditions/vitamins-and-minerals/vitamin-d. 19th July 2022.

Sky News. https://news.sky.com/story/amp/vitamin-d-overdose-warning-after-man-admitted-to-hospital-for-excessive-intake-12646798. 19th July 2022.

Eckhart Tolle: Tolle, Eckhart. The Power of Now: A Guide to Spiritual Enlightenment. London. Hodder and Stoughton Ltd., 2005.

EMDR: EMDR UK. https://emdrassociation.org.uk/a-inique-and-powerful-therapy/emdr-the-basics. 19th July 2022.

Empath: Raypole, Crystal. https://www.healthline.com/health/what-is-an-empath#high-sensitivity. 19th July 2022.

Endorphins: Eureka Alert. https://www.eurekalert.org/news-releases/756852# 19th July 2022.

Erica Spiegelman: Spiegelman, Erica. https://www.ericaspiegelman.com. 21st July 2022.

Ethanol: Arnold Clark. https://www.arnoldclark.com/newsroom/347-can-cars-run-on-alcohol# 19th July 2022.

E Vitamins: NHS. https://www.nhs.uk/conditions/vitamins-and-minerals/vitamin-e/ 19th July 2022.

Fact not Fiction: Lexico. https://www.lexico.com/en/definition/alchol. 20th July 2022.

Change.org. https://change.corg/p/boris-johnson-alcohol-truth-to-be-declared. 31st July 2022.

FAST: Gov.Uk. https://www.gov.uk/government/publications/alcohol-use-screening-tests. 31st July 2022.

Fertility: Your Fertility. https://www.yourfertility.org.au/everyone/drugs-chemicals/alcohol# 21st July 2022.

Meds Like. https://www.medslike.com/why-is-boozing-harmful-to-your-sexual-life/ 21st July 2022.

Fetal Alcohol Spectrum Disorders: Vorgias, Demetrios and Bernstein, Bettina. https://www.ncbi.nlm.nih.gov/books/NBK448178/ 1st July 2022.

Formaldehyde:

National Cancer Institute. https://www.cancer.gov/about-cancer/causes-prevention/risk/substances/formaldehyde/formaldehyde-fact-sheet. 21st July 2022.

Monakhova, Yulia B et Al. https://

pubmed.ncbi.nlm.nih.gov/22728807/ 21st July 2022.

Frank Ostaseski: Ostaseski, Frank. The Five Invitations: Discovering What death Can Teach Us About Living Fully. London. Bluebird, an imprint of Pan Macmilan, 2017.

Gabba: Pugle, Michelle. https://www.verywellhealth.com/gaba-5095143. 21st July 2022.

Genetics: Bevilacqua, L and Goldman, D. https://www.ncbi.nlm.nih.gov/pmc/articles/PMC2715956/ 21st July 2022.

Edenberg, Howard J and Foroud, Tatiana. https://www.ncbi.nlm.nih.gov/pmc/articles/PMC4056340/ 21st July 2022.

Glennon Doyle: Doyle, Glennon. Untamed. London. Vermilion, and imprint of Ebury Publishing, 2020.

Gold: Tolle, Eckhart. The Power Of Now: A Guide to Spiritual Enlightenment. The Parable of the Beggar: The Treasure You Seek is Within You. Page 9. London. Hoddon and Stroughton Ltd., 2005.

Government: Statista. https://www.statista.com/statistics/284336/united-kingdom-hmrc-tax-receipts-alcohol-duties-by-type/ 21st July 2022.

Gratitude: Baystate Health. https://www.baystatehealth.org/news/2019/11/gratitude-and-your-brain# 21st July 2022.

Grounding: Walters, Stephanie. https://pemfcomplete.com/do-we-have-electricity-in-our-bodies. 21st July 2022.

Gut:

Henderson, Rober. https://patient.info/news-and-features/the-digestive-system# 21st July 2022.

Bode, Christiane and Bode, J Christian. https://pubs.niaaa.nih.gov/publications/arh21-1/76.pdf# 27th July 2022.

Jones, Brandi. https://www.verywellhealth.com/types-of-cancer-caused-by-drinking-alcohol-513626. 21st July 2022.

Gut Health:

Mosley, Michael Dr. The Clever Guts Diet: How to revolutionise your body from the inside out. London. Short Books, 2017.

Collen, Alanna. 10% Human: How Your Body's Microbes Hold the Key to Health and Happiness. London. William Collins, an imprint of HarperCollins Publishing, 2016.

Gut Instinct: Tresca, Amber J. https://www.verywellhealth.com/enteric-nervous-system-5112820. 21st July 2022.

Habits: Blackmores. https://www.blackmores.com.au/everyday-health/how-long-does-it-really-take-to-break-a-habit. 21st July 2022.

Hangovers: National Institute on Alcohol Abuse and Alcoholism. https://www.niaaa.nih.gov/publications/brochures-and-fact-sheets/hangovers# 21st July 2022.

Heart:

Centre for Disease Control and Prevention. https://

www.cdc.gov/heartdisease/about.htm. 21st July 2022.

Murrell, Daniel. https://www.healthline.com/health/alcoholism/cardiomyopathy#symptoms. 21st July 2022.

Hippocampus: Queensland Brain Institute. https://qbi.uq.edu.au/brain-basics/memory/where-are-memories-stored# 21st July 2022.

Human Rights:

Melody, Sarah. ttps://www.samaritanmag.com/we-have-30-basic-human-rights-do-you-know-them# 21st July 2022.

Citizens Advice. https://www.citizensadvice.org.uk/law-and-courts/civil-rights/human-rights/what-are-human-rights/ 21st July 2022.

Hypothalamus: Top Doctors UK. https://www.topdoctors.co.uk/medical-dictionary/hypothalamus. 21st July 2022.

Hypothermia:

Brouhard, Rod. https://www.verywellhealth.com/hypothermia-causes-and-risk-factors-4161049# 21st July 2022.

NHS. https://www.nhs.uk/conditions/hypothermia. 21st July 2022.

I Am Woman: Song Lyrics from the song '*I Am Woman*' written by Ray Burton and Helen Reddy.

Identity Crisis: Elmer, Jamie. https://healthline.com/health/mental-health/identity-crisis#TOC_TITLE_HDR_1 21st July 2022.

Illicit/Illegal Substances:

World Science Festival. (122) Revealing the Mind: The Promise of Psychedelics - YouTube

Kelland, Kate. https://www.reuters.com/article/us-drugs-alcohol/drug-experts-say-alcohol-worse-than-crack-or-heroin-idUSTRE6A000O20101101. 21st July 2022.

Fitzgerald, Kelly. https://www.addictioncenter.com/community/why-alcohol-is-the-deadliest-drug/ 21st July 2022.

Inflammation:

Bode, Christiane and Bode, J Christian. https://pubs.niaaa.nih.gov/publications/arh21-1/76.pdf# 21st July 2022.

Cullins, Ashley. https://riahealth.com/blog/alcohol-and-inflammation/ 21st July 2022.

Intestines: Tresca, Amber J. https://www.verywellhealth.com/enteric-nervous-system-5112820. 21st July 2022.

Iron: Ballard, Harold S. https://pubs.niaaa.nih.gov/publications/arh21-1/42.pdf. 21st July 2022.

Johari Window: Self Awareness.org. https://www.selfawareness.org.uk/news/understanding-the-johari-window-model. 21st July 2022.

Kidneys: National Kidney Foundation. https://www.kidney.org/atoz/content/alcohol# 21st July 2022.

Kindness: Breazeale, Ron. https://www.psychologytoday.com/us/blog/in-the-face-adversity/201211/practicing-acts-kindness. 21st July 2022.

Korsakoffs Syndrome:

Martin, Peter R et Al. https://pubs.niaaa.nih.gov/publications/ arh27-2/134-142.htm. 21st July 2022.

Alzheimer's Society. https://www.alzheimers.org.uk/about-dementia/types-dementia/wernicke-korsakoff-syndrome. 21st July 2022.

K Vitamin: Iber, F L et Al. https:// pubmed.ncbi.nlm.nih.gov/3544923. 21st July 2022.

Language of Letting Go: https://melodybeattie.com

Lighthouse: UK SMART Recovery. https:// smartrecovery.org.uk/wp-content/uploads/The-Lighthouse-Analogy.pdf# 21st July 2022.

Limbic System:

Science Direct. https://www.sciencedirect.com/topics/ neuroscience/limbic-system. 21st July 2022.

Boeree, George. www.albertpeia.com/generalpsychology/ limbicsystem.html# 21st July 2022.

Liver:

Luo, Elaine K. https://www.medicalnewstoday.com/ articles/305075. 21st July 2022.

YouTube Link- What does the liver do? - Emma Bryce - Bing video

Lungs:

Mehta, Ashish J and Guidot, David M. https://www.ncbi.nlm.nih.gov/pmc/articles/PMC5513688/ 21st July 2022.

Lujan, M, et Al. https://pubmed.ncbi.nlm.nih.gov/20150202. 21st July 2022.

Living: Harris, José N. https://www.goodreads.com/author/show/4631437.Jos_N_Harris. 21st July 2022.

Mantras: Yoga Signs. https://yogasigns.com/difference-between-mantras-and-affirmations. 16th July 2022.

Maslow's Hierarchy of Needs: Cherry, Kendra. https://www.explorepsychology.com/maslows-hierachy-of-needs. 22nd July 2022.

Melody Beattie: Beattie, Melody. https://melodybeattie.com. 22nd July 2022.

Memory Loss:

Ling, J et Al. https://onlinelibrary.wiley.com/doi/10.1111/j.1530-0277.2003.tb04422.x 22nd July 2022.

Buddy, T. https://www.verywellmind.com/alcohol-damages-day-to-day-memory-function-62982. 22nd July 2022.

Milestones: www.recoveringkindredspirits.co.uk

Monkeys: Blanchard, Ken. One Minute Manager. Recalled from memory – date and publisher unknown to me.

Moon: Cowart, Kirsten. https://www.thespiritscience.net/2016/06/21/the-connection-between-the-moom-cycles-and-your-mood. 22nd July 2022.

Neural pathways: Great Minds Clinic. https://www.greatmindsclinic.co.uk/blog/what-are-neural-pathways. 22nd July 2022.

Neurons: Cherry, Kendra. https://www.verywellmind.com/how-many-neurons-are-in-the-brain-2794889. 22nd July 2022.

Oestrogen: Al-Sader, Hassen et Al. https://www.ncbi.nlm.nih.gov/pmc/articles/PMC3318874/# 22nd July 2022.

Old Brain: Open Libraries. https://open.lib.umn.edu/intropsyc/chapter/3-2-our-brains-control-our-thoughts-feelings-and-behavior/# 2nd July 2022.

Omega 3: Beck, Craig. Alcohol Lied to Me: The Intelligent Way to Escape Alcohol Addiction. Wroclaw. Amazon Fulfilment, 2019.

Pain: Farlex. https://medical-dictionary.thefreedictionary.com/pain. 23rd July 2022.

Pancreas:

Apte, Minoti V et Al. https://pubs.niaaa.nih.gov/publications/arh21-1/13.pdf# 23rd July 2022.

Pancreatic Cancer UK. https://pancreaticccancer.org.uk/information/just-diagnosed-with-pancreatic-cancer/what-is-the-pancreas. 23rd July 2022.

Pandemic: World Health Organisation. https://www.who.int/news-room/fact-sheets/detail/alcohol. 16th July 2022.

Peman Chodron: The Pema Chodron Foundation. https://pemachodronfoundation.org/about/pema-chodron. 23rd July 2022.

Perceptions: World Science Festival. (122) The Reality of Reality: A Tale of Five Senses - YouTube. 20th July 2022.

Pregnancy: Your Fertility. https://www.yourfertility.org.au/everyone/drugs-chemicals/alcohol# 23rd July 2022.

Prelapse: Robertson, Belle. https://www.tiredofthinkingaboutdrinking.com. 31st July 2022.

Psychodynamic: McLeod, Saul. https://www.simplypsychology.org/psychodynamic.html. 23rd July 2022.

Psychotherapy: American Psychiatric Association. https://www.psychiatry.org/patients-families/psychotherapy. 23rd July 2022.

Qi: Reninger, Elizabeth. https://www.learnreligions.com/what-is-qi-chi-3183052. 23rd July 2022.

Qigong: Qigong for Beginners - Bing video by Yogi Yoga and Qigong. YouTube. 26th July 2022.

Recovery:

Mental Health Foundation. https://www.mentalhealth.org.uk/explore-mental-health/a-z-topics/recovery. 23rd July 2022.

Jacob, K. S. https://www.ncbi.nlm.nih.gov/pmc/articles/PMC4418239. 23rd July 2022.

Recovery Dharma: Recovery Dharma. https://

recoverydharma.online. 23rd July 2022.

Reduce Gradually: With You. https://www.wearewithyou.org.uk/help-and-advice/advice-you/how-safely-detox-alcohol-home/ 23rd July 2022.

Relapse: DiscoverPoetry.com. https://discoverpoetry.com/poems/william-edward-hickson/try-again. 16th July 2022.

Retreats: Kadampa Buddhism. https://meditateinnorthants.com. 23rd July 2022.

Reward Pathway: Guy-Evans, Olivia. https://www.simplypschology.org/brain-reward-system.html# 23rd July 2022.

Rewired: Spiegelman, Erica. https://www.ericaspiegelman.com/rewired-program. 23rd July 2022.

Rosacea: NHS. https://www.nhs.uk/conditions/rosacea. 23rd July 2022.

Rose Elliot: Elliot, Rose. I met a monk: 8 weeks to Happiness, Freedom and Peace. London. Watkins Publishing, 2015

Self-Esteem Booster: Abrams, Allison. https://www.psychologytoday.com/us/blog/nurturing-self-compassion/201703/8-steps-improving-your-self-esteem. 23rd July 2022.

Self-Love: Brain & Behavior Research Foundation. https://www.bbrfoundation.org/blog/self-love-

and-what-it-means. 23rd July 2022.

Serenity Prayer: Buddy, T. https://verywellmind.com/the-serenity-prayer-62614. 16th July 2022.

Sex:

Yetman, Daniel. https://www.healthline.com/health/alcohol-and-erectile-dysfunction. 23rd July 2022.

Hampton, Scott. https://www.alcoholproblemsandsolutions.org/drinking-and-sexual-assualt-the-connection/# 27th July 2022.

Shame: Mental Health at Home. https://mentalhealthathome.org/2021/04/30/what-is-the-shame-compass. 23rd July 2022.

Sleep:

Breus, Michael. https://thesleepdoctor.com/alcohol-and-sleep# 23rd July 2022.

Lockett, Eleesha. https://www.healthline.com/health/healthy-sleep/stages-of-sleep# 23rd July 2022.

Sleep Apnoea: Simou, Evangelina et Al. https://www.ncbi.nlm.nih.gov/pmc/articles/PMC5840512. 23rd July 2022.

Smart Recovery: https://smartrecovery.org.uk . 29th July 2021.

Smile: OGN Daily. https://www.onlygoodnewsdaily.com/post/smiling-is-infectious# 25th July 2022.

Sobertown Podcast: www.sobertownpodcast.com

Solar Plexus: Gotter, Ana. https://www.healthline.com/health/solar-plexus-pain. 25th July 2022.

Spleen: Jackson, Whitney. https://www.msdmanuals.com/home/liver-and-gallbladder-disorders/alcohol-related-liver-disease/alcohol-related-liver-disease. 25th July 2022.

Statistics:

National Institute on Alcohol Abuse and Alcoholism. https://www.niaaa.nih.gov/publications/brochures-and-fact-sheets/alcohol-facts-and-statistics. 25th July 2022.

World Health Organisation. https://www.who.int/news-room/fact-sheets/detail/alcohol. 25th July 2022.

Stephanie Covington: Covington Books. https://stephaniecovington.com/books/bookstore/a-womans-way-through-the-twelve-steps. 25th July 2022.

Stress: Mind. https://www.mind.org.uk/information-support/types-of-mental-health-problems/stress/what-is-stress. 25th July 2022.

Story: Irons, Chris and Beaumont, Elaine. The Compassionate Mind Workbook: A step-by-step guide to developing your compassionate self. London. Robinson, an imprint of Little, Brown Book Group, 2017.

Sugar:

Santos-Longhurst, Adrienne. https://www.healthline.com/health/sugar-detox-symptoms# 25th July 2022.

O'Keefe Osborne, Corinne. https://www.verywellmind.com/sugar-withdrawal-symptoms-timeline-and-treatment-4176257. 25th July 2022.

Suicide:

Suicide Support - YouTube – Positive Living with Corinna. https://youtu.be/jyNLZoSYAbw 31st July 2022.

Stay Alive App

Sunlight: Skcin.org. https://www.skcin.org/sunSafetyAndPrevention/theFiveSsOfSunSafety.htm# 25th July 2022.

Survivors Guilt: Cherry, Kendra. https://www.verywellmind.com/survivors-guilt-4688743. 25th July 2022.

Taste:

Harding, Anne. https://www.livescience.com/47970-alcohol-taste-perception-genetics.html. 25th July 2022.

Graff, Steve. https://www.pennmedicine.org/news/news-blog/2017/april/effects-of-smoking-and-alcohol-on-smell-and-taste. 25th July 2022.

Thalamus:

The Human Memory. https://human-memory.net/thalamus. 25th July 2022.

Brain Made Simple. https://brainmadesimple.com/thalamus. 25th July 2022.

The Boy, the Mole, the Fox and the Horse: Mackesy, Charlie. The

Boy, the Mole, the Fox and the Horse. London. Ebury Press, 2019.

The Twelve Steps: Alcoholics Anonymous. https://www.aa.org/the-twelve-steps. 25th July 2022.

Thich Nhat Hanh:

Kandpal, Disha. https://www.hitc.com/en-gb/2022/01/22/thich-nhat-hanh-quotes. 25th July 2022.

McLeod, Melvin. The Pocket Tich Nhat Hanh. Colorado. Shambala Publications inc, 2012.

Time Out: Mecchi, Irene et Al. The Lion King. Produced by Walt Disney.

Timing: Prochaska, James O, PHD. https://www.prevention.com/life/a20429391/seven-stages-of-change. 28th July 2022.

This Naked Mind: Grace, Annie. This Naked Mind. Control Alcohol, Find Freedom, Discover Happiness & Change Your Life. London. HarperCollins *Publishers* Ltd., 2018.

Trauma:

Gillihan, Seth J. https://www.psychologytoday.com/us/blog/think-act-be/201609/21-common-reactions-trauma. 25th July 2022.

Mind. https://www.ming.org.uk/information-support/types-of-mental-health-problems/trauma/about-trauma. 25th July 2022.

Trust in the Process:

Rebecca. https://www.minimalismmadesimple.com/home/

trust-the-process# 25th July 2022.

Moggach, Deborah. (2011). he Best Marigold hotel. (film).

Unexpected Joy of Being Sober (The): Gray, Catherine. The Unexpected Joy of being sober. London. Octopus Publishing Group Ltd., 2017.

Units:

Alcohol Change UK. https://alcoholchange.org.uk/alcohol-facts/ interactive-tools/check-your-drinking/alcohol-units. 26th July 2022.

Roehm, Eric MD. https://www.nutritionheart.com/alcohol-drinks-grams-of-alcohol. 26th July 2022.

Vagus Nerve:

Fogoros, Richard N. MD. https/www.verywellhealth.com/vagus-nerve-anatomy-1746123. 26th July 2022.

Chmelik, Stefan. https://www.getsensate.com/blogs/news/ everything-vagus-nerve? 26th July 2022.

Vitamins:

Christensen, Stephen. https://healthfully.com/vitamins-depleted-by-alcohol-6843537.html. 26th July 2022.

Beck, Craig. Alcohol Lied to Me: The Intelligent Way to Escape Alcohol Addiction. Wroclaw. Amazon Fulfilment, 2019.

Roche, Dylan. https://livestrong.com/article/375909-what-are-the-effects-of-alcohol-in-vitamins-minerals. 26h July 2022.

Water: Helmenstine, Anne Marie, PhD. https://

www.thoughtco.com/how-much-of-your-body-is-water-609406. 26th July 2022.

Weakness: Mackesy, Charlie. The Boy, the Mole, the Fox and the Horse. London. Ebury Press, 2019.

Wernicke's Encephalopathy: Martin, Peter R, M.D et Al. https://pubs.niaaa.nih.gov/publications/arh27-2/134-142.htm. 26th July 2022.

Wernicke-Korsakoff's Syndrome: Cooper Tarry Partnership LLP. The Upstreet Project. https://Korsakoffs.org/home/what-is-wernicke-korsakoffs-syndrome. 26th July 2022.

Wet Brain Syndrome: Imonirhua, Michael. https://www.rehabclinic.org.uk/fundamentals-about-wet-brain-syndrome. 26th July 2022.

WHO:

World Health Organisation. https://www.who.int/news-room/fact-sheets/detail/alcohol# 26th July 2022.

Change. Org. https://www.change.org/p/boris-jphnson-alcohol-truth-to-be-declared. 1st August 2022.

Worry: Living Life to the Full. www.llttf.com. 26th July 2022

WRAP: North Staffordshire Combined Healthcare NHS Trust. https://www.combined.nhs.uk/person-centredness-framework/wellness-recovery-action-plans-wrap. 28th July 2022.

Wrong: Fitzgerlad, Kelly. https://www.addictioncenter.com/community/why-alcohol-is-the-deadliest-drug/ 26th July 2022.

X-Ray: Sampson, H Wayne, Ph.D. https://pubs.niaaa.nih.gov/publications/arh22-3/190.pdf# 26th July 2022.

Yin and Yang: Subtle Energy. https://subtle.energy/whats-the-difference-between-yin-yang-qi-energy. 26th July 2022.

Printed in Great Britain
by Amazon

42194956R00172